TALES OF POTOSÍ

TALES

OF POTOSÍ

Bartolomé Arzáns de Orsúa y Vela

Edited, with an Introduction,

by R. C. Padden

Translated from the Spanish

by Frances M. López-Morillas

Brown University Press

Providence

Brown University Press

Providence, Rhode Island 02912

© 1975 by Brown University

All rights reserved

Set in Janson by Dix Typesetting Company, Inc.

Printed in the United States of America

By Halliday Lithograph Corporation

On Warren's Olde Style

Bound by Halliday Lithograph Corporation

Designed by Richard Hendel

Library of Congress Cataloging in Publication Data:

Arzáns de Orsúa y Vela, Bartolomé, 1676–1736.
   Tales of Potosí.
   Translated selections from Historia de la
villa imperial de Potosí.
   Includes bibliographical references.
   1. Potosí, Bolivia—History. I. Title.
F3351.P85A8213 1975   984'.1'03   74–6574
ISBN 0–87057–144–3

Contents

Editor's Foreword / vii
Editor's Introduction / xi

PRIVATE LIVES

1598 • Floriana / 3
1602 • A Tale of Sound and Fury / 13
1604 • Blood for Blood / 20
1612 • The Strange Case of Fulgencio Orozco / 27
1616 • The Miracle of San Pedro / 33
1625 • The Hermit / 37
1646 • Don Juan in Potosí / 40
1647 • Of Love and Partisanship / 48
1648, 1649 • The Downfall of Don Francisco Chocata / 51
1653 • The Spook / 56
1653 • The Adventures of the Warrior Maidens / 58
1656 • On Rancor and Christian Charity / 71
1657 • A Virgin's Revenge / 77
1657 • The Wages of Sin / 81
1657 • The Twelve Apostles and Magdalene / 84
1658 • Honor Lost and Redeemed / 87
1658 • The Salvation of Antonio Escorrón / 91
1658 • The Fearless Avenger / 94
1661 • Big Gaspar / 97
1661 • Doña Magdalena / 103

1674 • *Claudia the Witch* / 116
1676 • *The Brief Engagement of Francisca Mirueña* / 127
1677 • *Sebastián and His Golden Spurs* / 137
1677 • *A False Alarm* / 142
1678 • *The Making of Ambrosio de Soto* / 145
1682 • *A Servant of God* / 148
1688 • *The Reformation of Don Francisco Aguirre* / 152
1688 • *The Trials of Doña Teresa* / 155

PAGEANTRY

1599 • *The King Is Dead* / 167
1600 • *Long Live the King* / 171
1687 • *The Fear of God* / 176
1716 • *The Triumphal Visit of a Viceroy* / 183

Notes / 201

Editor's Foreword

LIKE Potosí in its heyday, Arzáns's *Historia de la Villa Imperial de Potosí* is apt to evoke superlatives, whether because of its great size—nearly a million words—or its incredible wealth of factual data or its employment of the tales (*cuentos*) of Potosí, by which Arzáns innocently inaugurated a whole new Hispanic-American literary genre. The *Historia* is annalistic, being a year-by-year account of everything that happened in the city from the time of its founding until 1736, when death stayed the hand of the author. What saves it from the common fate of annals—that of being mined by historians but seldom read—is that Arzáns took as axiomatic the proposition that history not only teaches but also entertains, and readily recognized that most people would rather read of stunning exploits, acts of violence, wonders, scandals, and wars than the humdrum of peaceful and orderly existence. Therefore he took pains to depict both the sensational and the prosaic in the *Historia*, hoping that the reader might be moved to abhor the vices and crimes and imitate the virtues, and deduce from his reading the rules by which to live the good life. Potosí was Arzáns's canvas, but the human condition was his subject.

It was this aspect of Arzáns's work that persuaded me to undertake the present English edition and that suggested the rationale of selection. The most stirring episodes of Potosí's history as well as the exploits, trials, and tragedies of many of its citizens found their way into a folk history of the city that for the most part was maintained orally until committed to paper by Arzáns; one finds these legendary tales, both written and oral, verified and questionable, strewn throughout the *Historia*. Once separated from their matrix and provided with a suitable prologue they present an extraordinary human pageant, a distillation of humanity that transcends Potosí and the barrier of time, achieving the universality, if not the language, of *Don Quixote* or *Hamlet*. The reader will find some of the tales better than others; while a few rival the most exquisite novellas, others fall far short of the literary mark, understandably because Arzáns was neither Cervantes nor Shakespeare and was concentrating on history rather than fiction. What is important is that, literary merit aside, the tales provide us with a dimension of Spanish colonial life seldom before seen or imagined. This English edition is thus more than simply a translation of selections from Arzáns: by using this Foreword, the Introduction, and the notes to the text the American reader has it in his power as never before to lift the veil and recreate in his own mind the society of the Potosinos at its peak of florescence, to walk the city's streets and plazas, to enter its homes, and to witness the foibles and passions, failings and triumphs of its people.

I have divided the selections into two groups, the first dealing with private lives and the second with public life as it was expressed in formal pageantry. The latter portion generally lacks the novelistic qualities of the former but yields, nevertheless, a collective portraiture that is indispensable to a fuller comprehension of individual lives in Potosí.

Arzáns had been dead for well over two hundred years before his *Historia* was published in its original Spanish and in its entirety. On the basis of a rare manuscript copy of Arzáns's original work, now at Brown University, and under the joint editorship of Lewis Hanke and Gunnar Mendoza, a three-volume edition of the *Historia* issued from the Brown University Press in 1965. Since that edition is the one to which the interested reader of *Tales of Potosí* must necessarily refer, the present English edition is based upon that text. Notes have been kept to a minimum, with most of the background information that the general reader may need supplied in the Introduction. The reader of Spanish will find the three-volume edition comprehensively annotated, offering a running guide to historical sources and critical evaluation, and furnished with the most complete bibliography on Potosí to be found anywhere. I hasten to express my admiration for the scholarship and erudition with which Lewis Hanke and Gunnar Mendoza accomplished their task and my indebtedness to them for the role they played by means of that accomplishment in my own researches on Potosí and in the preparation of this English edition.

The quickest way for the reader of *Tales of Potosí* to find his place in the Hanke-Mendoza edition is to correlate the date at the head of each tale with the date at the top of each page of the Spanish text. I have not indicated omissions or chapter breaks within narratives, simply because it did not seem worth the bother. Almost invariably omission is employed to spare the reader excessive and repetitious moralizing or the interruption of a tale for the purpose of cramming into the text the miscellaneous data that is required to fill out the account of a given year. For the sake of clarity as well as reading ease, I have taken liberties both with Arzáns's oftentimes complicated sentences and with Frances M. López-Morillas's translation of them. Although Arzáns's work generally lacks the more abstruse stylistic convolutions of the baroque, his idiosyncrasies with the pen—and the fact that his manuscript was unedited at his death—suggested a need for considerable emendation. This is always risky business, but it is especially necessary in editing a work like that of Arzáns in which historical and historiographical contexts frequently provide subtleties of shape and meaning to the text that translation in itself may not yield. Ultimately my endeavor was to bring the labors of author, translator, and editor together in a faithful and readable rendering of the subject and in a form most suitable to the purposes that moved the enterprise in the first instance.

Editor's Introduction

Potosí

PICTURE, if you will, a graceful, conical mountain, dark red in color, rising some two thousand feet to a perfectly symmetrical peak, majestic in its domination of the horizon— a surrounding sea of broken peaks and crags. This is high country, the backbone of the Andes. The mountain appears to rise from the edge of an escarpment that slopes downward from east to west, following the lay of the land in its gradual but tortuous descent to far distant Pacific shores. The lower slopes of the mountain and its lesser hills spill out over the escarpment, forming a threshold that is nearly fourteen thousand feet above sea level. The mountain is called Potosí, named by whom we do not know, nor are we certain of the language from which the name was derived. Some believe it to have been Quechua, others Aymara. The name could be one of those occasional outrageous Spanish corruptions of a native word that defy analysis. Obviously we cannot be certain of its meaning. Spaniards argued the point in the sixteenth century, with one persistent tradition holding that it meant something like "high place."

What distinguished Potosí, aside from its natural beauty, was the fact that it embraced one of the largest and perhaps richest silver lodes ever found on earth. All was hidden except for a massive outcropping of ore three hundred feet long and thirteen feet wide—50 per cent pure silver—that had been uncovered by centuries of erosion. It appears likely the Incas knew of it; they were efficient in maintaining precise knowledge and control of the gold, silver, lead, copper, tin, and mercury deposits within their realms. Their silver mines of Ccolque Porco, about twenty miles from Potosí, but at a lower elevation, were well developed and very rich. Since their use of precious metals was essentially artistic and decorative, and gold and silver lacked the intrinsic value assigned to them by European cultures, the Incas were content to exploit the more accessible deposits for the limited quantities they required. Besides, Potosí was located well above timberline in the barren region the Indians called the *puna* ("the uninhabitable") because of its thin and icy air. Altitude, awesome storms, freezing temperatures, and bitter winds were effective barriers to human habitation. Thus, the brooding silence of the puna was broken mainly by the shrieking of winds and the snapping of frost-cracked rock, while the fabulous silver treasure of the High Place remained untouched as it had been for untold centuries.

The Spanish conqueror Francisco Pizarro dethroned Atahuallpa, the Inca, on 15 November 1532, assuming sovereignty at Cajamarca and founding Spanish Peru. Recognizing the Europeans' obsession with silver and gold, and thinking to save his own life, Atahuallpa vowed to fill a room with treasure for the conqueror, a task requiring several months for completion. While the Inca raised his ransom, his captors followed to their origins the main trails over which silver and gold treasure appeared—one leading them up to ancient Cuzco and its incredible riches—and otherwise occupied themselves in spying out the land. By the following July Atahuallpa had become a political liability and his room was very nearly filled, whereupon both the Inca and his treasure—worth something near two million pesos[1]—were liquidated, the former by execution, the latter by being melted down and distributed in shares to everyone who had taken part in the emperor's capture.[2] One year to the day after Atahuallpa's overthrow the Spanish intruders took up residence in Cuzco, where gold and silver works of art were gathered, admired, and then melted down. Meanwhile, efforts were also made to find the primary sources of the precious metals. The Indians were helpful in pointing out mines and deposits they knew about, so that for the Spaniards it was a matter of revelation, rather than discovery. But, as in Mexico a dozen or so years earlier, when the Indians subsequently found themselves forced to slave in the very mines they had revealed, other Indians took the hint, and soon the common tendency was to conceal rather than to disclose. By 1543, however, the rich silver mines of Ccolque Porco had been placed under Spanish management, and now the intruders were but twenty miles from the treasure of the High Place.

The inevitable occurred in April, 1545. In the preceding decade, as Spain's newly sovereign conquerors went about establishing new cultural and economic imperatives, thereby transforming local societies, the Indians had found silver to be no less attractive and useful than it was to their mentors in the new life. Many Indians claimed and worked their own mines, while others simply worked deposits not yet claimed. And so it happened that surreptitious exploitation by an Indian of the outcropping on Potosí came to the attention of the principal Spanish mine operators of Porco, who investigated and hastily filed claims to what was showing on the mountain—and the rush was on. Word of Potosí spread on the wind and nearly emptied the newly settled Andean communities of Porco and La Plata[3] of Spaniards and their Indians; shortly the entreaty, "Please God, take me to Peru," was to echo throughout the Caribbean.

José de Acosta, commenting in 1598 on the city that had grown out of the original mining camp on Potosí's threshold, was struck by the hostility of its natural environment. On his own experience and the recorded observations of others he declared the High Place to be colder and more wind-swept than any plateau of Old Spain, and judged that its complete lack of vegetation, its sterility, should have rendered it uninhabitable. "But the power of silver," he surmised, "which through greed summons to itself all other things, has peopled that Mountain with the largest population in the whole of the Indies and has made all manner of viands and luxuries so plentiful that there is nothing to be desired that is not found in abundance."[4] The good padre did not exaggerate: at the time he wrote, Potosí was nearing the zenith of its size and opulence. By 1611 it would have a population of 160,000, making it not only the largest city in the New World, but larger than most of the urban centers of Europe and Asia. It was also one of the world's highest cities and probably the richest. Its name had become legend and was universally employed to express the quintessential idea of unlimited and inexhaustible wealth. Most expressive, perhaps, was the motto that appeared on Potosí's coat of arms:

> I am rich Potosí,
> Treasure of the world,

The king of all mountains,
And the envy of all kings.

And so the human history of Potosí began with the silver rush of 1545. The Spaniards of Porco, having laid claim to what was popularly called the Discovery Lode, were promptly joined by 175 eager countrymen from La Plata, with 3,000 Indians in their service.[5] Winter was just beginning, allowing them scarcely enough time to establish claims and then move their camp down to a more habitable elevation, where they appropriated the houses and shelters of the Indians who happened to be living there. The next move was to force the former occupants to provide most of what was necessary for the maintenance during the winter of the intruders and their repartimiento Indians—and for the building of their town at the foot of Potosí, come spring. In spite of the displaced Indians' resistance and open rebellion, the Spaniards gained their objectives, and within eighteen months twenty-five hundred houses had been thrown up on Potosí's threshold to shelter some 14,000 people. There was neither planning nor regulation, largely, one suspects, because the silver was not expected to last: boomtowns are never built to endure. Perhaps the closest approach to planning was the deliberate laying out of crooked, narrow streets to break the freezing winds.

Nothing was of greater moment than the production of silver, and all things were bent in that direction. Experience had already indicated that black slaves could not withstand the rigors of physical labor at such altitudes and such low temperatures. Therefore, everyone who held Indians in encomienda employed them, but they represented no more than a fraction of the labor force necessary for development of an industry. Since there were too few local Indians to support a general repartimiento, the mine owners had no choice but to rely on a free labor market throughout the early period.

Free Indians, like Spaniards, flocked to Potosí to get rich, and many did so in the mining or in the smelting of *tacana*, the Mountain's ultrarich ore. Spanish smelters faced a crisis when they found the ore "too hard" to be melted; they repeatedly increased the heat, and then helplessly watched the silver content of the superheated ore burn and volatilize instead of melting and running as expected. Inca metallurgy, on the other hand, was superior; the Indians had long ago learned to add a measure of lead to the ore to induce melting and had learned how to maintain more precise control over smelting temperatures. They had invented a portable wind oven (*huayra*, or "wind," in Quechua) that was carried to a hill and loaded with charcoal. When it was ignited, small perforations in the walls of the fuel chamber caused the wind to create a blast-furnace effect. Temperature control was achieved by estimating wind velocity and then moving the oven up or down the hill to get the correct draft to produce the desired degree of heat. When the oven was operated by an experienced smelter, the silver quickly melted and ran. The product of this first extraction was taken by pack train down to lower elevations for two more refining operations by Indian smelters whose techniques, arcane to the Spaniards, produced ingots of pure silver.

By mutual agreement (*concierto*) Indian smelters delivered to the mine owners a specific amount of refined silver per hundredweight of ore delivered to them, keeping the remainder for themselves. Many free Indian laborers in the mines similarly paid the owner an agreed amount of silver each week, based on their own production, and in that way acquired large amounts of ore, which they then refined for themselves. Apparently it was an exceedingly profitable arrangement all around. Garcilaso de la Vega estimated that up to fifteen thousand wind ovens could be seen operating at one time, so that after dark the slopes of Potosí shone like some marvelous new galaxy. Through opportunities afforded by the free labor market and their monopoly of silver smelting and refining, many Indians grew so wealthy that enterprising Spaniards attempted to compete. They built foundries with large furnaces, to be fanned by oversized bellows, and experimented with horse-driven wind wheels. But their technical innovations failed, even as they vainly sought Indian smelters willing to desert their own enterprises to work for daily wages. The Indian monopoly on smelting would hold until the discovery and implementation of a new chemical method of extraction, the amalgamation process, but that was not to come until 1571.[6]

In spite of Spanish fears of Indians' getting rich, the mine owners were doing very well for themselves. Near the end of the colonial period Baron Alexander von Humboldt estimated, from royal treasury records, that Potosí produced over 127 million pesos during the first eleven years.[7] There are no reliable figures on production in the early period because there were no royal treasury agents living in Potosí and keeping records prior to 1556, nor was there effective local administration. The area was under the rule of the corregidor of La Plata,[8] whose deputy collected the *quinto*, or royal fifth, in Potosí every Saturday and indiscriminately mixed it with royal income from the mines of Porco. Moreover, informed contemporary commentators on the colonial scene were unanimous in estimating that Spaniards regularly paid the quinto on no more than a third to a half of all the silver they took from the earth. The Indians almost never paid the royal fifth, so that official records, even if complete, would account for but a fraction of total production. Some therefore believe Humboldt's estimate to be low, while others think it too high. But all would probably agree with the Spanish inspector in Concolorcorvo's *Lazarillo* when he declares to a native: "The Spaniards extracted more silver and gold from the entrails of this land in ten years than your countrymen did in the more than two thousand in which they were established here, according to the calculations of the most judicious men."[9]

It was not only the miners who achieved wealth in the early years. Every mouthful of food, whether for man or beast, every barrel stave, every beam—everything consumed or used in the High Place—had to be brought up from below. From the very beginning Potosí was, in an economic sense, a vacuum that would not be filled, given the swelling torrent of silver that fed insatiable demands. The fertile, watered valleys that girdled Upper Peru—the Bolivian plateau in today's geography—had already been settled by Spaniards whose farms and herds bespoke a comfortable, if isolated, way of life. With the sudden materialization of Potosí as a market for their meat, fodder, vegetables, fowl, cereal crops, fruit, and timber, their fortunes were made, and grants of land and encomienda increased tenfold in value almost overnight. Merchants of La Plata, already supplying the mining communities of Porco and Beringuela, expanded their operations to include Potosí, and within a few years La Plata counted among its population some of the richest Spaniards in the Indies. A measurement at the vortex, Potosí's central market place, is afforded by contemporaries who estimated that in 1549, when the city was hardly four years old, the daily volume of trade ran from forty thousand to eighty thousand pesos.[10] In spite of prodigious wealth, life in Potosí was primitive by any standard. Houses and buildings were cramped; ceilings were made low and rooms small to conserve heat. Windows were few and unglazed. Even rich miners lived in wretched shacks that were cruelly ventilated by cracks and fissures. Severe cold was expected in winter, but on the balmiest of summer days the temperature never rose above fifty-nine degrees Fahrenheit. The burning of charcoal in poorly vented fireplaces or simple braziers was the principal protection from the eternal chill and offered its own peril in the form of carbon monoxide poisoning, which was chronic. So rigorous was life in the early period that during the first fifty years not one child born in Potosí of European parents survived for more than two weeks. Women learned to go down to the lower valleys for confinement and to stay there with the child for its first year of life before returning to the High Place.[11]

The hostility of the natural environment was not always the chief problem in the earliest years. The erstwhile partners in the overthrow of the Inca empire, Francisco Pizarro and Diego Almagro, had fallen out over the division of spoils and had died in the ensuing warfare, which dragged on for a decade. In 1546 Gonzalo Pizarro, Francisco's brother, rebelling against reforms ordered in the New Laws of 1542, beheaded Charles V's first viceroy and crowned himself king of Peru. The settlement at Potosí was just getting started, and many of Porco's Spaniards, most of whom were now leaders in Potosí, were royalists. In addition, the silver of Potosí was like a magnet to Pizarro, who sent his field marshal and captains on regular pillaging expeditions. Potosí suffered substantial losses in the raids and from strife between royalist and rebel factions of its small but growing population. Not until 1548, after Gonzalo Pizarro's overthrow and execution, could the building of Potosí be pursued without interruption.

With violence and intimidation halted, silver production soared. But by the middle of 1566 the more accessible veins of tacana, the ultrarich ore, had been exhausted, and fortunes began to fade. Inferior ores were not suitable for smelting, and the silver they yielded was devalued because it retained much of the lead used in the smelting process. Scores of mines were now faced with closure because the prevailing technology could not compensate for the diminishing quality of the ore. Meanwhile, Potosí's sudden and dramatic decline did not go unnoticed in Spain. The Habsburgs had grown accustomed to receiving a million to a million and a half pesos annually in quintos from Potosí.[12] Already goaded by the civil war and rebellion in Peru and by what appeared to be dangerous instability in Mexico, Philip II initiated a sweeping investigation of the administration of the American empire with two fundamental reforms in view: to centralize royal authority and make it more effective, and to increase substantially the flow of revenue by stimulating the production of precious metals. The king convened a special junta to deal with the problems of Peru. One of its members, Francisco de Toledo, was subsequently sent out as Philip's viceroy, well armed with comprehensive plans and instructions, together with wide discretionary powers. Toledo's tenure lasted from 1569 until 1581, during which time he earned lasting fame as the founder of Spain's colonial system on the southern continent.

When Toledo arrived, in November, 1569, he found a general Andean economic depression and Potosí on the verge of collapse. He quickly surveyed the state of affairs and then moved to confront what he evidently took to be the major problems posed by a free labor market and inadequate technology. The viceroy had apparently brought from Spain a conviction that the decline of silver production, and consequent depression, was in part caused by the traditional reliance upon a free Indian labor force. The Indians worked or not as they saw fit, and always within the terms of their concierto with mine owners. Indeed, with the Indians' monopoly of extraction and refining, control of the production of silver had never rested in Spanish hands.

Before leaving Spain the viceroy had doubtless been briefed on the discovery in Mexico in 1554 of a new method of amalgamating silver ores with mercury. As originally invented, this was a cold chemical process for the extraction of silver from low-grade ores. In 1558 Enrique Garcés, a Portuguese long resident in Peru, visited Mexico and learned the new method—

there known as the "patio process" from the paved courtyard in which it was carried on. He subsequently returned to Peru, and in 1566 discovered the first of several large mercury deposits at Huancavelica, about 140 miles southeast of Lima. Experimentation with local mercury and Peruvian ores followed, and Garcés obtained a twelve-year monopoly of the new extractive process, which he must have brought to the attention of Viceroy Toledo upon his arrival.[13]

Toledo convened a junta to discuss the question of compulsory Indian labor in the mines, and in October, 1570, the junta reported its opinion that compulsory Indian labor in the mines was justifiable on the basis of the public interest. Meanwhile, Toledo took two related actions: he expropriated the Huancavelica mercury mines and ordered a census to be taken of all the Indians of Peru between eighteen and fifty years old. The census found 1,677,697 males liable for service. Toledo now decreed that henceforth the Indians must pay their tributes in silver. In order to get the silver with which to pay their taxes, every village was to submit to a general labor levy: every year one-seventh of its male population was to be made available for a four-month term of paid labor in mines or on other projects. Theoretically, the individual so drafted would work for a period of 121 days no more often than once every seven years. Wages and working conditions were stipulated, and relevant mining ordinances were issued and inspectors appointed. Thus began the infamous *mita* of the mines, its victims the *mitayos*.

However it appeared in theory, the mita proved to be disastrous for the Indians, who were commonly forced to work beyond their term of service if they survived its perils; they were not always paid, and when they were, their wages were far below free market levels; villages were commonly forced to send more than their allotted number of laborers, and more frequently than specified. A summons to labor in the mines came to be viewed as a virtual death warrant. Excessive labor under the most adverse conditions, an inadequate diet, disease, accidents, and, above all, what must have been spiritual suffocation contributed to soaring mortality among the mitayos. The worst conditions, perhaps, prevailed in the state-owned mercury mines at Huancavelica. There the discomforts and dangers suffered by all miners—semidarkness and air befouled by sweating bodies and human waste, the smoke of candlewick, and toxic molds and dusts—were compounded by mercury poisoning and its implacable and hideous course.[14] The Incas knew quicksilver, but had no uses for it. Because of its toxic effect on those who mined and handled it, they prohibited its mining and, as a true measure of the totalitarian state, simply ordered it to be forgotten. Its name was obliterated from the language and there was no ready word for it when it was rediscovered by Garcés, in 1566.[15]

It should be understood that mitayos were not the only Indians who labored at mining. A detailed report of 1603 on the mines of Potosí shows that out of 58,800 Indians employed, only 5,100 were mitayos. There were also 43,200 free day laborers and 10,500 *mingas*, or workers who labored on a contractual basis. However, the most killing labor in the mines was that of carrying on one's back a large and heavy basket of ore, climbing up hundreds of feet through narrow, precipitous tunnels, clutching at ropes and finding toeholds in notched logs, struggling, antlike, to reach the mouth of the mine, where one's exhausted, sweating body would be blasted by freezing winds upon emergence. This was the work four-fifths of the mitayos were forced to do; of the 10,500 mingas, only 600 would contract to do it. Not one free Indian laborer of the 43,200 who worked in and around the mines would volunteer for it.[16]

The mita was intended to be a formal assignment of Indian labor for all types of enterprise, and it was so used, but it never incurred elsewhere the odium that it did in mining. There, the nature of the crown's fiscal policy and its administration, and the greed of mining entrepreneurs made the mita what it was. In the beginning and over the years the mita was forcefully attacked by moralists and jurists, but nothing really happened to change the system. Garcilaso de la Vega stated the ultimate case succinctly in commenting on the aborted section of the New Laws of 1542 prohibiting Indian labor in the mines— which had cost the king's first viceroy his head when he attempted to implement them in Peru: "With regard to the law against putting Indians to work in the mines, I have no comment to offer, except to refer to the Indians who still today in 1611 work by orders of the governors in the silver mines of the hill of Potosí and in the quicksilver mines in the province of Huanca; if they ceased to do so, neither the silver nor the gold of the empire would be brought every year to Spain."[17] If, in the long view, it was the mines that made the Spanish colonial societies and, eventually, the nations that followed, surely it was the bodies of the Indians that made the mines.

The new amalgamation process was successfully adapted to local ores, and Toledo dictated its general employment in Peru on 20 August 1571. This revolutionary advance in metallurgy required a whole new approach to the operation of the extractive and refining industries. The viceroy had the technology, the mercury, and the labor, and now he determined to go to the High Place and take personal command of its reorganization.

Upon his arrival in Potosí in November, 1572, Toledo summoned the leading mine owners to a meeting in which he proposed construction of a vast refining and processing complex within the city, together with development of a new water supply that would serve the domestic needs of Potosí and simultaneously provide hydraulic power for grinding ores and the large amounts of water necessary for extractive and refining operations. Taking advantage of existing springs and natural drainage areas above the city, plans provided for a series of dams and catch basins to store runoff from summer rains. The water was to be conducted to the city by means of a natural arroyo, sections of conduit dug out of the rock where necessary, and an aqueduct where there was no other way, finally spilling into a canal that would terminate at the refining site. Both projects were undertaken, and the water system was completed in 1576 at a cost of some 900,000 pesos. The refining center was not completed until the following year. It consisted of 132 walled and fortified refining and processing plants, each having a residence for the owner, a chapel, kitchens, maintenance shops, and living quarters for its many Indian workers, slaves, and domestics. This, then, was the famous Ribera, virtually a city within a city. The complex was built at a cost of 10 million pesos and, as the reader will see for himself, was owned and operated by a unique aristocracy.[18]

While these considerable projects were under construction, Toledo turned his attention to the city itself. The population had by now passed the hundred thousand mark, and urban chaos was resulting. As Governor Pino Manrique observed in

1786, Potosí was in its origin "a city raised in pandemonium by greed at the foot of riches discovered by accident."[19] All was done by Toledo that could be done to mitigate the errors of the past: he widened and straightened streets wherever it was possible to do so; he directed construction of a stone flood-control canal, thirty feet wide and three miles long, bisecting the city from east to west and crossed by twenty-two bridges. In addition to controlling the flash floods of summer, the canal would also carry any surplus water from the Ribera. The viceroy also constructed the new Plaza del Regocijo, eight hundred feet long by four hundred feet wide. It was a typical Spanish Renaissance plaza, its western side being an extended portico that served as an imposing entrance to new halls of municipal government. Drinking water was piped into the plaza from springs above the city. Toledo personally laid the cornerstone of a new cathedral facing the plaza and initiated construction of the royal mint and new treasury buildings.[20] To the older Plaza del Gato, which remained as the central market place of Potosí, he added row upon row of stone benches.

In addition to his many public works that produced the streets, buildings, bridges, plazas—even the benches—that one who reads *Tales of Potosí* will come to know, Toledo issued ordinances for the improvement of housing and sanitation. Building materials were always scarce, especially with so many public works under way, so that private housing tended to lag for a time, but eventually it caught up. Improved living conditions lessened infant mortality, and Don Nicolás Flores, born in 1598, was celebrated as the first Creole to be born in Potosí.[21]

During the early mining period lesser ores, called *negrillos*, were found together with tacana, and both were carried out of the mines. The tacana was melted and the lesser ores rejected. Over the years piles of negrillos grew mountainous. With the introduction of the amalgamation process, the negrillos could be made to yield wealth, and this led to an increase in the production of silver even before the Ribera was completed. Of course, the Indian monopoly on smelting had disappeared with the tacana, and the mita effectively terminated participation in the free labor market for those Indians whose labor it claimed. Increasingly their welfare would be subordinated to the conscienceless dictates of what their rulers determined to be economic necessity, and in the new order of things there would be far fewer opportunities for Indians of humble means to achieve wealth and status in Spanish eyes. Rich and powerful mine owners now sought to deny the Indians what had become a traditional right to possess and trade in silver. Viceroy Toledo opposed them successfully, and so there would always be some rich Indians who lived and moved about as they pleased, but in the post-tacana age even a free laborer would not be able to earn in a week or more what he had formerly produced in a single day.[22]

The racial and social discrimination implied in Toledo's labor policies was made explicit when he declared, upon completion of the Ribera, that henceforth the Indians would continue to live on the southern side of the canal that now bisected Potosí, while the Europeans would reside on the other. The Indian side was the original town site, under the very shadow of the Mountain. Most of the new residential construction followed Toledo's design, and the European population congregated in the northern section and its suburbs. The Indian quarter, already old, rapidly succumbed to urban blight, becoming a ghetto where poor Indians and Europeans were joined by fugitives, criminals, prostitutes, homosexuals, and alcoholics—outcasts all. But the twenty-two bridges joining the two worlds carried heavy traffic. Many of the neighborhoods and suburbs of the Indian side, like El Arenal, Cebadillas, El Ttio, San Clemente, Contumarca, and Carachipampa, were favored by Potosinos as places in which to stage their battles, gang fights, duels, and assassinations. Many amorous adventures, as well, took place in those same haunts, which provided both setting and plot for much of the human drama that fills the tales that are to follow.[23]

Philip II's income from the Mountain was 177,275 pesos in 1570. By 1585 the annual quinto had risen to 1,526,455 pesos, and it maintained or exceeded that level, as a general rule, for over sixty years. Nothing better demonstrates the monumental success of Toledo's policies, at least in terms of the rather narrow scope of the goals that had inspired them. Some Peruvian aristocrats, looking back on the long reign of silver in Potosí that was nearing its end in their own eighteenth century, would hail Toledo as an "immortal hero" for having joined the trinity of ore, technology, and Indian labor.[24] Completion of the Ribera had turned Potosí's stream of silver into a mighty river, and beside the older aristocracy of mine owners and merchants grown rich there appeared a new breed of millionaire, the refiners, who emerged as a powerful group by 1590. The upward economic surge engineered by Toledo brought Potosí to its peak of material and demographic wealth. By 1611 the city had a population of 160,000, including 3,000 peninsular Spaniards, 40,000 presumably non-Spanish Europeans,[25] 35,000 Creoles (including many mestizo children of Spanish-Indian unions), 76,000 Indians, and 6,000 Negroes and mulattos and other persons of mixed blood.

In the new flood of wealth, exaggerated ostentation became almost normal: a beggar, seeking alms in the right place at the right time, might be given ten, twenty, even thirty thousand pesos; a man gained renown by spending ten thousand pesos for a single fresh fish; daughters were dowered with hundreds of thousands of pesos, even millions; one bride in 1597 brought her husband 2.3 million pesos in dowry; weddings and funerals were occasions for conspicuous consumption; public offices were purchased for great sums; once in office, municipal officials staged opulent celebrations featuring lavish hospitality, and employed pages, all dressed in splendid livery, to attend them; churches were extravagantly endowed and were provided with the most elaborate silver service and ornamentation; public occasions provided opportunities for personal display of wealth bordering on the orgiastic; public celebration of royal weddings, accessions, births, and deaths cost millions, and in addition the Habsburgs had received over ten million pesos in gifts by 1670. Personal fortunes were immense; Don Antonio López de Quiroga died of old age in 1699, leaving a fortune in excess of one hundred million pesos.

Potosí had scores of gambling houses and hundreds of professional gamblers, but they were far outnumbered by prostitutes, some of them celebrated for their splendid houses and lavish entertainment of their clientele. There were dancing schools and fencing schools; apparently everyone wanted to be taken for a hidalgo. Even the tradesmen, mechanics, Indians, Negroes, and persons of mixed blood dressed in silks and satins, wore diamond studs, and sported like silver barons on feast days. "He who was a peasant in Spain takes on airs of gentility," wrote Arzáns, "and the commoner tries to look like a noble. He who in his past had never amassed a hundred pesos spends that much in Potosí for a good meal, and he who has but ten pesos squanders them on a snack. If this is out of keeping with prudent conduct, it is but an indication of the lordly spirit this city engenders."[26]

Visiting Potosí during the great boom, a French merchant, Acarète du Biscay, noted that the common people "live much at their ease, but all are proud and haughty, and always go very fine, either in cloth of Gold and Silver, or in Scarlet, or Silk trimmed with a great deal of Gold and Silver Lace. The Furniture of their Houses is very Rich, for they are generally serv'd in Plate."[27]

Apparently there were few luxuries that could not be had for a price. Wealthy Potosinos fenced with the best Toledo blades and stabbed their enemies with fine German cutlery; their ladies dressed in luxurious fabrics from Tuscany trimmed with Milanese silver and gold laces, and wore hose from Naples and laces from Flanders; they chose between the most exquisite Chinese, Calabrian, and French silks; they wore perfumes from Arabia, American pearls, and precious stones from India and Ceylon. Their homes were furnished with ironwear from Spain and Germany, Portuguese and Dutch linens, rich wall tapestries and embroideries, laces, elegant mirrors, and carved desks from Flanders; Florentine satins, Tuscan embroideries, and fine Italian paintings graced their walls, Venetian glass and Chinese lacquerware and carved ivory their tables. They trod on rugs from Persia, Cairo, and Turkey. Against the cold they all wore English hats and woolen coats or sported expensive beaver hats from France.[28]

Profits of 1,000 per cent were common among the suppliers of Potosí, and they made imposing fortunes. As for Potosinos themselves, commercial venture was extremely attractive, not only because of the money, but also because it was an ideal way to dispose of illicit silver. If, as tradition has it, they declared no more than a third to a half of their silver, they needed a way in which to utilize the part on which they had evaded payment of the quinto. Some luxuries and necessities found their way to Potosí via the only legal route provided by Spain's mercantilistic system of control; that is, upon being discharged at Cartagena or Portobelo, cargoes were packed over the isthmus to the Pacific and transhipped to Callao, then down the coast to Arica, where they were loaded on animal carriers and packed up to Potosí. Shipments of legal silver and the royal fifth went out over the same route in reverse. Inasmuch as the material needs of Spain's American colonists were seldom, if ever, met by her merchants holding the trading monopoly, smuggling was an omnipresent fact of colonial life. There was a large contraband trade with Manila via galleon and the fairs at Acapulco, but a far larger flow of contraband reached Potosí from Buenos Aires via the Río de la Plata.[29] This trade embodied Padre Acosta's image of silver summoning to itself all other things. Endless shiploads of forbidden wares unladen at Río de Janeiro, Montevideo, and Buenos Aires made their way up the river system through lowland forests and rising highlands, finally emerging on the high, broken tablelands of the Altiplano, where, through established channels of commerce, they were made available to the patrons of Potosí's markets. It is reasonable to assume that contraband was most often paid for with illicit silver, supposedly with officialdom none the wiser—excluding, of course, its bribed minions—and everyone the richer. We do not know how much illicit silver flowed down the Río de la Plata and into the waiting hands of international contrabandists. Arzáns estimated that during the period of highest silver production in Potosí, over half a billion pesos in unregistered silver found its way out by that route.[30] The Potosinos' insatiable appetites supported a clandestine traffic that dominated the economic life of a continent.

If Potosí was one of the richest cities in the world, it was also one of the most violent. Having set the physical and historical stage on which this turbulent and unruly society is to reveal itself, it remains to provide some understanding of how and why violence, especially the organized kind, came into such prominence. In this, Spanish medieval history played a part. During nearly eight centuries of frequent participation in wars against the Moors and each other the Spanish kingdoms were reinforced in their incipient nationalism and its concomitant rivalries and jealousies. When Isabella and Ferdinand joined their kingdoms, they initiated a centralization of political authority that was bitterly resisted, and while both Charles

V and Philip II further reduced the independence of the powerful feudatories of Spain's kingdoms, this only heightened the latter's jealousy of the newly risen power of the state that was superimposed over the older, but still fervent, regional rivalries. Throughout the Spanish Indies, therefore, traditional animosities between Basques, Estremadurans, Andalusians, and Castilians often provided a ready-made basis for local post-conquest political alignments, subject, of course, to individual variables of ambition and greed. Moreover, one distinct advantage of being in the Indies was that of escaping the crown's centralized authority and, accordingly, being able to impose one's own will to the very limit of one's power. As a political catalyst, this was a factor to be reckoned with.

As for events in Peru, the Pizarro clan hailed from Estremadura, and Almagro was a Castilian. Their deadly vendetta was waged primarily over treasure and territorial rights, but the old element of regional rivalry was always implicit and served explicitly in the gathering of partisan support. By the time Gonzalo Pizarro was overthrown in 1548 his disruptive tactics had contributed to a severe shortage of food in Potosí. Andalusians and Estremadurans cornered the available maize and other staples, whereupon they were opposed by Basques, Creoles, and Portuguese. Before the fighting was over and the issues were resolved, forty men had been killed.

There does not appear to have been a consistent pattern to violent rivalry in Potosí until after construction of the Ribera and the spectacular rise of a new and influential aristocracy of silver refiners, whose ranks included a disproportionate number of Basques. The latter had swiftly increased their number by bringing in their countrymen and setting them up in businesses of their own. Basques were traditionally considered to be clannish by other Spaniards, and this was more painfully felt by Potosí's Creoles because of the special contempt in which the Basques held all American-born Spaniards. By the 1590s non-Basques viewed the scene with alarm, for the Basques now held the lion's share of refineries and a growing number of other enterprises; they were taking over the most influential offices in the municipal hierarchy and the royal administration; they were using economic and political power to gain still more advantages and to silence those who opposed them, even to the point of corrupting the highest officials in order to influence political and judicial decisions. When protests and appeals failed, the losers turned to violence, reprisals nearly always provoking bloodshed on both sides, in chainlike reactions that often continued long after the original causes had been forgotten.

By 1612 the Basques had set their sights on gaining possession of some of the larger mines, and now the non-Basques determined to organize and to resist with arms what recourse to law and the pen had failed to halt. Andalusians, Estremadurans, Castilians, and Creoles joined in a formal alliance against their common foe, but the Basques would not be deterred from pursuit of their objectives. In 1615 violence was widespread; by 1620 it was epidemic. The allies agreed to be known as "Castilians," rather than by individual regional designations, and adopted brightly colored vicuña hats with a distinctive band and device as a means of ready identification. A sanguine and tragic "War of the Vicuñas" was finally joined that ravaged Potosí intermittently from 1622 until 1625, ultimately ending in mutual exhaustion rather than a signal victory for either side.[31]

After the war was over and large-scale organized violence had been suppressed, individual crimes of passion and those prompted by ambition and greed—eclipsed somewhat during the civil war—once again came into prominence. Arzáns tends to dwell on violent crime in Potosí, but because he is a moral didactician his treatment of criminal behavior tells us less than we should like to know. He mentions 260 homicides between 1671 and 1702, of which it appears only 26 were followed by prosecution. On the other hand, Corregidor Juan Velarde Treviño hanged 96 men in a three-year term of office at midcentury. Evidently, much depended on the inclination and effectiveness of the ruling corregidor. But, in any case, to what extent may a given record of prosecution be taken as a reliable index of criminal activity? It reports only public crimes. How many remain secret? Arzáns elsewhere mentions that when old buildings were torn down or fields dug up, bodies of murder victims were commonly found stuffed in the walls or buried under the rocks.[32]

The early chroniclers of Potosí always mention, with frequent lamentation, the unruly behavior of soldiers and fortune seekers. Apparently miners, merchants, traders, and gamblers were as ready to fight, and the plazas of Potosí witnessed daily brawls, not uncommonly with death resulting. Harried municipal councilmen and magistrates—who themselves wore armor and carried weapons to work—passed laws prohibiting onlookers from taking sides in private disputes. When those measures failed, they tried to get fighting off the streets and plazas by decreeing that those who fought must duel, formally choosing seconds and agreeing upon a field of honor, preferably somewhere out of town. Dueling became the rage, and "eight fencing schools were opened to teach men how to kill each other. Some fought in shirt and trousers, and others naked to the waist, with utter disdain for a shield; some wore carmine taffeta shirts so that the blood from their wounds should not be noticeable, and others put on chain mail or metal breastplates. Some fought with pistols. They fought on horseback, on their knees, or in any other position out of the ordinary."[33] Many failed to observe such formalities and accordingly went about prepared for capricious homicidal encounter. Acarète du Biscay declared most mestizos to be "idle, apt to quarrel and Treacherous, therefore they commonly wear Three or Four Buff-wast-coats one upon another, which are proof against the point of a Sword, to secure themselves from private stabs."[34] Such an observation from a foreign visitor, together with contemporary documentation resting in Potosí's archives, suggests that Arzáns did not exaggerate the violence that ruled in Potosí.[35]

The Empedradillo, frequently mentioned in the tales, was a section on the eastern side of the Plaza del Regocijo that was set aside for testing the swordsmanship and courage of male Potosinos. A gang or partisan group, taking up a position there, would taunt and challenge every armed male who attempted to pass through its ranks more than once, and force him either to fight his way through or retreat. Many failed and not a few were killed, while some, evidently, were recruited by the gangs. Arzáns referred to this tradition as "one of the insanities wrought by the men of this city."[36] All of this would tend to support the conclusion that Potosí's bloody fights and brawls constituted "a recognized social activity."[37] But the reader will have ample opportunity to judge that for himself.

The Author and His Work

Bartolomé Arzáns de Orsúa y Vela was born in Potosí in 1676. His father had come out from Spain as a boy, in 1643, at the height of the boom. Apparently he failed to achieve material success in Potosí, and there were few advantages for his children. Arzáns accordingly grew up without the benefit of formal education; he educated himself, like many Creoles, and did it well enough to make his living as a teacher in later life. He married a woman considerably older than himself and, according to the scant biographical data we have, lived a rather prosaic life, never achieving the wealth and status that would have put him in touch with persons of power and influence. He lived his entire life in Potosí and died there in 1736 in his sixtieth year.

As a self-taught man Arzáns was widely read and, at the same time, apologetic about his lack of literary and historical training. In his *Historia de la Villa Imperial de Potosí* one sees the stylistic and thematic influence of those writers who most impressed him, especially Cervantes, whose exemplary novels are suggested everywhere. Like most untraveled Creole authors, Arzáns suffered from a certain lack of cultural confidence, to overcome which he made slavish reference to classical authors and theologians. One suspects he knew the latter more intimately than the former.[38]

Just as Arzáns was influenced by other writers, so was he shaped by the times in which he lived. Early in the second half of the seventeenth century Potosí's long prosperity began to falter, then decline. The Mountain was being mined out, as evidenced by diminishing production and quality of ore. More immediately, Spain and her overseas empire were suffering the effects of the later Habsburg decline, and it would require a tremendous effort on the part of the Bourbons to restore the economic vigor of the colonies in the eighteenth century. Population, like silver production, was a reliable barometer of Potosí's economic well-being. By the beginning of the eighteenth century, as Arzáns was starting to write his *Historia*, Potosí's population had shrunk to about 60,000. The 132 refineries of boom times were now 60, and the Ribera, with its abandoned buildings, fallen roofs, and jutting, skeletonlike walls, smelled of decay. Many of the surviving refiners were in financial difficulty through indebtedness for mercury. Scores of mines had closed down, and those still producing yielded none but inferior ores. In good times shipments of registered silver to Spain had run to many millions of pesos annually. The year before Arzáns's death, in 1736, they amounted to but 660,000 pesos. Arzáns's generation, therefore, lived in a state of interminable crisis that was to color not only his *Historia* but his very conception of history. "Everything is finished," he wrote, "all is affliction and anguish, weeping and sighing. Without doubt this has been one of the greatest downfalls ever to overtake one of the world's peoples: to see such diversity, such incomparable wealth turn to dust, to become nothing."[39]

So cataclysmic a decline cried out for explanation. According to Arzáns, "Experience invariably shows that abundance of material things occasions in man a forgetfulness of God and the breaking of His divine precepts. Such has been experienced in this imperial city of Potosí, for the greatness of her riches has always been the occasion of her offenses to God and, for this reason, the cause of her calamities."[40] In his interpretation of the history of Potosí, Arzáns thus assumes the stance of a social critic and a moralist. His social criticism largely speaks for itself, but his moralizing requires illumination. It is most important to recognize Arzáns for what he was, a self-trained neoscholastic whose views of life and reality were thoroughly Augustinian. He saw man as being suspended between life and death, heaven and hell, ever tormented by the necessity of choosing good or evil—and usually succumbing to the latter, only to be punished for it by a vengeful deity. In his view, sex and sin are coterminous, if not synonymous, and the illicit satisfying of bodily appetites is the surest way to eternal damnation. Public and private sins of the flesh, stealing, homicide, and worship of the silver calf are held sufficient to bring down the wrath of God, and Arzáns shaped the whole of his *Historia* on this theme. Divine vengeance was visited upon Potosí in three installments: the War of the Vicuñas in 1622–25; a terrible flood caused by the failure of the dam retaining the waters of Lake Caricari in 1626; and a devastating devaluation of Potosí's silver and coinage in 1650, made necessary by the ex post facto discovery of a scandalous debasement. In Arzáns's mind, the fall of Potosí was intelligible only because the working of God's will and history's goal were perceived as one and the same, which was man redeemed from sin. In such a view, history is enmeshed in a teleology that extends quite beyond the compass of history itself. Indeed, the philosophical aspect of Arzáns's redemptive historiography is so overpowering that to him a historical source would be empty of meaning without it.

Arzáns was appealing to an absolute, timeless, and unchanging horizon of reality, and it is worthy of our notice that he did so in order to communicate with the readers of his own generation. These were baroque times and people, far removed from the age of conquest and their own beginnings. Early in the sixteenth century, as Spanish conquerors and settlers took control of man and land, and fashioned their societies, the mendicant orders instituted civilizing and evangelizing missions as remarkable for their cultural diversity as for their geographical span, and invested enormous amounts of energy and material resources in the founding of a colonial church. But in the course of the century, while the missionaries of the orders continued to work among the Indians in expanding the frontiers of empire, their leadership within the colonial church was assumed by a proud and ambitious secular clergy, an establishment whose efforts at shaping a colonial faith were based upon more widely ranging objectives. By the seventeeth century the Indians were vastly reduced in numbers, having fallen victim to plagues and exploitation. The idealistic and juridical debates of the previous century over the status of the Indians and the implications for them of European entry into the New World were largely spent, and growing Spanish and mestizo populations found other interests. It was almost as though the disparities and inequities of colonial existence had been brought to a point of irreducibility and had achieved common acceptance as the greater part of reality. Spain's colonial church turned—in expiation, perhaps—to a singularly abstract glorification of God, achieving in its attempt the familiar baroque splendor of the Silver Age.

The missionary orders historicized their glories of the sixteenth century, giving rise to a literary movement in which the miracle achieved an eminence that overflowed into secular traditions, finally vesting itself in the symbolism of the elite and in the pragmatic questing of the masses. In effect, this was an atavistic welling up of the miracle from the early Middle Ages to a position of prominence in American baroque culture. A second approach to the glorification of God was through the renunciation of materialism, with its mystical denial of the flesh. The Augustinian polarization of good and evil was central by virtue of the implication of choice and its attendant consequences. Nowhere does Arzáns reflect the Silver Age more eloquently than in his elevation of sins and miracles to dramatic heights.

And yet this denial of materialism and the flesh induced unbearable tensions within baroque culture.[41] In its daily life, as portrayed by Arzáns, the society of the Potosinos contradicted by its actions nearly everything it professed to believe. Arzáns is troubled to explain an almost limitless toleration of mayhem, rape, and murder by a society that consistently upheld the most formidable of canons against them. One is given the impression that the greater the departure from the ideal, the louder the ideal was proclaimed and the more ominous the punishment threatened. But to little avail. Machismo had its way in Potosí, and the generating of life and the taking of it were as two sides of the commonest coin in the realm. One who reads the *Historia* from the vantage point of a society such as our own that has for generations sought its identity in the achievement of social and political justice, however imperfectly realized, is likely to ascribe to Arzáns's society a shallow hypocrisy. But that would be to miss the point. Contradiction was the very essence of the baroque, to which Quevedo's mordant satire eloquently bears witness.[42] As for the matter of justice, in Arzáns's world divine justice reigned but did not rule. In everyday affairs justice was a temporal matter and closely associated with personal vengeance. At the end of this life, in which the flesh too often sated itself while materialism overmastered renunciation, God's greatest glory resided in His infinite mercy. "Justice is all right for saints," an old saying goes, "but men require mercy." Intercession was the key, the means by which man could yet be saved, and to this fact the cult of the Virgin owed its central position in the baroque church. Perhaps nowhere in the New World or the Old was the Virgin invoked more than in Potosí, where Arzáns, as one might well guess, was her unflagging propagandist.

There is some irony in all of this. It was Columbus's opening of the New World and Spain's penetration of it that produced the first major cracks in the old Augustinian world view, especially after much of its traditional wisdom had been contradicted by experience in the New World. Intellectually, Europe was never to be the same again. In the course of the seventeenth century, as Europeans moved still further away from the Augustinian destiny of man—notwithstanding the continuing vitality of Christocentrism, as suggested in the writings of Bunyan, Bossuet, and Milton—the old view was revived and crystallized in baroque Spain and her empire, essentially as a spiritual and cultural defense against the changing world and Western man's perceptions of it. Thus, even though in Potosí man and his silver were in fact the measure of all things, the prevailing philosophy denied it, and in Arzáns's day Copernicus had yet to overcome the Ptolemaic universe to the satisfaction of a great many Potosinos. The old view generally held its own against the Enlightenment, at least popularly and among a significant portion of the ruling aristocracy; subsequently it was redefined in ways compatible with independence and the new nationalism of the nineteenth century, and it is only now falling before the vast intellectual and spiritual alienation that is transforming the decolonized world of the twentieth century.

From a purely historiographical point of view, there is a serious problem of which the reader needs to be made aware in Arzáns's use of source materials. It appears that Arzáns read and used everything available to him that had been written by Potosinos about their Mountain and its city. He also consulted some local archival material, such as reports, religious and financial records, and legal documents, and he was widely read in the printed works of a general nature concerning his own colony as well as the greater Spanish Indies. His primary sources, however, were Potosí's oral and written historical traditions, and he was relentless in searching them out; herein lies the nucleus of the problem. The five authors whom Arzáns most frequently cites as sources are Antonio de Acosta, Bartolomé de Dueñas, Pedro Méndez,

Juan Pasquier, and Juan Sobrino. Of the five, the historical existence of only one, Juan Sobrino, has been established, even though his much-cited work has never been found. Neither have the works of the remaining four been discovered, nor is there any documentary evidence *in hand* that would give them historical reality. However unlikely it might appear, it is entirely possible that Arzáns invented these sources for reasons of his own.

What could those reasons have been? We have no certain answer, largely because the necessary research that can be done only in Potosí has not yet been carried out. However, we do know from Arzáns's own testimony that during the thirty or so years that he worked on the *Historia* he was harried and pressured by people who feared that his work would reveal scandals in which they or their kin had been involved. Unheeded warnings were followed by blunt threats of death, delivered with conviction sufficient to send Arzáns into hiding, and more than once. There were attempts to buy his unfinished manuscript. He lived in fear that his work would be seized and destroyed; therefore, he always kept it well hidden, and from time to time loosed rumors to the effect that the manuscript had been sent to Spain for publication—anything to throw the hunters off the scent. Because of the public nature of his research, in the course of which he investigated oral traditions through interviews with participants and witnesses or their kin, his lines of inquiry could not remain secret, and his opponents must have known what he was doing most of the time.

Arzáns frequently omitted the names of his subjects in order to spare living relatives certain embarrassment; he sometimes suppressed all but the "least scandalous" data in a given account. It is possible that some of his frequent errors of name, place, or date represent deliberate attempts to escape certain retaliation, rather than careless mistakes. On the day of Arzáns's death the *Historia* was unfinished, unedited, and still lay hidden, presumably because of the continuing opposition of Potosinos who feared the book's revelations.

If, as some believe, Arzáns did invent the works of Acosta, Méndez, Pasquier, Dueñas, and Sobrino, and perhaps other sources as well, he might have done so in order to relieve himself of much of the opprobrium and retaliation that disclosure promised to bring. If the oral traditions were presented as the work of others rather than his own, his own culpability, in a public sense, would have been vastly reduced. On the other hand, if these men really did live and write, as Arzáns would have the reader believe, it is possible that they were subjected to the same pressures and opposition of which Arzáns complained and that their works were successfully suppressed. Only through extensive research, yet to be undertaken, will we find definite answers to these intriguing questions.

The ultimate problem conceals the ultimate blessing. To insert the unreal into the real, the fictitious into the factual, did not have the significance for Arzáns's generation that it does for our own. Contemporary readers may be bothered by Arzáns's historiography—if not by the possibility of his having manipulated sources, then by his willingness to exercise scrupulous honesty and accuracy in recording hard facts on the same page with descriptions of supernatural events, wonders, and miracles, all then to be subjected to moral reflection and interpretation. But to concentrate on these seeming disparities is to miss entirely the historical value of the unhistorical aspects of Arzáns's work. Both the man and his work are artifacts. Moreover, in compiling this brilliant collection of oral traditions, admittedly for his readers' moral edification, Arzáns provided us with a unique social portraiture of the Potosinos in their history. What served as grist for the moralist of yesterday is grist for the behaviorist of today.

Although Potosí's silver has long since vanished, the Mountain continues to yield wealth, at the present time in the form of tin mined some three thousand feet below her threshold. But after the tin disappears, as it surely will, all that will be left, once again, is the colossal human drama that unfolds in Arzáns's tales. Who is to say that this is not the most enduring treasure of them all?

PRIVATE LIVES

1598 · Floriana

In their writings Captain Pedro Méndez, Don Antonio de Acosta, and the poet Juan Sobrino (the latter in elegant verses) all tell the story of the loves and remarkable experiences of the incredibly beautiful Doña Floriana Rosales. According to these authors her parents, Don Alvaro Rosales Montero and Doña Ana Quintanal, were noble Estremadurans who came to these Indies after having been united in the bonds of holy matrimony and took up residence in this city. They brought from Spain two small sons, Don Pedro and Don Martín.

Little more than a year after their arrival in this imperial city Doña Ana realized that she was pregnant, and when the time approached for her to give birth, fearing the rigors of the climate, she decided to retire to the valley of Tarapaya, which, though it is cool, has a better climate, and life is more enjoyable there; it also has the advantage of being near Potosí. There a daughter was born to the couple and named Floriana, both for her mother and for the child's great beauty, like that of a tender and lovely flower, and because she was born on the day of Christ's nativity. There she was nurtured until she reached the age of three, the perfection of her beauty increasing daily. Then she was brought to this city, which she thenceforth recognized as her home.

As soon as she had passed her twelfth birthday, many noble, rich, and highly placed men began to concern themselves with courting her. And although her parents and brothers were importuned by many of them to bestow her hand, none was successful in his suit, because the parents knew full well that their daughter had no intention of entering the married state, for she had been trained in the virtue and shelter of her home. She kept close watch over herself, avoiding occasions on which she might herself see and be seen by men, for sometimes an imprudent glance makes us love that which we would not choose to love and begins the forging of that chain whose first link has the shape of an eye and whose last link is often eternal damnation: thought follows upon sight, amorous desire upon thought, consent upon amorous desire, the deed upon consent, habit upon the deed, necessity upon habit, despair upon necessity, and damnation upon despair for the man who is lost deliberately (because he did not guard his eyes so as not to see and shut them so as not to perceive).

But although this beautiful girl avoided seeing and being seen, this very circumstance further inflamed the minds of her suitors because their intentions toward her were honorable. Among those who pressed their suit most determinedly was Captain Rodrigo de Alburquerque, a person who, in his desire to serve the king in Chile, had come to Potosí to raise troops at his own expense, and for whom a marriage had already been arranged in La Plata with a maiden who was his equal in every respect. Ambition is a disease, and the desire for honor, esteem, reputation, and greater riches grows easily in men's minds; both in this desire and in amorous pursuits the suitor often proceeds blindly, heedless of the outcome of his desires. The other persistent suitor was the governor of Tucumán,[1] who had stopped in Potosí on his way to Los Reyes[2] to consult with the viceroy and had remained to court Floriana (after having seen her one feast day in a church); yet another suitor was Don Julio Sánchez Farfán, the corregidor of Porco. In addition to these outsiders Floriana had other admirers who were residents of the city, and all of them haunted the street where the beautiful maiden lived, hoping for a glimpse of her.

Floriana's life was so retired that she was unaware of their intentions until one day the neighbors told her parents, and they their daughter; and although they had great confidence in her virtue, yet they redoubled their care in keeping her safe, to the point that she went out to hear mass only on feast days, and then only at daybreak. But even these precautions proved inadequate, for one day a paper was placed on top of a writing desk in her house (it was never known by whose hand), and when she picked it up and looked at the signature, it was seen to read: "Your grace's servant, The Governor." Previous authors do not divulge the contents of the letter, for they all say that it contained only lewd suggestions lacking any honorable intent; and because it deserved nothing better, Floriana angrily consigned it to the flames of a brazier conveniently at hand. She did not wish to disclose the matter to her parents, for they had little regard for the governor. She replied to the letter briefly and sensibly in the following terms: "I have been told that Heaven denied you noble birth, and, indeed, I can believe it on the evidence of the gross message you have sent me; but it suffered a well-merited fate, for such wantonness deserves nothing but the flames."

The governor was so angry at this reply that, supposing her father to have informed his daughter that he was an unworthy suitor, he decided to fight a duel with him: a fine way, indeed, to attain his goal, for if he had meant to abandon his hopes of her, such action would have been in no way remarkable; but it was madness to think of injuring the father and then taking his pleasure of the daughter. Nevertheless, the governor resolved to do it, and as he knew that Don Alvaro went nearly every day to the field of San Clemente, he rode there, spurring his horse cruelly, to await him. Don Alvaro, unaware of the governor's intentions, arrived a short time later. The governor revealed his desires; Don Alvaro refused to listen to him and upbraided him for his effrontery, further argument ending when the two drew their swords and attacked each other.

This happened in the month of January, 1598, and since in that month many women were accustomed to go to that place for picnics and dances (and still are to this very day), owing to a spring of excellent water that is there, as luck would have it, two ladies were present although it was only two o'clock in the afternoon. When they saw the two men fighting nearby, they approached and very courageously interposed themselves between the two, so successfully that, having intervened, they prevented each from attacking the other again, although Don Alvaro was very eager to do so because he had been superficially wounded early in the encounter. Then more people arrived and there was nothing for the combatants to do but each to go his own way.

When Don Alvaro returned home he reproved his daughter bitterly and at length; she, furiously angry, first exonerated herself and then determined to punish the insult personally. She sent a polite and carefully dissembling message to the governor telling him to wait for her the following evening in a certain shop to which she had access through a little door that opened out of one of the rooms in her house, for she wished to speak to him where no one could overhear. The governor (as Captain Pedro Méndez tells us) received messenger and message with the utmost joy, for since love is blind, so are all its effects; he replied that he would be there at the appointed hour. That day the governor donned his richest clothing, for in this regard he was exceedingly vain and fond of dressing magnificently in the company of women. Now, excessive luxury in dress, though it is somewhat more tolerable in women, is an abominable vice in men who seek out exquisite colors and materials that are perhaps excessive even for women of easy virtue, and the vice is all the more reprehensible in these unhappy times when Spaniards are so eager to wear foreign fashions. For all classes of society to affect the wearing of silk is to follow in the footsteps of Heliogabalus, who, according to Herodianus, scorned Roman and Greek garments because they were of wool and wore gold and purple and precious stones in the Persian style, as Lampridius attests. Nowadays we rarely find a man who wears the same kind of cloth or color that his father or grandfather wore.

Punctually at the hour indicated the governor was at the specified place, and Floriana soon entered, bearing among the beautiful flowers of her visage the poisonous serpent of her anger. The would-be lover who had offended her virtue had arrived in a state of great excitement, hat in hand, and said to her, "My lady, you see before you your slave and true lover; I should rather say, the man unworthy of your love, for I have doubly insulted you." But just as he spoke these words, Floriana, without allowing him to proceed, took out a broad, sharp knife that had been hidden in her sleeve and as fiercely as a lioness rushed at him and attempted to slash his face, showering him with insults. The governor, seeing himself attacked by that prodigy of beauty and fury, quickly fended off her blow with one hand, thus avoiding a face wound, but the knife pierced the space between his thumb and the palm of his hand, cutting it to the bone. And in stepping backward in order to protect his face he stumbled over a billet of wood that was lying on the floor and fell; realizing that he was wounded and that she was about to deliver a second blow, he rose to attack Floriana as a treacherous enemy. He drew a dagger he was wearing, and Floriana, realizing the danger she was in, thrust a bundle of blankets that was lying on the floor into his face, successfully impeding both his view and his arm, for some of the cloth became entangled with the dagger. This gave her time to seize a heavy piece of wood that was fortunately lying nearby, and, wielding it with both hands, she struck the governor such a blow across his chest and head that he fell senseless.

Alerted by the commotion, some of Floriana's servants entered through the connecting door, followed by other people from neighboring shops; seeing the governor stretched out and bloody from the blow, all concluded that he was certainly dead. Floriana ran back to her house, and her parents, overcome with grief and fright, tried to hide her. But it was too late, for the corregidor [of Potosí], whose house was close by, had already been summoned and came in haste, and Floriana had time only to run to an upper room and jump out the window into the street. The window was not high, but her leap might have resulted in the greatest misfortune, for as she fell her petticoat caught on a beam that protruded from the window frame and she was left hanging there head down, unable to help herself or make an effort to tear the petticoat, since if she had fallen to the ground headfirst she might have been killed.

By this time nearly everyone had heard of the affair and many persons had rushed to Floriana's house; because one of the maidservants knew Don Julio and was aware that he was in love with her mistress, she told him to go into the alley behind the house to look for Floriana, for some time had passed since she had jumped out of the window. Don Julio went out at once; meanwhile Captain Alburquerque, when he saw the maidservant and Don Julio speaking privately together (for lovers are quick to observe the actions even of the servants of those they love), followed him into the alley without being detected.

Don Julio, therefore, arrived just as poor Floriana, in deadly fear, was calling for help and crying that she was choking. The lovestruck gentleman approached her and, stretching out his arms, seized the maiden by the shoulders. He gave a sharp tug (tearing her petticoat in the process) and she fell to the ground and, under the weight of her fall, Don Julio with her. Just then Captain Alburquerque came rushing up and with loving and compassionate words covered Floriana with his cape and raised her from the ground. When Don Julio saw this, he leaped to his feet in a burning rage and, drawing a dagger, attacked the captain, calling him a boorish traitor for making such advances to Floriana before his very eyes. When the captain heard these insults and saw Don Julio rushing at him so furiously, he drew a dagger and leaped at his attacker. As they clashed, the captain received a grievous wound in the chest and fell to the ground, calling for a priest. Hearing this, Floriana cursed her ill fortune and fled from the scene before some Indians who were approaching.

 Don Julio followed her, and when the girl saw this, she begged him to turn back so that her honor would not be damaged by loose gossip more than it had been already. The gentleman refused, saying that he would prefer to lose his life a hundred times than to leave her in that predicament. But the delay merely afforded the corregidor time to come looking for the aggressors; and Don Julio, as soon as he caught sight of him, took the girl by the arm and hastily led her out the other end of the alley, where there was a dunghill. There he left her, telling her to crouch down so that she could not be seen while he decoyed the corregidor into going in another direction. And so Don Julio, sword in hand, made his way to another street, where, finding himself pursued by some of the corregidor's servants, he turned and charged them. When they saw the fury of his attack, they scattered before him, and he took to his heels and fled to safety. He returned by a circuitous route to the place where he had left Floriana, who, as anxious to flee from Don Julio as from the officers of the law, had followed the banks of a stream that ran nearby until she reached one of its bridges; she crossed it and entered the dwelling of some Indian women, where she was received with great kindness. There she awaited the dawn, which was not long in coming, and then sent word to her father to let him know where she was; he had also gone into hiding that night because the corregidor wanted to arrest him. Floriana learned that the lives of the two wounded men were not despaired of, which pleased her no little, because the whole city was blaming her for what had occurred and she knew that they would absolve her of guilt by stating the facts.

 The governor had a nephew who was a quicksilver refiner; he brought a formal complaint against Floriana before the corregidor and insisted that she be found and imprisoned. When this news reached Floriana, she decided to change her clothing and leave the city. She donned Indian dress (any costume merely enhanced her beauty), and just as she was about to mount a mule in order to escape, someone informed the corregidor, who (although it was nine o'clock at night and very dark) came at once and very courteously told the frightened maiden that she must accompany him to his house.

There are some who say that as the corregidor gazed upon her she seemed to him (even in that garb) the most beautiful woman he had seen in his life; that blind boy who goes by the name of Love did not waste the opportunity that was offered him to vanquish the soul of this man like other men (though a prudent and conscientious judge) and enter it upon the list of his trophies. And so, it is said, Love crept up to the corregidor and loosed his terrible dart, which pierced his heart through and through. Since Love is invisible, he could do this very easily, for he comes and goes as he pleases, and no one can call him to account for his actions.

The corregidor, therefore, took her hands in his and, consoling her with loving words, led her to his house. And how sweetly Floriana allowed herself to be led to the prison of love! He gave her a suitable room and retired to his own; but he could not rest all that night for thinking of the beauty of her who had become the mistress of his heart. As soon as it was dawn he went to visit her, and when he saw her by the light of day she seemed more beautiful than ever. He gave her all sorts of explanations (trying to justify the fact that he had imprisoned her in his own house), but Floriana immediately realized in what direction they were leading. She answered him with great circumspection and was forward in nothing but her gratitude. The corregidor's visits were so frequent that after Floriana had been there only two days she would have preferred to be shut up in a dungeon with the usual discomforts suffered by prisoners rather than to receive these special favors and marks of affection that were being offered for evil purposes. When a man loves to excess, he withdraws his love from others who are equally worthy of love and runs the risk of not being loved at all; and he who does not take heed of this becomes odious to many, for he shows an excess of love toward a single person.

From his hiding place Don Julio had learned the circumstances of Floriana's captivity in the corregidor's house, and, filled with jealous rage, he wrote to the girl expressing his love for her. She replied, trying to dissuade him from the course he was planning, both for his own sake and the corregidor's, although she did implore him on his honor as a gentleman to help her escape from that prison. Don Julio agreed to all of Floriana's suggestions, and in secrecy they arranged that one night (after the corregidor had gone to bed) Don Julio would wait for her under a balcony and she would slide down a rope and he would then take her to Chuquisaca. The plan having been made, the night agreed upon arrived; it was the night (according to Captain Pedro Méndez's account) when Floriana had falsely promised the corregidor that she would accede to his lascivious desires. Since it was a Friday in Lent, all the corregidor's servants had been sent to hear a sermon at the Jesuit church, and Don Julio was thus able to see Floriana and arrange for the hour and manner in which their plan was to be carried out.

When ten o'clock had struck, which was the hour when the girl was to go to the corregidor's bedroom, she went out on the balcony and, tying the rope securely to it, slid down into Don Julio's arms without anyone's being the wiser. Floriana informed Don Julio that she would not take a single step until he swore to respect her person and her virginity. This he did, and just as he was untying the rope that she had placed around her waist, the corregidor appeared on the balcony; since Floriana had not come to his room, he had gone to see what she was doing. When he saw her beneath the balcony with a man, he went back inside, calling upon his servants to come and catch them. The girl was so upset by this that, although Don Julio urged her to flee before the corregidor emerged from the house, he was unable to persuade her to take a step. Realizing the immediate danger both were in, Don Julio hoisted Floriana over his shoulder and ran with her toward the Plaza del Gato. When he reached the stone benches of the plaza, he was dripping with sweat and sat down to rest on a bench, and (as Captain Pedro Méndez reports), whether because of exhaustion or some internal weakness, or whether in some mysterious way that God alone knows, he suddenly fell dead.

When Floriana saw this she supposed it to be a fainting fit and hastened to him to place his head in her lap. But on realizing that he was dead, she jumped up in terror, fearing that if she were caught there it would be thought that she was in some way responsible for his death. Taking up Don Julio's cape, sword, and hat, she put them on and ran to the cemetery of San Agustín, where, after recovering herself slightly, she began to walk toward the neighborhood of San Lorenzo and the home of a friend of her mother. She knocked on the door and was immediately recognized, and they opened the door and let her in.

Let us leave her resting there and return to the corregidor, who, realizing that he had been deceived when he stepped out on the balcony and saw Floriana in the street with a man, called his servants and set out to overtake them. But they were unsuccessful, because Floriana and Don Julio had gone toward the Plaza del Gato, while the corregidor had started off along another street where he heard voices that he took to be theirs. He and his servants soon discovered that this was not the case, and as they returned to the Plaza del Gato they heard some dogs barking among the benches. They went toward the sound and found Don Julio's dead body, to the great astonishment of the corregidor and those who were following him. Lights were brought, and the body was recognized as Don Julio's; since the corregidor knew that he was one of Floriana's suitors and that it was he who had wounded the captain on the night that Floriana, fleeing from the law, had hung head down from the window, he leaped to the conclusion that she must have killed him. He ordered a search made for her among the benches and in all the nearby streets, but since she could not be found, he ordered the corpse taken to his house. They searched the body for wounds, naturally supposing that this must have been the cause of death. But they found none, which was not what they expected, and in consequence the corregidor persuaded himself that Floriana must have poisoned him in some way. Upon this assumption he called in several doctors to look at the body as soon as it was day, and they gave it as their opinion that neither poison nor a blow had been the cause. The corregidor made every effort to lay hands on Floriana, but she was so well hidden that during the rest of his term of office he did not hear a word about her.

A few days after the sudden death of Don Julio, Captain

Rodrigo de Alburquerque also died of the wounds that Don Julio had given him, for all efforts to cure them were in vain. The governor returned to Los Reyes at the end of that same year of 1598 and upon his arrival in La Paz fell ill with a severe bout of fever that carried him off in a few days. In this manner ended the lives of all three of Floriana's suitors, while she, since her only aim was to serve God, emerged from her hiding place as soon as the corregidor Lopidana had left office and from that time onward lived a very reclusive life in her parents' home and preserved her virginity all her life long. And Don Juan Pasquier says that she died at an advanced age and was held by all to be a great servant of God.

1602 · A Tale of Sound and Fury

WHEN the corregidor Don Alvaro Patiño[3] realized how powerful were the members of the Basque nation in wealth and arms, he determined to join them in order (as Captain Méndez and Acosta tell us) to persecute the Creoles, Andalusians, and Estremadurans, for whom he had a mortal hatred. The aforesaid authors (as well as Don Juan Pasquier, Bartolomé de Dueñas, and Juan Sobrino) report the official posts, wealth, and power held by the Basques in the year 1602: they tell us that of the 132 heads of refineries in the Ribera 80 were of that nation; the posts of honor in the city (judicial positions and offices in the mint and exchequer) were in the main administered by them. This gave rise to a very arrogant attitude on their part, scornful of all other nations, and for this reason the peace and calm of the inhabitants of Potosí were totally lost; the situation worsened daily until it gave birth to new misfortunes. The Basques' arrogance swelled until it burst and their pride was brought low with notable injuries, deaths, and destruction, as we shall see.

Those who occupy the heights are farther from the lofty knowledge of God than those whose way lies at the lowest levels if they do not surrender themselves to God and try to follow in the footsteps of His virtues. Vainly do they aspire to enjoy honors, high office, and wealth if they are arrogant in the loftiness of their position and act as if the authority exercised were theirs and not God's. But His Divine Majesty punishes and destroys them because of this arrogance.

When the corregidor Patiño observed the strength of the Cantabrian nation, he attempted to get into the Basques' good graces and carry out his purpose, which was (according to the authors I have mentioned above) to punish some of the rich men among the Andalusians and Estremadurans (as well as the Peruvians, or Creoles) because they opposed many of the manifestations of his greed and ambition. And while the corregidor was very happy to have gained the Basques' good will in order to achieve his aim, they also were happy because they believed that no one would now intervene in their factional fights and brawls; and Captain Pedro Méndez even says that the Basques reminded him [Patiño] of the lamentable death of his nephew, Don Mendo Patiño, and others of his servants at the hands of the Andalusians, Estremadurans, and Creoles (during the resistance against him in the year 1600, as I have described) and urged him to vengeance by promising their help and appointing him head of their faction.

By this perverse procedure they so provoked the opposing nations, performing acts of insolence toward some of their number, that those nations realized that the corregidor was not acting as a judge but rather as the leader of a gang, and so they determined to break with him and with the Basques. They elected Don Justino Botello as their captain, or chief, for, our authors say, he had firmly opposed the corregidor for several years and was seeking a means of revenge. Both sides provided themselves with weapons and horses, and thus matters stood for two months, without an open confrontation, each faction fearing the other because they were nearly equal in arms and numbers of men. The corregidor's band was composed of 180 Basques and Navarrese and a few Catalans. Of these, 50 were provided with brave and well-trained horses, 80 had harquebuses, and 30 muskets, while 20 were pikemen; in addition, there were slaves, servants, and pages, all armed with pistols and swords. Botello's side was composed of 200 Andalusians, Estremadurans, Creoles from a number of cities in Peru, and a few youths who were natives of this city. Of these, there were 40 who had horses, 100 armed with harquebuses, 20 musketeers, and 40 pikemen, not to mention mestizos, servants, and slaves armed with short pikes, pitchforks, and a few fowling pieces.

The city was in such an uproar that work had to be suspended both in the Mountain and in the Ribera; the tradesmen and artisans closed their shops; some, not daring to appear in public, hid in their houses, others left the city. All longed for the day when the battle would be joined once and for all, because no supplies were reaching the city; they had been seized by the servants and rabble belonging to the two opposing armies (if a handful of madmen on each side could be called an army). By his evil actions the corregidor caused all these and many other injuries, including the loss of his own life; and as for the loss of his soul, only God knows. Nothing is more important or more difficult for a man than to make good use of his life, and to do so successfully is such a grave matter that if he commits one error he is lost. Life is not something that, once expended or lost, can be recovered. Possessions, honor, health, all that we hold most dear, can be regained if they are lost, but life and time cannot be restored.

Don Justino Botello determined to challenge the corregidor by appointing the following day for the battle. The corregidor accepted and, ordering the alarm to be sounded, was the first to sally forth to the field between El Arenal and the hill of Munaypata.[4] There he left his men under the command of the licentiate Juan Ramírez de Salazar, all in great discomfort because it was the month of March and there had been considerable flooding that year and the horses had neither straw nor barley to eat. He told them not to stir from that spot until the following day, and he himself returned home, where he slept the last sleep of his life. His adversaries were more sensibly lodged in the home of Captain Botello, where they supped well and slept even better. Not so the corregidor and his men, for at eight o'clock in the evening it began to rain so hard that the Biscayans, after receiving a thorough wetting and realizing that the rain was not going to stop, mounted two men on each horse and went around to the other side of Munaypata at the end of the Ribera and took shelter in the ore refinery of a Basque named Sancho Aranzoaga; since they had to do this in two relays, the horses were completely exhausted, for the distance was a quarter of a league[5] and each horse had to carry two men at a time.

As soon as day broke on Wednesday, the twenty-sixth of March, 1602, the two squadrons went to take up their positions in the appointed place. The corregidor Patiño emerged from his house with an escort of thirty halberdiers, astride a powerful horse with no more ostentation than a saddle embroidered in gold, with many pearls and diamonds, and a plume of varicolored feathers over his brow. He wore no uniform or other touch of elegance except for a red sash, all embroidered with pearls, diamonds, emeralds, and rubies, over the very fine armor he was wearing; his lance was long and thick, and his buckler heavy and gilded. Captain Don Justino

Botello was equally well armed but more elegant, for over his armor he wore a rich overgarment, or tunic, of brocade the color of mother-of-pearl, with many diamonds and emeralds sewn to it and many loops of pearls, which made his appearance extremely elegant and colorful. Over his helmet flew a large number of green, red, and white plumes. His lance was enormous and had two steel points, one of them more than a handspan in length and the other shorter. His buckler was of well-tempered steel, with a long spike, likewise of steel. His horse was strong, heavy, and high-spirited, and wore trappings of pearly brocade with many loops of pearls and a diamond within each loop. Hanging on its chest from two gold chains was a shining sun made of the same metal; its plume was of many-colored feathers, and its mane decorated with ropes of pearls. In short, this gentleman was determined to display his wealth as much as his valor.

At about seven o'clock in the morning the two squadrons drew up within harquebus range of each other; since the hill of Munaypata was very broad on the side overlooking the field, it was covered with a vast crowd of people, men and women alike, all awaiting the outcome of that bloody encounter. When the battle was about to begin, the ecclesiastical vicar of the city arrived accompanied by all the clergy, together with the rector of the Society of Jesus, and placing themselves between the squadrons they earnestly pleaded with the captains or leaders not to carry out their plan, since the fight was between Christians and for so small a cause, or for none at all; and they begged each captain to consider the state in which death might surprise him. These and other arguments were presented by the priests, but all efforts to dissuade the captains from carrying out their design were fruitless; thus, the priests were forced to return to Munaypata, grieving that their appearance and their pleas had accomplished nothing.

The licentiate Ramírez, whom the corregidor had left in charge of the disposition of his squadron, had very skilfully drawn it up in the shape of a half-moon (for, according to Captain Méndez, he was expert in arms as well as in letters). On the right flank were forty harquebusiers, ten musketeers, and ten pikemen; these sixty men were all Basques. On the left flank were the same number of men similarly armed, and these were a mixture of Navarrese and Basques. In the center or main body of the squadron were ten Catalan musketeers in the first rank and behind them fifty horsemen, each with two pages and servants on either side, armed with swords and pistols. Many slaves brought up the rear on both flanks, armed with spears, cutlasses, and swords. Don Justino Botello disposed his squadron in two wings, dividing the infantry equally and leaving forty horse at one side because, since all were new to battle, he feared that they would panic when they heard the first explosion of gunpowder. He also placed the mestizos and servants at some little distance, in reserve. All were well armed, and he ordered them to be on the watch so as to help out at points of greatest danger.

The signal to attack was given, and Lieutenant Ramírez rode out with his fifty horse and the servants and pages, fiercely charging the section of the enemy's line manned by Andalusians and Creoles; in an instant they were routed, with some dead and most of the others wounded. This accounted for about eighty men. The remainder fled in disorder to the other wing, which was also losing because it was being attacked on both sides by infantry and cavalry together. Botello then rushed forward with his forty horse, which, since both mounts and riders were very skilful, not only stopped the rush of the lieutenant and his cavalry but also killed four men, and the lieutenant was gravely wounded by two lance thrusts administered by Botello. So fiercely did the latter's men press their advantage that most of the wounded fell to the ground and the rest fled, for their horses were so exhausted that they could no longer move; there were some who left their horses in the victors' hands and fled on foot. Meanwhile the foot soldiers and servants of both sides were fighting like lions, with the Basques getting the better of it in the initial encounter until Captain Botello returned from pursuing the fleeing horses and, attacking his adversaries with thirty-five horse (for the Catalan musketeers had killed the other five), began to cause great havoc among them.

The corregidor (up to this point he had been stationed slightly to one side, observing the battle with his halberdiers) realized that luck had turned in favor of his adversaries and that his side was in danger; he now came to aid them at a half-gallop. Botello was informed of his arrival, and although he was very tired he left the scene of battle accompanied by a few musketeers, who fired some balls at the corregidor's halberdiers, causing them to flee in terror. Botello's men held their fire on his orders, and riding out to meet the corregidor he angrily inquired, "Wretched captain, why have you stayed so quiet while your soldiers have fought like heroes and lost their lives, and only now you appear again to try to stop my last effort to secure the victory?" The corregidor, without speaking a single word, rushed fiercely at Botello, intending to finish him off with the first thrust of his lance. Botello had no time to swerve, and thus he took the blow on the lower part of his buckler; it was knocked aside by the blow and he was gravely wounded in the arm and chest. The corregidor fell back and again charged Botello, who had time neither to counterattack nor to avoid another thrust from his adversary's lance, which wounded him a second time under one rib. Then, swearing and cursing his ill fortune, he turned his horse around, thinking to flee from death (as was later concluded); when he had galloped some distance, he came to himself and realized what a dishonorable thing he was doing. In recovering himself he wheeled his horse around and fiercely charged the corregidor, who was following him at a trot; in the encounter he gave him a lance thrust under his shield that, notwithstanding his heavy breastplate and mail coat, wounded him severely in the region of the left kidney. Botello's lance broke under this blow; turning his horse to give himself room to draw his sword, he approached the corregidor and gave him a savage thrust that struck his shield and easily went through it, piercing the mail coat and shirt and stopping at his jerkin without breaking the skin. When Botello saw his adversary so close at hand, he spurred his horse and administered a powerful sword thrust on the right side that opened a mortal wound.

 The unfortunate corregidor fell to the ground, and when his men saw this, ten harquebusiers rushed to help him, just as Botello was leaping from his horse and advancing on the corregidor to give him the *coup de grâce*. The harquebusiers, more interested in the trappings, rich saddle, and jewels worn by Botello's horse than in their commander's peril, rushed upon the animal and ripped off all his adornments. Meanwhile Botello had time to wound the corregidor once again, this time fatally. But he had no time to rejoice in his victory, for the greedy harquebusiers killed him also with two volleys from their weapons, and as quickly as they had looted the horse they stripped Botello naked.

This signaled the end of the battle, for there was very little advantage on the part of the Andalusians, Estremadurans, and Creoles, since the number of dead and wounded was almost the same on both sides. All the Catalans (about fifteen in number) and nearly thirty of the Basques and Navarrese were killed. Of the other nations who took part in the combat, twenty-four also died. The corregidor's lieutenant, licentiate Juan Ramírez de Salazar, had three dangerous wounds; and there were sixty wounded on both sides. All the spectators came down from Munaypata to the scene of the battle, where, seeing so many lifeless bodies, they began to lament to high heaven, especially the women, because among them were daughters, wives, and relatives of the dead men and mothers as well. They soon attempted to carry off the bodies and bury them, and those who lived nearby were appalled to see such pitiful tragedies as took place every day. After a few days the licentiate Ramírez was declared to be much improved, and as soon as he was able to get out of bed he was carried to the cabildo on men's shoulders, where he was installed as the lieutenant corregidor of this city, which he tried to calm with much prudence. In this task he was successful, and Potosí had some respite from its quarrels during the short time he held that office.

1604 · Blood for Blood

AFTER the bloody battle between national factions that took place in 1602, in which sixty-six men including the chiefs of the two factions died—most of whom were related to each other in some way—the hatred of both sides became more and more inflamed and both had a still greater desire for vengeance. However, owing to the heavy losses on both sides, encounters between squadrons in battle array no longer took place, though there were many quarrels and private fights, with dreadful destruction and death among the city's inhabitants; and because this imperial city has always been, and continues to be, the common home of the sons of nearly every nation on earth and because, if those of one country are lessened in number, others come to fill their places, therefore, at all times in its history the city has had innumerable inhabitants who have traveled thousands of leagues, attracted by the lure of silver.

To continue with the battles and challenges between persons of both high and low degree, it happened that in January, 1604, there occurred a very scandalous fatality having to do with the love affair of a noble married lady. Truly it was, and is, very necessary for judges to restrain that unchastity of highborn women that wreaks so much havoc in kingdoms, provinces, or cities and prevents so much good; and thus it is only right that judges should exercise severe discipline. Who can persuade the highborn that nobility must not be a sanctuary for sinners but rather a tacit example of virtuous behavior and that God deals harshly with those who, though they enjoy the highest positions by virtue of their class and ancestry, repay Him with insults, especially those who rashly display the vice of sensuality?

The lecheries of this lady, therefore, led to a duel between Jorge Carrizales, an Estremaduran, and Sancho Burgoa, a Basque, on the field of San Clemente. Both fought fiercely, and Carrizales downed Burgoa. The victor was utterly without pity: as the Biscayan lay stretched out on the ground, with three mortal wounds, he pleaded with Carrizales not to finish him off until he had made his confession, and so he begged him for our Lord Jesus Christ's sake to bring him a confessor and summon his brother, Sebastián de Burgoa, to arrange the disposition of his estate. But the perverse and barbarous Estremaduran refused to extend him the slightest charity and, carried away by the devil, drew a dagger and administered the *coup de grâce*. And piling cruelty upon cruelty he mounted a mule and went to the home of Sebastián de Burgoa, the dead man's brother, and, craftily feigning sorrow, told him that his brother had received mortal wounds and was lying at death's door in that place and that Sebastián must accompany him posthaste to the place where he had left him, without rousing the people of his house.

When the Basque received this sudden and shocking piece of information, he naturally had no thought that any harm could come to him and, taking only his sword, set out on foot with the evil Carrizales following. Approaching the corpse, he began to call his brother by name, and when he did not answer, Sebastián turned to Carrizales and said, "My brother is dead: who, sir, has killed him?" Then the cruel Estremaduran, without dismounting from his mule, answered him, saying, "It was this blade that took his life," and quickly unsheathing his sword he let go a savage slash at Sebastián's head and wounded him severely. Burgoa was stunned by the blow but quickly recovered and drew his own sword, saying to Carrizales, "Only you, traitor, could have done this evil," and rushing toward him (for the murderer was about to strike again) the Biscayan dealt him so powerful a thrust that the point of the sword went in low through his genitals and came out his rump. He collapsed, mortally wounded, and called out to Sebastián, pleading with him not to be as cruel as he himself had been to Sebastián's brother and briefly recounting the inhuman treatment he had meted out to Sancho. He asked to have word sent to his house so that they might call a confessor, or, if he lived long enough, that they might take him away from there in order to make his will. "For I wish," he said to his adversary, "now that my cruelty has deprived you of the estate that your brother would have left you, through my having denied him time enough to convey it to you in writing, I wish to give you all I have so that you will forgive me and receive everything that God has given me; and I ask only that you have care for my soul and that of your brother."

When Sebastián heard this, he mounted the wounded man's mule and went to inform his household, and he himself retired to San Francisco to wait and see how the affair turned out, also sending friends to bring his brother's body home and prepare it for burial. All was done in a short space of time: the wounded man was taken home, was confessed, and received the viaticum; he made his will just as he had promised Sebastián, making him the sole heir to a very large fortune, specifying only that he left to Sebastián's good will the task of caring for his soul and that of his brother Sancho (whose large estate was promptly adjudicated by the corregidor in his capacity as judge of estates without his admitting a single demur). Four days later Jorge Carrizales died like a Catholic and a Christian, and his heir, Sebastián, making use of several Creoles, went one night to the place where Jorge Carrizales's fortune was kept and removed it without the knowledge of anyone and then quietly left the city, for the Basques had demanded of Burgoa, as soon as they learned the amount he had inherited (more than 100,000 pesos) that he use it to continue the warfare and destroy their enemies. Sebastián de Burgoa escaped from the whole situation by taking his wealth to the city of Arequipa, whence he returned to Spain to enjoy those riches in perfect tranquillity.

This episode infuriated the Estremadurans all the more, and they declared that it had not been an inheritance at all but plain robbery. And when the Basques heard of it, they made plans to gather all their forces and destroy their enemies. With this aim in mind they took advantage of the accursed custom of Shrovetide revels,[6] forming two squads of thirty men each with an admixture of Navarrese and a few non-Spaniards; and as there was a partisan banner flying from the balcony of a house in the Plaza de la Cebada where many Andalusians, Estremadurans, and Creoles were carousing, the Basques arrived in a gang, tore up the banner, and entering the house without giving its occupants time to defend themselves, killed four men and a well-known lady from the city of La Plata who had been the mistress of one of the Basques. The Andalusians' and Estremadurans' servants and slaves defended their masters so bravely that two Basques were also killed and another had his leg severed by a cutlass. The carnage would have been greater had not the Estremadurans and their allies been encumbered by the meal that was in progress, in which a great many toasts had also been drunk.

The Basques emerged from the house, leaving dead and wounded men behind them, and as they were making their way toward the place called Las Cebadillas, they met two young Creoles, sons of Andalusians, and knifed both of them to death. The whole city was aroused by these murders and rose up in arms, which brought the city to the point of disaster; the Andalusians, Creoles, and Estremadurans who had not been in the house where the fight took place gathered in the Plazuela del Rayo as soon as they heard the news and with their harquebuses and fowling pieces set off in search of the Basques.

The corregidor Pedro de Lodeña, realizing that if the two groups met it would be a disaster for the city, raised his voice in the king's name; many Castilians and Creoles rushed to his side together with most of the clergy and their vicar, who out of Christian charity hastened to put out the flames of discord. This they attempted to do undeterred by their family relationships or friendships among the opposing factions. To observe the divine precept of loving one's enemies is also an imitation of God, Who makes the sun to shine on the just and the unjust. And although the man who loves his enemies performs a godlike act by withholding neither the light or sun of his love nor the effects of his charity, yet it is very difficult to love what is hateful or to return thanks for insults. But the prize is so great and the aim so divine that all is made easy for him who knows how to appreciate it, as did these priests of God: among the men who died by shot and steel many were their own fathers and brothers, yet they did not fail in charity, not even toward the murderers themselves.

At last those venerable priests succeeded in detaining the vengeance seekers in a street, and so successful were their arguments that they persuaded them to go into a house, although six of them, brandishing their weapons threateningly, went off in search of the Basques, who were also armed with harquebuses, fowling pieces, and pistols. They caught up with them behind the parish church of San Lorenzo, and in the exchange of shots between the two groups the six men killed four Basques and the Basques five of them. The one man who escaped fled into a house, climbed to its rooftop, and from that vantage point killed two more of the Basques, the first with a ball through his chest and the second after hastily reloading his weapon. When the remaining Basques, who were running up the street, saw what he was doing, they entered the house; as they were climbing the staircase leading to the roof, the sharpshooter (who was an Estremaduran) was about to effect an escape by dropping down onto the roof of another house; but he was unwilling to lose an opportunity to do evil, and aiming his harquebus, he killed the first man to reach the top of the stairs. The others jumped down from the staircase, two of them injuring themselves in the process, and only then did the Estremaduran leap from rooftop to rooftop until he was lost from view.

By this time it was about six o'clock in the afternoon and raining so hard that it was impossible to move through the streets, but despite this (says Captain Pedro Méndez) the thunder of harquebus fire could be heard in many streets of the city, and women and children shrieking in others. Here men dashed about with swords or harquebuses in their hands; there others half-dragged, half-carried the dead or wounded; the church bells nearly cracked with their appeals to heaven; the clergy went about the city, running and stumbling in their efforts to help the wretched men who were dying, carrying the Most Blessed Sacrament to one spot, the oils of extreme unction to another; and thus Potosí underwent the most disastrous day and night in its history, making Shrove Tuesday of that year, the day on which this fateful tragedy occurred, memorable forever.

On the following day, Ash Wednesday, all the inhabitants of the city were horrified to see and learn the particulars of the many atrocities that had been committed everywhere, for there had been more than fifty deaths, men and women alike, and more than eighty had been wounded; many well-known ladies who were visitors to Potosí had had their faces, ears, and legs slashed, and even the Indians and other members of the servile class had used the occasion to revenge themselves on their enemies, for many of them were also killed and wounded. In the end neither the holy season that was just beginning nor reason nor justice sufficed to assuage the general fury. Only the magnitude of the destruction brought it under control, for there was scarcely a house where some tragedy was not bewailed. The corregidor, grieving to see the city on the verge of ruin, went about most solicitously, attempting to calm the nobles in the hope that the common people would desist from their folly if they saw that their betters had ceased to fight. But he was unable to calm them completely, and so not a day passed without battles, wounds, and deaths.

Peace is the offspring of justice, and the one cannot obtain where the other is not meted out. But Potosí was in such a state that justice could not be administered with safety. The outrage that aroused the most scandal happened on Maundy Thursday of this Lententide when, after darkness had fallen, some Andalusians and Estremadurans who had just taken part in one of the processions and were still dressed in their robes murdered two Basques named Pedro de Alava and Sancho de Allendona as they were performing the stations of the cross, having had nothing to do with the disturbances.

On the night of Holy Saturday a gang of Basques went to the home of Don Fernando Arzáns Dapífer y Toledo, an executive of the guild of quicksilver refiners, where the Andalusian killers had taken refuge because he was a person of great importance. At about eleven o'clock that night Don Francisco Nicolás Arzáns, Don Fernando's son, a young boy who had secretly stolen out of the house through a postern without his parents' knowledge, was returning home; seeing (though from some distance) that the Basques were raising two ladders against the wall of the refinery, he quickly gained entry, and as soon as the postern was opened ordered the servants to see who might be on the rooftop or the thatch. They looked up and saw that more than twenty men were on the rooftops and walls, occupied in letting down ladders; but since the walls were higher on the inside, the ladders did not reach. The servants shouted out the alarm, rousing their master and mistress and the stewards (who were Creoles), along with the Andalusians and Estremadurans who were the target of the intruders' revenge. All armed themselves, and taking aim with harquebuses, fowling pieces, and pistols—and the Indians who worked there (of whom there were more than a hundred), with slings and stones—they all fired on the

Biscayans simultaneously, with such skill that four of them went rolling down the roof and two never rose again. The Basques fired their harquebuses all at once, and luck favored them, for they killed one of the overseers and wounded two servants. Meanwhile the owners of the house opened the doors and the Indians went outside, and from an alley (the same one by which the Biscayans had approached) they loosed a shower of stones that wounded or knocked to the ground so many of the intruders that the rest fled, some of them throwing themselves off the bridge.

Such was the behavior of the wretched inhabitants of Potosí in their insane gang warfare. Many were the fights and brawls engaged in by twos, by fours, and by groups of ten and twenty on a side during the course of that year. And in them (as Captain Pedro Méndez and Don Antonio Acosta tell us) many noblemen of both Spain and the Indies perished.

1612 · The Strange Case of Fulgencio Orozco

IN 1610 there arrived in this imperial city of Potosí a hidalgo named Fulgencio Orozco, of the kingdoms of Spain. He was fifty years of age, strong of body, severe of face, and terrible of glance; he lacked worldly goods and because of that had set out to improve his condition. The charitable inhabitants of Potosí helped him, as they are wont to do, and after having satisfied his most pressing needs they procured employment for him as foreman of an ore refinery so that by his own efforts he could not only earn his bread but also try to save some money. He went to work with great enthusiasm but in vain, for his misfortune was such that he could acquire nothing useful for his worthy purpose. He worked hard at other employments, projects, and attempts to earn money, but in none was he successful; this must have been for his own good, since God's divine majesty invariably bestows on every man that which is appropriate for him.

After a year and eight months of unproductive work, seeing that he had not saved anything, he became so desperate that (behaving as though he were no Christian) he shouted a thousand blasphemies and loosed as many curses; and refusing to accept good advice or to discuss the matter reasonably he went to the royal hospital. It appeared from the dreadful threats he made that he wished quickly to end his life, either because he was suffering from some illness or because of his very rage and despair. When he began to curse Christ our Savior and the holy saints, all who heard him thought that he was merely raving and that his curses were a madness inspired by the devil. Apparently the evil spirit spoke to him in secret, and the sick man seemed to be listening to him, for he screamed out, "What do you want of me? I am doing what you command, I have fulfilled my promise to you, yet you have done nothing of what you promised me."

When those who were present heard him say this, they

supposed him to be possessed and went to call the Very Reverend Padre Maestro Fray Antonio de la Calancha (who at the time was chief preacher in his monastery, that of our father San Agustín, and was much admired in this city for his great virtue and learning) so that he might try to subdue the man. He came at once, accompanied by other priests, and they found the Spaniard still blaspheming and repeating horrible expostulations. The Reverend Padre Maestro Fray Antonio tried to induce him to submit but could not make him cease his ravings either by arguments or by pleas. At that time Padre Juan de Vega, of the Society of Jesus, was commissioner of the Holy Office, and when he learned what was going on and that Padre Maestro Fray Antonio was with the stricken man, he sent orders as to what he must do, begging him for charity's sake not to abandon the sufferer. So great a crowd gathered to see the man they believed to be possessed that the noise prevented him even from hearing the good monk; and the commotion was so great that there was no way to calm him. But at last the officers of the law (who had also come to see what was going on) forced the crowd to be still.

The sick man became very angry with Padre Fray Antonio, telling him not to wear himself out, because he was going neither to confess to Christ nor to cease to abhor Him eternally, and that he was already a lost soul and could see from his bed the bonfire prepared for him in hell. The good father made several adjurations to him, but none could calm him. When a crucifix was placed before him, he turned his face away from it or else merely uttered blasphemies. Once he snatched the crucifix from the friar and threw it at a well-intentioned woman who stood nearby insisting that he be exorcised, and the blow wounded her in the forehead. As he uttered each blasphemy a great howl went up and the faithful who were present outdid themselves in zeal, and neither force nor the persuasion of the law could budge them from the spot. Rather, more and more people crowded to the scene and the confusion increased, with everybody invoking the most holy names of Jesus, Mary, and Joseph. An attempt was made to exorcise him as one possessed of a devil; the priest and Padre Fray Antonio exorcised him twice, and the sick man yelled, "I do not have the devil in my body but here at the head of my bed. He has deceived me with promises and has worn me out with lies and oppression. Leave me alone," he shouted, "for very soon I will go down into hell."

The preaching father Fray Antonio, with an expression of great tenderness in his eyes, sweetness in his words, and great charity in his undertaking, sought to prove to him that it was all an illusion of the devil and a despair that was not hopeless, promising him heaven if he would repent; and when the sick man answered that this was impossible because he had spoken so ill of Jesus Christ and hated Him so much, Padre Antonio explained to him how vast is the mercy of our Redeemer and how merciful is His patience. He also begged him to consider the false deceits of the devil who was afflicting him, and sometimes the sick man implored Padre Fray Antonio to insult the devil, for he said that the devil seemed pained by his presence; but he soon began to repeat his blasphemies.

When the reverend father had worn himself out in trying to persuade him, he asked the Spaniard why he hated his Creator so much and why (being noble and of a family of hidalgos) he was raving like a heretic or a Judaizer. The stricken man, raising his voice so that all the crowd of people who were present heard him, said, "I abhor Christ because He gives riches to worthless men and common folk, while He afflicts me, a gentleman whose obligations are heavy, with poverty; since I came to this Peru to earn money for my daughter's dowry, He has repeatedly taken away everything I have earned, forcing me to witness with my own eyes others earning money where I have lost it. Is there anyone in this city who has worked as hard as I and yet acquired nothing? And when I am witness to the fact that with less effort than my own, in less time and more easily, many have succeeded in laying hands on thousands? But what have I gained except greater poverty and in the end the hell that awaits me? But what offends me most at this moment is that a man who lent me money, trusting in my word, is going to think I am a scoundrel; I would rather go to hell than stay in this world."

Oh, human misfortune; oh, false sense of chivalry! But oh, what abominable laws there are in the world when a man is more reluctant to lose the trust of another than to scorn the Faith and lose respect for God! For we see that humans take advantage of God because He suffers us to do so, and we offend Him because He honors us. Oh, if only our blindness would choose a debt in money rather than a debt to the Creator who nurtured us, redeemed us, and sustains us, to a Father and Lord who waits for us, and to a Judge who grants us all we ask before demanding payment from us!

Padre Fray Antonio asked him how much money he owed and what he would need to provide a dowry for his daughter. The sick man replied furiously, as if this made him even angrier with God, "I am all the more infuriated because it is so little, for since I left Spain I have only asked Him for two thousand pesos to provide my daughter's dowry and eight hundred more that I owe to an honorable friend who lent me that sum; I have half killed myself working ever since I came to this Peru and this Potosí, and everything I have earned with my labor Jesus Christ has spitefully taken away from me, enriching vile men who have no obligations and bringing me to this miserable condition. I tried to have recourse to the devil, and he has promised me thousands in benefits, but he has always lied to me. And now he has cast me aside; and showing me the place that awaits me among the flames of hell he has forced me to curse Christ and despair of God and His mercy, telling me that there is no hope for me and that I am damned."

Having spoken, he turned his face to the wall, and all who heard him were so confused, frightened, and terrified that no one said a word. Padre Fray Antonio forced him to turn his face away from the wall and told him that his little faith and confidence in God had made the Lord angry with him ever since his departure from Spain and that He was punishing him for previous sins in not helping him to obtain a dowry for his daughter; or perhaps what God had done was best for the salvation of both his daughter and himself, that God's secrets were reserved to His infinite knowledge; and not all worldly goods were given to rich men by the Lord, because some were wont to steal them, while others acquired them by trickery and usury, and that many kept monies entrusted to them, either as borrowers or as testamentary executors. And thus wealth was not a gift of God, nor should he have been angry with God because He did not give him such worldly goods; rather, he should be grateful to Him, and when the devil told him that there was no salvation for his soul and that he was damned, he should have taken it as a great lie like the devil's promises and gifts, which the Spaniard admitted were lies; and so that he might see the immense mercy of Jesus Christ, those who were at his bedside would make him a free gift of the twenty-eight hundred pesos, for they wished to please Jesus Christ by saving his soul.

Even before the Reverend Padre Fray Antonio had finished making this offer, each of eight or ten Basques and Asturians who were there as representatives of the Holy Office offered to give the whole sum, most particularly Martín Pérez, who said that this was a work of charity in which all wished to participate; and four or five of them went to the assaying office not only to arrange for that sum but also to find out how much it would cost to send the money to Spain; they also added many pesos to say masses for the man.

While they were gone to obtain the money (which they brought at once, for the office was but one street away), Orozco fell silent and then said, greatly amazed, "Oh, Christian charity, oh, wretched man that I am! Frighten away this demon who is trying to choke me; throw holy water on him, for that will make him go away. Is it possible," he asked, "that I can be pardoned and Jesus Christ will have mercy on me?" So tender were the bystanders' prayers and tears of joy that it seemed a heavenly tumult. The ecclesiastics who were there did as God had inspired them to do.

The silver was brought in sacks, and when Orozco saw it he began to weep, and seizing the crucifix he abjured his heresies and rejected his blasphemies, calling himself a filthy, wretched, ungrateful, mad, barbarous, and faceless excommunicate. The venerable priests told him that because it was part of his confession he must name the man to whom the silver was to be delivered, so that it could be sent to Spain on his behalf; he designated a certain man, and the silver was delivered to him.

This was at six o'clock in the evening, and the struggle had begun at about three-thirty. Early in the evening the Spaniard began to confess, following in every particular the instructions given him by the commissioner of the Holy Office: "Go, deceitful enemy," he said to the devil, "for all that you tell me is a lie. Leave me, for I have returned to my Redeemer."

He performed signal acts of repentance, calling on the Most Holy Virgin to help him. In a few hours he had lost the power of speech, but his lips remained glued to the figure of Christ; and between three and four in the morning he died, leaving everyone greatly consoled and confident of his salvation.

1616 · The Miracle of San Pedro

Among the very miraculous images of Most Holy Mary that are venerated in the sacred temples of Potosí there is the very beautiful Lady of Candlemas in the parish church of San Pedro, the refuge and help not only of the city's inhabitants but also of the Indians and miners when they are in the frightful bowels of the Mountain, where it is particularly efficacious in helping those in peril. The miracles wrought by this beautiful image as well as by other images in the city are innumerable. Among them I shall recount those that have been investigated and are confirmed by sworn and written testimony, in the belief that the material of my history is the same as that contained in many other ancient and modern books that recount what happened in a given place, and that each reader of such books can suit himself as to how much he believes; and in those instances where I do not quote authoritative texts and cite remarkable happenings verified by high ecclesiastical officials or certificates and written testimony, such cases still have the credit that is owed to upright churchmen and to others whose reputation for veracity is sound, and to the strength of continuing traditions.

Now, the greater part of what this history tells with regard to miracles is taken from conventual archives and has been looked into and ascertained by persons both lay and clerical, choosing what seems most truthful and probable. Moreover, it is given to all who have been born into this world to write under the same conditions under which I write, for since the beginning of the world a multitude of different miraculous occurrences have been described and written about; besides which, no one has a greater obligation to the truth of history than to relate things as he knows them, and each reader will then believe them to the degree that common prudence demands; and if a person lacks this prudence he will believe whatever he wishes to believe without the historian's either gaining or losing authority on this account. The historian takes warning that in these grave matters a God-fearing Christian must recount nothing that he holds to be a lie and that the wonderful favors granted to men by God are not fictitious tales or books of poetry. In like vein I must warn my readers that if I call something a miracle or refer to someone as a holy servant of God (for it is incumbent on me to declare the virtues of some good persons that have heightened the greatness of this illustrious city), I employ the name conferred on them by the people of Potosí and not that which can be conferred only by the Supreme Pontiff, whose authority I abjectly adore and at whose feet I fall, subjecting myself in all things to the correction of our Holy Mother Church. If I relate miracles of Christ our Lord, of His holy Mother, or other canonized saints and of some whose lives have been just and admirable (even though their deeds have not been officially attested by the Church), I do so pending investigations by competent authority and the Church's judgment on them. With this word of warning I shall gladly relate the following miracle and others that will appear in the course of this history.

The beautiful image of our Lady of Candlemas, of the parish church of San Pedro in this imperial city, was made by the hands of a man named Juan de Miranda, a marvelous sculptor so favored by this divine Lady that it would appear to have been created by angelic rather than human hands; for it is both a miracle of beauty and an astonishing source of miracles. The first miracle wrought by the image was in the year 1616 in those deep workings (which in this rich Mountain have yielded so many millions in silver) formerly owned by the chief of mines Don Pedro Zores de Ulloa, a wealthy refiner in the Ribera of this city.

Now, it happened that the great cave-in at this mine occurred in April, although it was preceded by another very serious one in the Discovery Lode in which 186 Indians perished. There was no such loss of life in the one we are describing, but after the cave-in 8 Indians and a small boy were trapped, and from outside the owners could find no remedy for the disaster nor any way to rescue them. Several days passed and all hope was lost that they were still alive; thus, many masses were said for their souls. The tolling of the bells ceased after eight days had passed, and there was not even hope of extracting their bodies because the cave-in had taken place so far inside the mine. And although 20 Indians were working night and day to reopen the passage that had collapsed, they could not reach the seam where the Indians had had the misfortune to be trapped; God's will disposed matters in this way so that His marvels would shine all the more.

On a certain Saturday sixteen days after the men had been entombed, while the priest was in his church of San Pedro celebrating the mass of the Mother of God, those who were in the church became very excited over news that the Indians who had been buried had miraculously emerged from the mine. At once the bells began to peal; the whole city rushed to the church, and within less than a quarter of an hour the rescued Indians arrived, surrounded by a great crowd of people. They entered the church and went to the main altar where, beholding the most holy image uncovered, they shed many tender tears and gave thanks to the sovereign Virgin, addressing a flood of affectionate words to her in their own language. Words of endearment in the Indian tongue (especially in this land of Peru) are so sweet and abundant as to be most touching, and when the Indians spoke them, mingled with their tears, it caused all who heard them to weep.

The priest finished saying mass and in the presence of all the people who had come to see them asked the survivors how they had escaped and how they had managed to live for so many days without the sustenance necessary to this human life of ours. They replied, "When we were working in the mine that night, there was a sudden cave-in very close to us, and realizing the great danger we were in as soon as we heard the noise, we called on the most holy Virgin of Candlemas of San Pedro, and that Lady helped us in everything: first, because the cave-in did not catch any of us, and even though it covered the exit, we did not lose our trust in her but continued to hope that the Virgin would lead us out of that place; and, second, because a candle end we had with us did not go out, nor was it used up between that night and this very morning. The third miracle performed by our Lady and Mother was that we had not so much as a bit of bread to eat and were beginning to feel the pangs of hunger, and so we earnestly begged the Virgin for something and suddenly found beside us some loaves that were better than white men's bread, so tasty and nourishing that one mouthful was enough to last us all the days we spent there; even the water was a miracle, for we had not a drop, and when we got thirsty, water began to trickle out of a seam in the rock, and we drank it. And so we stayed there well content, always pleading and hoping that the Mother of God would help us out of that place.

"Pedro and Cristóbal, two of our companions, awoke once from a nap they had taken in order to rest and told us that they had dreamed and the Virgin had told them that on Saturday, at the very hour mass began in San Pedro, we would get out of the mine; but we did not know what day it was or which would be the day of our deliverance. At last we suddenly saw through a small hole that had remained when the mine collapsed a light so bright that it seemed to be the sun; we began to follow it, and the way opened miraculously before us. We followed the light (for it went before us), and in its brightness our light was consumed and went out. That light seemed to precede us, and in a moment we found ourselves outside the mine; but we did not see who had borne that bright light because it was soon lost from sight. But we knew very well that it belonged to the same Lady who had revealed the day of our escape to our companions. As soon as we were outside we asked what day it was, and they told us, Saturday. We were astonished when they asked us how it was that we had not died in the sixteen days that we had been buried, for it seemed to us to be five days at the most that we had been in the mine."

When the Indians had finished recounting the miraculous occurrence (with much weeping), all gave hearty thanks to God and to His most holy Mother; and as an act of thanksgiving the custodians of this sovereign Lady offered a sumptuous novena.

1625 · The Hermit

THE Lord says: "Be ye not like the hypocrites who make show of what they are not and use tricks to make it seem that they fast and, feigning sanctity, secretly give rein to vice." O monstrous tricksters, hermits in appearance and devils in deed! How well was it said by the poet who compared you to the prodigious mountain of Catania[7] in the following lines:

> Hypocritical Mongibello,
> Displaying snow, hiding your fire,
> If mountains can dissemble,
> What cannot humans hide?

And that is what hypocrites are: mountains (like Mongibello) covered with the white snow of feigned virtue; but within, what are they? Let that mountain speak, for it is a mouth of hell according to its acts. The following case is also an illustration of this, an example of how a rancorous breast can hide its terrible and abominable deeds.

In the year 1625 there died in this city of Potosí a man who was well known as a hermit and who for twenty years had wandered through its streets dressed in a sack or tunic, wearing a long beard and carrying a skull in his hand. To all he gave the impression of being a good and penitent man, and such was he held to be and as such was he venerated. Since he always walked with the skull in his hand and sometimes stopped and looked at it very fixedly, all supposed that he was contemplating the fact of death. His usual dwelling place was among some dilapidated buildings behind the parish church of Santiago.

As I have said, his life came to an end, and he died provided with all the sacraments of the Church. After he had expired, those who were with him took up the skull as he had requested, and inside it they found a paper on which was written in his own hand the following message:

I, Don Juan de Toledo, a native of this city of Potosí, son of a gentleman of very good repute in this realm ever since he came from Spain in an official capacity, wish to make known to all who have known me through sight and speech in the city and to all who would like to know about me in the future that I am the man whom all took to be a hermit because they saw me always clothed in a sack, and the more intelligent considered me to be virtuous and weary of the things of this world; and I was generally acclaimed in all this city as a just man.

I am none of these, for I am the most evil of all the wicked men that have ever been in the world. Know that my garb was not the mark of virtue but of damnable malice. And so that you may all know of it I will say that a little more than twenty years ago, because of grievous wrongs inflicted on me by the Spaniard Don Martín de Salazar, in which he defamed all or at least the greater part of the honor God had given me, I stabbed him to death; after he was buried I found a way to enter the church by night, open his tomb, and take out his body, and I opened his breast with a dagger, took out his heart, and ate it (oh, my enormity!). After this I cut off his head and skinned it, and having reburied the body, carried off the skull. I donned a sack such as you have all seen me wear, and taking the skull in my hands I have walked about with it for nearly twenty years, never letting it out of my sight either on my table or in my bed.

Everyone has taken me for a good and penitent man, but I deceived them when I gazed upon the skull, for they supposed that I was contemplating death; but, indeed, it was the opposite, for just as men become beasts through sin, I became the most terrible beast of all, a fierce and cruel crocodile. They say this beast groans and weeps over the skull of some unhappy victim whose flesh it has devoured, not because it has killed him but because it cannot eat him again; thus did I (more bloodthirsty than the very beasts) contemplate the skull of my enemy whose life I had taken, and I was sorrowful to see him dead, for had he risen again a

30 ※ The Hermit

Perforation in pp. 165-180.

ve killed him again as many
ith this cruel rancor for
being able to abandon my
n myself up to this very
of my life; but in this moment
ne and pray God to pardon
pardon for me from that
ayed for those who crucified

ter. Take note, O Christian
rea

1646 · Don Juan in Potosí

THE year 1646 saw the conversion of a great sinner who became celebrated in Potosí and La Plata for his bravery and notable exploits (as Acosta, Pasquier, and Juan Sobrino relate), and I shall briefly recount what those authors say about him. His name was Francisco Verazano (though Pasquier calls him simply Vera), he was a native of this city of Potosí, and his excellent lineage was that which Seville has given to its sons, for his parents were from that city, the capital of Andalusia. Don Juan Pasquier is the writer who describes this young man's escapades most fully, and he complains of his boisterous ways, saying that his bad company ruined his own son, Don Pedro Pasquier, for in their childhood and youth the two were very close friends.

This author begins his account of the deeds of Francisco Verazano by relating that one Shrovetide afternoon when he was only twelve years old he was strolling with the writer's son, Pedro, in the place known as Las Cebadillas and there saw a beautiful half-breed girl to whom he took a great liking. In a word, he fell in love with her; and although the matter was carried on half seriously and half in jest, all three (Verazano, the girl, and Love) being children, it was Love who had the last laugh. In order to win the girl over, Verazano gave her some pieces of eight, realizing (though he was inexperienced in such matters) that the hope of gain is very powerful. But just as she was answering him with a few suggestive words interspersed with laughter (which cost women little and obtain much) four young men of the kind vulgarly known as pimps approached her and angrily and contemptuously asked the lads what they were doing with the girl. Verazano answered by denying that he had done them any wrong in speaking to her.

The force, compulsion, and jealous pangs of love cannot be restrained by any law, nor is any injunction strong enough to mitigate them, for they are easily capable of knocking down and trampling upon honor, respect, and reputation; propriety is overruled and life and property are imperiled. And so, in a jealous rage one of the youths rushed at the half-breed girl and began to beat her with his fists. Verazano was also feeling anger and jealousy, and when he saw this, he reacted with courage more appropriate to a man than a child. He drew his dagger and, stammering out a few words (for his anger prevented him from speaking clearly), attacked the young man who was abusing the girl and succeeded in giving him a severe wound on one hand. The others then turned on the two boys, Francisco and Pedro; they fell back a few steps, and Pedro picked up a stone and threw it with such force that the fellow closest to him received it full on the forehead and fell senseless to the ground. Pedro then seized his downed adversary's sword and joined Verazano, and the lads again rushed at the two remaining pimps. They fled the scene, and Verazano took the half-breed girl away with him to the valley of Mataca. There, a year and a half later, while crossing a river whose swift current runs through that valley, the girl was drowned before his eyes. Just after that he returned to Potosí.

When he was eighteen, our Verazano was married in this city to a merchant's daughter, a beautiful maiden of his own age who brought him a dowry of twenty thousand pesos. They had been married a year when a certain Basque fell in love with her great beauty and, since both Verazano and his wife were so young and inexperienced, succeeded in seducing her; this situation arose from the great friendship her husband felt for this Basque, who was in truth a virtuous person, as was the girl; but many risks lie in frequent communication of men with women (though they be saints) and also of women with men.

In the beginning Verazano had but vaguely suspected some offense to his honor, but with the continuation of the adulterous affair he gradually found his suspicions confirmed. What most enraged him was the shamelessness with which they wrought his dishonor. At length the wronged husband, one night catching his rival in the act of entering his house by means of a ladder in order to visit the adulterous wife, shot him, and the Basque fell dead at his very door. Verazano then entered the house to kill his wife, but she had already escaped. He had to leave the city as a result of this murder, for although he could have claimed that right was on his side, the minions of the law made great efforts to capture him, for the dead man was rich and had powerful relatives. Nor did the arguments for exoneration that Verazano sent from his place of refuge serve to dissuade them.

Finding himself so avidly pursued, Verazano fled to the city of Cuzco, and after he had been there a short time the news reached him that his wife had died. With this, he determined to return to Potosí, where there are so many people that no one notices who comes in or leaves. He stayed in this city for eight months, never daring to show himself in public. After he had been a widower for ten months, he was walking one day in the street of Santo Domingo when he saw at a window an exceedingly beautiful young girl, the daughter of rich and noble parents. Enraptured by her beauty, he sought her ardently. For her part, she looked with favor on Verazano's dashing figure and his persuasiveness, and in the course of his amorous visits her own libidinous desires increased. But it was impossible for this girl to let her lover into the house, for her family was large and her parents watched over her with great vigilance; as a result, her health began to suffer.

Love has always been held to be a very cruel torment, and never is it more unbearable than when it must be concealed; for when the heart tries to hide it, love increases with ever greater fury and traces of its fire break out in blushes on face and mouth, a truth the girl learned by painful experience. With much patience and good sense she tried to resist, pitting her feeble strength against the overpowering and ever increasing affliction; but the only result of her valiant resistance was that she took to her bed, utterly vanquished. Believing that if matters went on like this she would surely die, she solved the problem by making use of a manservant who helped Verazano get into the house. This servant brought Verazano to her bedroom without anyone's knowledge, and the mere sight of him restored her health; and after that he continued his visits until at last the lovers found it impossible to give up seeing each other every night.

Besides her father, this young woman had an uncle and a brother, all of them living together, and to get out of the house she had to pass by the beds of her father and brother, which meant that she ran a great risk that they might see her. At this point the girl was preparing to flee from her home because she knew that she was pregnant. She left her bedroom one night to meet her lover in a corridor that she had chosen as the safest place in the house. Since a person cannot always be lucky in this life, it happened that her father was lying in bed awake, and when he heard a noise he opened the bed curtains and saw that it was his daughter, who, in her shift and with only a shawl around her shoulders, was crossing the room to go to the corridor.

Realizing that her father had heard her, she hastened to Verazano's side and tearfully made known to him the terrible danger they were in. But the youth showed not the slightest sign of alarm; he quickly locked the door of the room from the outside and, taking the girl by the hand, went out to the street; there, noticing that she was barefoot and her terror such that she could not take a single step, he slung her over his shoulder and carried her to the Plaza del Gato.

All this took place in the short time that her father and brother were furiously beating down the locked door. They quickly emerged on the street with weapons and servants, and since there was no lack of bystanders to tell them where the guilty pair had gone, they hastened toward the plaza. Verazano turned around and saw them in angry pursuit. Now his fear was great, for finding himself so suddenly vulnerable and with little chance of escaping from his predicament, he almost decided not to defend himself; but since in moments of difficulty and peril a generous and lofty spirit shows greater strength and courage, Verazano called up those qualities. The danger was so close at hand that he had time only to cover the girl with his cape and hide his dear treasure among the stone benches in the plaza, then turn with rare courage to stop his pursuers with a sword and a shield that he was never without.

When the raging father and the members of his household saw him (though without recognizing him) they attacked savagely, and Verazano took them on. His first act was to flatten one of the servants with a great blow to the head; and then, seeing that his lady's father was pressing him mightily, he boldly rushed at him and gave him a bad wound in the shoulder. At this juncture the watch making its rounds happened on the scene, and Verazano thought it prudent to slip away and hide until he could see what was going to happen next. Everyone departed, the lady's seriously wounded father being carried away, and Verazano went back to look for his love in the place where he had left her. Not finding her there, he returned home sighing unhappily (for, to make matters worse, dawn was approaching) in the belief that her father had taken her away, and swearing to kill him for it.

Just after daybreak a note was brought to Verazano, sent by the girl from a house where she was staying; it said that the night before, while her father and his household were fighting with Don Francisco, she had crept to the gate of the Jesuit cemetery, where she remained, naked and with only the cape covering her body, until dawn. Then, seeing someone open the door of the nearest house, she went inside and wrote from there to beg him to see her and to make the best arrangements that he could. He was much cheered by this news and went to see her, taking her some clothes. They discussed what they might do and decided to flee without delay, and two days later did so, departing for Cuzco in disguise. On the way (as the first fruits of their relationship) she gave birth to a beautiful baby girl.

After having lived in that city for two years, the beautiful lady came to recognize what the state of her soul must be and made up her mind to enter one of the convents in Cuzco as a nun. In effecting this plan she turned into good fortune the evils that had cost her so dearly. Nor did Verazano stand in the way of so praiseworthy a desire, and so before she entered the convent he gave her the greater part of the required dowry, the rest being contributed by her women friends in this city, because her father, who had made his will immediately after being seriously wounded, had completely disinherited her.

Verazano then took the habit also, completed the necessary studies, and sought ordination, although he did not receive it because the deaths he had caused made him ineligible. He returned to this city in clerical garb, where the devil again got him into trouble through the lust to which he was always too much given, following the example of brute creation and indulging excessively in this vice. Any man with such a failing is incapable of understanding the spiritual gifts of the Lord; the man who shuns the reason of a Christian is very like a brute in his actions: he cannot quite persuade himself that

Don Juan in Potosí

there are other riches greater by far than those that glitter in the sun and are purified in the flame, nor that there are other true delights, other sweet rewards and bounties than those that feed his belly and ruin health and life.

Having returned to Potosí, Verazano took up with a lady who was very notorious in the city, and who was being kept by a very rich man. This woman gave him access to her house and surrendered herself to him. He stayed in the house for several days, until the rich man learned what she was up to. Verazano and the woman were sleeping one night when four men entered the house from the roof, together with her rich man and two manservants, so that altogether there were seven of them. As soon as they entered, three were sent to watch the doors to the hallway and the street, in case Verazano had the keys and could open them, thus to make his escape. The two servants were given orders to kill him if he tried to escape through the window, and the former lover, with another man, began to break in the doors of the bedroom.

On hearing the noise and suspecting what it must be, our Verazano quickly dressed and armed himself; he ordered the lady to dress and hold fast to his sash in order to follow closely every movement that he made, so that he could simultaneously defend himself and attack his enemies till they reached the doors, where one or the other could open them and so escape with both their lives. The lady got dressed and, once she had obeyed his orders, Verazano opened the doors of the bedroom before the others had time to break them down. He stepped out into the courtyard, attacking those who were at the doors like a lion, dropping them with terrible slashes of his sword. The servants who were nearby also attacked him, and he defended himself from them all and wounded and downed them in turn. In this way he reached the entrance hall of the house, where those who were guarding the street door defended themselves with more fear than courage, so that after Don Francisco had cut them up somewhat they fell back, and Verazano, opening the doors, emerged from them with his lady.

After the couple had spent several days skulking in uninhabited parts of the city, fleeing from those who had been wounded in the fray but who had now recovered and were searching for them, Don Francisco was in the Campo de San

Clemente with the lady one day when she suddenly fell dead at his side. The man was so shocked and impressed by this event, which brought much of the past to his mind, that he determined to impose penance on himself; and so he withdrew from the world and entered the Order of San Francisco in the monastery of Chuquisaca. Don Juan Pasquier says with certainty that he had been ordained a priest when he was in the city of Cuzco and that he was a priest at the time of this affair; but Bartolomé de Dueñas confirms what I stated above, that he had not been ordained owing to his bad conscience. Having assumed the habit of that order, he lived very quietly as a lay brother for some time, until obedience to his superiors brought him to this city to collect funds. He reached Potosí at Lententide, 1646, and the devil again snatched him from his tranquility and did not let go until Don Francisco was utterly lost.

Easter Sunday was approaching, and one day, tempted by our constant adversary, he told another monk who was a friend of his (and a man as full of virtue as he was of learning) that on the night of Holy Saturday, Easter Eve, he was going to give the other the pleasure of going abroad through the streets in his company, and that for the purpose he would supply him with lay clothing. The worthy religious took it as a joke and mere talk, and thus accepted in that vein. When the day and the night had finally arrived, Verazano reminded the monk that it was the night they were to go out together as he had arranged. His companion, taken aback, asked him if he had truly suggested such an abominable thing; Don Francisco's answer was that since they had agreed upon it he had everything arranged; and so strongly did he urge him that in the end the other monk consented to dress as a layman and the two left the monastery together, the learned companion going rather with the purpose of protecting the other from harm than to imitate his wicked behavior.

Grave temptations and dangers that assume the appearance of laudable zeal often assail those who dedicate themselves to the things of the spirit. May God favor us in all our doings, for we have a common enemy who is most subtle in deceiving us and putting us on the road to our perdition. Fray Francisco Verazano took his poor companion to a certain very dangerous house, belonging indeed to a madam whose beauty and unchastity attracted the solicitations and accommodated the lusts of many men. The two religious entered, therefore, in lay clothing and with swords and shields, and had no sooner sat down than four men came in. Seeing them there, the four drew their swords and in a matter of moments had killed the good religious, Fray Francisco's companion, who had never before been in such a situation, for (as Pasquier says) he had been raised in the monastery since childhood.

Witnessing this bizarre turn of events, Fray Francisco fell on the four laymen ferociously and after a short struggle killed them all; and then with a dagger he cut off the head of the dead monk and took it with him so that the body would not be recognized. He ordered the madam to leave the city and never show her face in Potosí again, and she obeyed him. Fray Francisco went to his monastery and, in utter secrecy, told the whole story to the prelate and gave him the head of his fellow monk. The prelate, a prudent man, made no other move for the time being except to send Fray Francisco to his cell.

On the following day the whole strange happening became news in the city because officers of the law had found five dead men in the house; four of them could easily be recognized, but not the one whose head was missing. The investigations that followed were exceptionally thorough but all in vain, because there was not a shred of evidence. The father guardian of the monastery went to the corregidor and requested the dead man's body, saying that since no one knew who he was, he wished to perform an act of charity by burying it in his church. The corregidor gave him the body, and it was carried to San Francisco and buried, and the same was secretly done with the head. Fray Francisco tried to do penance for his faults by leading a new life, to the great consolation of his spirit; for no one can deny to my satisfaction how great is the pleasure, joy, and delight felt by the soul when it enjoys a good conscience. Verazano lived for only a few months more and then departed this life with many proofs of repentance.

1647 · Of Love and Partisanship

Doña Mariana de Osorio, a native of this city, a most virtuous maiden who was envied for her beauty, famed for her chastity, and applauded for her admirable intelligence, had reached the age of eighteen. Among the many suitors for her hand in holy matrimony were Don Jerónimo de Atienza, a knight of the Order of Calatrava and a native of Potosí, and Don Sebastián de Arzúa, a Basque. The girl's parents (who were Andalusians) had first arranged their daughter's marriage to Don Jerónimo, but because of some unfavorable allegations made against him by members of the Basque nation the negotiations were broken off and arrangements were made for her to marry Don Sebastián de Arzúa, to the great satisfaction of himself and all his nation.

The Creoles were especially nettled by this slight and sought revenge, but Don Jerónimo dissuaded them and decided upon another plan, which was to secretly win the love of the beautiful girl. He succeeded in this design with the aid of the foremen of her father's ore refinery, for he was a refiner of mercury and had entrusted the management of his affairs to Creoles. The maiden was sensible and more than commonly intelligent (most women being by nature subject to the trivialities of flirtation and concerned only with looking beautiful, sating their pleasure, living in comfort, and having as much money as possible); this maiden preferred to live simply, enjoy less comfort, not to overvalue her beauty, and to spend her life with domestic tasks, helping the man who would become her husband rather than wasting day and night in sweet words.

She well knew that Don Sebastián would give her all she could want and more, for he was a very wealthy gentleman, and she was not unaware that she would experience privations as the wife of Don Jerónimo, for he had no money to waste on vanities. But considering the whole matter with her natural intelligence she accepted Don Jerónimo; and in the course of their chaste meetings they agreed that at the moment when the blessing was given during the ceremony she would offer him her hand in marriage and that his friends (for he had many) would be at hand to prevent any outbreak of violence.

There came a feast day in the month of April, and all the nobles of his nation went to the principal church to accompany Don Sebastián, well armed for anything that might occur. Don Jerónimo was already in the church, in disguise, and his friends were deployed in a number of houses in the plaza, in secret as the occasion demanded. When Don Sebastián and the beautiful Mariana had arrived, the vicar began the traditional ceremonies, saying, "Señora Doña Mariana de Osorio, do you take Don Sebastián de Arzúa for your lawful husband?" And the maiden answered, "I do not wish Don Sebastián, but Don Jerónimo de Atienza" (who had stepped in beside her) "for my lawful husband, and to him I freely give this hand," and Don Jerónimo reached out his hand and took that of the one who was now his wife.

All the witnesses of this event were frozen with astonishment while the vicar, continuing the ceremony, pronounced the benediction. Who could possibly describe the rage and fury of the Biscayans and the effect on Don Sebastián? It was so terrible and he was so blinded by anger that he was almost ready to end his life, for he thought it infamy to go on living without the lady of his heart; he resolved upon the last, worst, and most desperate course that his unhappiness (or his recklessness and folly) could possibly have dictated. Moreover, the men of his nation, disregarding the sacred place in which they were, spoke very insultingly to the Creoles, and one of them went up to the bride and said that she was a slut and that she was marrying her lover; he went even further than this and tried to cut her face. But at this point Don Jerónimo, her husband, attacked the Biscayan (who was a servant of Don Juan Fernández de Oquendo) and, seizing him by the collar, dragged him to a place outside the cemetery and opened a great wound in his head by knocking it against a post.

At this time Potosí was in danger of total disaster, for there was great hatred on both sides. Creoles and Basques attacked each other like cruel barbarians; the plaza was filled with shouts and cries; large numbers of men rushed to the defense of their friends; and neither the officers of the law nor the many priests who were present could stop the savagery. Everywhere there were cries of "Kill them, kill them," which was precisely what happened, for the Creoles (since they were more numerous) killed four of their adversaries, and more than thirty men were wounded on one side and the other; and the carnage would have been still worse had not the priests intervened at the risk of physical injury. It was this encounter that ever after made the Peruvian nation so hated by the Basques; and for many years the almost daily shedding of blood led to many other tragedies.

However, Don Jerónimo and Doña Mariana were indeed married, though against the wishes of her parents. She received a dowry of eighty thousand pesos in addition to two ore refineries that, with their Indians and mines, were worth much more than that sum. Don Sebastián de Arzúa, filled with grief and despair after having seen Doña Mariana married to his rival, returned to his home. Two days later a certain woman with whom he had been carnally connected for some time came to see him by night and was foolish enough to taunt him about the affair; this caused him to become still more enraged, and he attacked her, strangling her with a scarf; then he had her body carried secretly to her home. Three days later this Biscayan was found dead in his bed in the morning, with clear indications that he had taken a terrible poison, a circumstance that gave rise to a great deal of scandal.

1648, 1649 · The Downfall of Don Francisco Chocata

In 1648 there lived in this city one Don Francisco Chocata Sapa, an Indian by race and a native of Potosí who, once having been a servant to Don Gaspar Martín de Vargas, secretary of its illustrious cabildo,[8] had become quite Europeanized; and in addition to having considerable natural gifts he behaved with great arrogance. This Indian was rich, for a mine that another Indian had disclosed to him had earned him more than 100,000 pesos in a very short time; as a result he struck up a friendship with the new corregidor, Don Juan Velarde, whom he honored with frequent spendid banquets and costly gifts. A son was born to this Indian, and he asked the corregidor to stand as godfather. Because of this relationship Don Francisco was always at the side of his friend the corregidor. He dressed richly in clothing of Spanish style and always wore a large and costly gold chain that fell upon his shoulders and breast. The rich respected him and the poor feared him.

Since it is very true that no one is ever satisfied with his lot (for even though that lot be good he always wishes it to be better) and greed and ambition are very old in the world and among all conditions of men, Don Francisco Chocata Sapa, not content with what he had, wished to obtain power in addition to his wealth. But he did not succeed, and his persistence brought about his ruin. Now, it happened that Don Pedro Cusipáucar, governor of the Indians,[9] had died suddenly and intestate. The office being a hereditary one, the governorship passed directly to his natural son, Don Juan Cusipáucar, for his legitimate sons were dead. Don Francisco Chocata was related (though distantly) to the dead man's wife, and for this reason alone he desired the office. He made every possible effort to obtain it, but his solicitations were fruitless despite the considerable aid he received from his friend the corregidor, for since there was a lawful heir his claim was not valid.

Chocata, seeing that it was impossible to obtain the office legally, tried to acquire it by guile. Instructed by the devil and his own greed, he called upon a Spaniard to whom he confided his intention and, promising him a sum of money, told him to seek out two other accomplices and with them to kill Don Juan Cusipáucar. The Spanish assassin (whose name it would not be proper to reveal, since his descendants live in magnificence today) accepted for the sake of the money, which was five hundred pesos for each man.

Now, premeditated murder is forbidden by all three divine laws, natural, written, and evangelical. Life itself, clearly, is the most to be desired of all things that exist among the gifts of Nature, on which Christ our Savior established the demonstration of love displayed by him who dies for another that is his friend when He said, "Greater love hath no man than this, that a man lay down his life for his friends." The man who kills another despoils and steals away from that man this gift; and since God is the master of life and death, the murderer, by killing one who was made in His image and likeness, usurps and destroys that which comes from God.

This sin was committed by the Spaniard who, having in his greed found others to help him, spent a whole day with his companions searching for Don Juan Cusipáucar; as they could not find him, they waited until nightfall so that when he went home to bed they could more easily kill him. It was about eleven o'clock at night on Sunday, February 20, 1649, and the assassins were lying in wait at the bridge of San Sebastián, just where he had to pass by, when the noble Indian arrived all unsuspecting. They set upon him barbarously, as though he were some bloodthirsty enemy, and administering twenty-seven wounds they thought him dead and dragged him as if he were a corpse and threw him off the bridge into the river. Then they went gleefully to their homes, fearing neither God nor human justice.

When the good Indian governor, whom God kept alive though bleeding copiously from many wounds, had come to himself a little, he managed to crawl out of the water where he might well have drowned had not God disposed that he fall with his feet in the water and his head out of it. Then, in continuation of the divine favor watching over the innocence of that good Indian, God disposed that some neighbors who had heard the noise come to his rescue and mercifully bear him off to their house. The Indian had clearly seen and recognized his assailants, and so he immediately sent for General Velarde. As soon as he learned of the affair, rather than being stunned into inaction, the general set off as swiftly as a flash of lightning in search of the assailants. He seized them and, clapping them into prison (except for one who slipped away), put them to judicial torture, whereupon they confessed the whole matter, consistently laying the blame on his close friend Chocata.

Chocata had already been informed of what was happening, and so in that very short space of time he hid a great deal of money, wrought silver, gold, and jewels. But by the divine will he failed to conceal a writing desk containing some letters from the viceroy in response to others written to him by Chocata informing him of General Velarde's dishonest actions and how he was in a sense an accomplice in the minting of the debased coins that were being issued and that this was the reason why he did not punish the guilty officials.[10] The general went to arrest his friend Chocata and seize his property (up to this point giving friendship its due). But when he opened the writing desk expecting to see many jewels there, he found instead those letters that were so damaging to his reputation. Furiously angry with the Indian, he went to the prison to lodge a complaint against him. Subsequently refusing to grant either acquittal or appeal, he had the case brought up promptly and thereupon sentenced Chocata to die on the scaffold along with the two Spaniards.

This Indian's treachery was particularly evil, for it was perpetrated against his friend and benefactor and a respected judge, a man who had been criticized throughout the city for maintaining a friendship with him. But what could be expected from a perverse, ill-intentioned, arrogant, and ambitious man? We will have to agree that ungrateful men eventually despise their friends, their parents, their country, and God himself, and that ingratitude is commonly associated with effrontery, the greatest of all infamies. It seems that even the beasts are ashamed to be ungrateful and are inclined to gratitude, and that many men (like this Indian) are wholly lacking in it; but he received his just deserts, and the corregidor combined justice with revenge.

The whole city interceded to beg that Chocata's life be spared, but all attempts to soften the corregidor's sentence failed. The Indian's Spanish friends, seeing that there was no hope for him, secretly arranged to have the ropes frayed so that they would break and the Indian would fall before he choked to death; then more than 150 priests and monks who were privy to the plan would take him and carry him to the principal church. On a certain Tuesday, according to the sentence, Chocata and the two Spaniards were taken to the place of execution, the Indian still hoping that he was not to die. They ascended the steps of the scaffold, and the executioner hanged Chocata. While all believed that the rope would break and he would fall alive and be rescued, by divine intervention that did not occur, for the ropes had been accidentally switched.

The Indian hung there dead, and the matter became even more lamentable because it was obvious that he had not prepared himself for death as he should have done, owing to the hope he had been given. But when God is angered, there is no refuge on earth from the bolts of heaven unless it be the just man's virtues and the mercy of God, which commonly quenches the fire of His justice. They hanged one of the Spaniards, and he too died. They did the same with the other, but the weakness of the rope that by luck had fallen to him became apparent: he fell to the ground unharmed, and immediately the priests rushed forward shouting, "This one belongs to the Church!" They carried him in their arms to the mother church despite the thousand armed men who came forward to assist the royal justice; behind closed doors they hid him in the baptistry in a sedan chair.

General Velarde lived in the plaza (he was the first to inhabit the buildings where the corregidors have their residence today), and as soon as he looked from his balcony and saw so great a commotion he came down filled with rage and went straight to the church, followed by a crowd of men. He caused the doors to be opened, and they went inside; when after an unsuccessful search they were about to leave, a little boy told them where he was. (Oh, would that he had not done so, for his descendants suffer that dishonor to this very day!) General Velarde took the Spaniard from the church (for he had already been divested of the habit of the Order of

Mercy),[11] and as he dragged him toward the gallows the cries and confusion among both priests and laymen, the knife thrusts and wounds, were remarkable to behold, for some wished to return him to the church and others to carry him off to the scaffold.

At last the corregidor, seeing the great effort the priests were making to defend him, ordered his men to stab the Spaniard to death. This they did by wounding him in the heart, and at the height of the conflict they tied one end of the rope around his neck, threw the other end over the crossbeam of the gallows, and pulled on it, and all saw him hanging there. The corregidor ordered Chocata's body to be quartered and his head placed on the bridge where the crime had been committed at his instigation. There it remained for many years.

1653 · The Spook

There lived in this city of Potosí a Negro named Antonio Bran de Brizuela, a native of the town and the slave of Don Pedro Brizuela, a rich ore refiner of the Ribera. This Negro disturbed the peace of the whole town with his evil-doing and depredations. He was called "the Spook" [El Duende], for when the townspeople least expected it he would enter their houses and cause great losses. He was reckless to the last degree, fighting equally well on foot and on horseback, and for this reason was feared by the Spaniards. The unfortunate womenfolk of the town dared not stir out of their houses from seven o'clock in the evening onwards, for he had raped many on the streets.

One day when President Nestares was standing on his balcony in the public square he saw that this Negro, the Spook, was beating a poor Peruvian, a stranger to the city; he became very angry, shouting that the Negro must be killed and that he commanded it in His Majesty's name. At once more than two hundred men of various nations appeared in the plaza with swords drawn to attack him.[12] But the Negro (whom everyone believed to be an agent of Satan) defended himself against all those Spaniards with a huge sword he carried, stabbing at all he could reach and moving back step by step until he gained sanctuary in the church of the Society of Jesus. The chief magistrate as well as lesser magistrates had already issued proclamations against his life, for one night he had attacked them all and put them to flight.

At last, when God the supreme judge was weary and no longer willing to suffer the abominations of this sinner, He caused the Negro to pay for them with his life by falling into the hands of the law. And so it happened that one night he plotted with a maidservant for her to hide him under her mistress's bed without the knowledge of anyone so that when all were asleep he might kill that noble lady and steal everything that was in the house.

By divine intervention while the lady was lying in bed and

before she had fallen asleep, she heard a noise under the bed; suspecting some evil (but under the pretext of feeling unwell), she got up in her nightgown, went out to the patio, and swiftly and secretly called for the aid of some neighbors; for though this lady was married her husband was away from the city on that occasion. Several men went in and, not knowing who was there, surrounded the bed with weapons in their hands, whereupon the Spook attacked them like a fearsome wild beast, with dagger in hand, threatening death to the white men. They struck at him again and again and at last captured him; tying him hand and foot, they notified the chief magistrate, Don Luis Pimentel, who came posthaste and took him to jail. After providing him with a confessor the chief magistrate had him garroted. At daybreak his body appeared hanging from the balcony of the cabildo, to the considerable satisfaction of the whole city.

1653 · The Adventures of the Warrior Maidens

Don Juan Pasquier—in his *History of Potosí*, which he wrote with such elegance of style—gives an eyewitness account of the exploits of two noble Peruvian maidens of this city. In this chapter I will follow his account, along with those of three venerable old men who are still alive today and who knew those ladies by both sight and speech. This is the manner in which it all happened.

In this imperial city of Potosí there lived Captain Antonio de Souza, a noble Portuguese, and his wife, Doña Leonor de Meneses, a native of this city; their children were Don Juan, the elder, and Doña Eustaquia, a singularly beautiful little girl. Their home was near Munaypata; and in the same quarter of the town lived Don Pedro Urinza, an Andalusian gentleman, and his wife, Doña Plácida Lezama; they had a daughter, Doña Ana, who was their only child and an unusually beautiful little girl. Doña Plácida died when the child was very small, and within the space of two years her father, Don Pedro, died also, leaving the child in the care of Don Antonio de Souza so that she might be reared with Doña Eustaquia, who at the time was also four years old. As soon as Don Juan de Souza, Eustaquia's elder brother, reached a sufficient age, his father had him taught to handle and make use of arms, both steel and fire, for he had all sorts of such weapons in his home. Eustaquia and Ana greatly enjoyed watching that sport and were even sorry they were not men so as to be able to use them.

Those who do not think that it is easy for a woman to succeed in whatever she attempts are mistaken, for many women have surpassed men in valor, in the use of arms, and in knowledge. In the use of arms there have been three Corinnes, two Aspasias, a Hortensia, a Sappho, a Zenobia, a Cornelia, and a Praxilla, not to mention others such as Arete, Proba, Eudocia, Istrina, and Cassandra; and in valor a Pantasilea, a Zenobia, an Artemisia, a Cleopatra, and the Castilian queen Isabella the

The Warrior Maidens

Catholic, heroic among famous women and a singular miracle of strength and prudence in the world. No one need be astonished to see such excellence in women, for neither are they of a different nature from men nor are their souls less perfect (insofar as essential perfection is concerned). With such examples of women before me I think it is no less than fitting to state that those whose story I tell in this chapter had the same qualities, and I am sure that no one will be surprised by the events I shall recount concerning them.

The uncertainty and misery of this life are always great and the proof of this is always with us; thus, it happened that just as Don Antonio de Souza had relied upon a particular means to advance his son in life the same means brought about his greatest grief. For it happened that one day when Don Juan de Souza was fencing with a fencing-master and sweating from his exertions, he asked for a pitcher of water; and having drunk it, within twenty-four hours he was dead, to the great sorrow of his parents; he was but fifteen years old. At this time the two maidens, Eustaquia and Ana, were in their thirteenth year and were more inclined toward the exercise of arms (because they had seen Don Juan use them) than to the needlework proper to their sex; whenever their parents (as Doña Ana also called Don Antonio and Doña Plácida, because they had reared her) were away from home, the two girls amused themselves in learning to shoot firearms and make use of other weapons.

Not much more than fifteen months after Don Juan's death his mother followed him, and Eustaquia and Ana were left alone with Don Antonio. They had been reared with such circumspection and kept so closely within doors that scarcely anyone knew of their existence, not only in the town at large but even in the quarter where they lived. There was an oratory in their house where they had heard mass, and they had gone to church only ten times a year; and their father continued to rear them in the same way. Don Antonio kept a young man-servant, and it was he who told them all about the fiestas, theatrical performances, bullfights, balls, and other entertainments that took place in the city, and all this increased their desire to get out of their house to see such things.

Still leading this quiet kind of life, they came to the year 1653 (which was also the fourteenth year of their age), and realizing that they were likely to be shut in for a long time they longed merely to see the streets of their native city; for this purpose they determined to go out one night in men's clothing to take a turn about the town and come back home; they also confided in a faithful Negro serving-woman. One night after supper they went to their bedroom when their father was already asleep and soon armed themselves and dressed in garments quite different from those they usually wore. Over their fine linen undergarments they put on doublets, and over these, mail shirts of the finest workmanship, under which they wore short tunics of fine scarlet brocade reaching to their knees, hose of the same color, and white shoes; over the mail shirts they placed jackets of Castilian buckskin, and over these, short skirts of scarlet cloth; then they donned white beaver hats, scarlet capes adorned with gold stitchery, swords, stout bucklers, and a pistol for each.

I have mentioned these trifles in order not to omit everything that Don Juan Pasquier recounts in connection with this feminine exploit, for he gives a great many small details, and I will try to include some of them. The maidens went out into the street dressed in this elegant and dashing clothing, leaving their father asleep; they ordered the Negress to await them at the door, promising her that they would return very shortly, even as she begged them not to get lost. When they had walked the length of a street or two, wishing to reach a corner where a food shop was still open, they met a young man who was going to such a place. He stopped to admire the dashing appearance and elegance of those two persons, and when the girls saw that he was so close to them, they asked him where he was going and if he had much to do. He replied that his parents had sent him to buy bread and that whatever they commanded him he would do with a good will. They told him that they wished to have him accompany them, for being strangers to the town, they did not know the streets and wanted to stroll about.

"Señores," said the youth, "I also am a stranger and have not been long in this city. But I know enough to tell you that the town is dangerous; for if by day men are killed like dogs in the street, by night it is even more common, and that is why the magistrates go on patrol at night, and it may be we will meet such a patrol. But I will accompany you if you like, for your elegance of person and the fact that you are armed for any encounter inclines me to follow you; and indeed all that I see in your persons is new and strange to me, especially the fact that your faces are covered. Be so good as to tell me who you are, and in return I will tell you that I live on this street, that my family is not lacking in nobility, and that my parents were Andalusian nobles in Spain. They died and left me in Mexico —for I am from that realm—and from thence I came to Potosí, this fount of all riches, refuge of strangers, hospice of the poor, homeland of the brave, requital of the ill-treated, and free exchange of firm friendships. Here in Potosí I live with Juan Bravo, who has received me into his house as if I were his own son."

The girls responded to the young man's speech with courteous words and told him that they would satisfy his curiosity as they walked along. When he heard this offer the lad (whose name was Diego Melgarejo) told them to wait for him, that he would leave at home the things he was carrying and return immediately. They agreed to this, and the young man shortly returned, wrapped in a cape and with a dagger at his side. They thanked him for coming back so quickly, and young Diego again implored them to tell him who they were. Because they were grateful to the youth they decided to lay the truth before him, and so they told him their names, true sex, and of their fancy to dress as men. Our youth was considerably disturbed by this but by no means unwilling to have such company, for when they uncovered their beautiful faces, their agreeable appearance left him in no doubt that both were equally attractive, especially when he heard them speak with the sweetest of voices and became convinced of their liveliness of mind. In addition to this, their weapons, their rich clothing, their behavior, their sweet smell, and their grace and elegance made him throw caution to the winds.

He led them down several principal streets without incident, but on their way back they met in the Plaza de San Lorenzo the servants and Negro slaves of the chief magistrate, Pimentel, who, with the excuse of going out on patrol, often set forth by night to perform many acts of effrontery, setting upon workmen or Indians to snatch or steal their money. As soon as these men saw the maidens, realizing how valuable were their clothes and swords, they surrounded them, with the aim of stealing all their possessions. But the valiant Eustaquia, seeing their boldness, said to the one who, as ringleader of the gang, had come closest, "Stand fast, for if you come closer I will fire this pistol whether you like it or not," and showed them her fierce weapon. The man raised his sword arm to strike her, and Eustaquia fired her deadly pistol; the bullet struck him in the chest and he fell senseless to the ground. Not to be outdone, her friend Doña Ana also fired her pistol, though to no effect, because the others turned and fled, leaving their comrade dead.

Then the brave girls laid hands on their swords and tried to follow them, as they surely would have done had not Diego, their youthful guide, told them that they had better leave the spot, for on hearing the cries of the other servants, not only the neighbors but also the officers of the law would rush to the scene. And so they had to follow the young man, retreating as though on wings. Eustaquia and Ana returned home, found the slave waiting for them at the door, and went in without their father's hearing them; Diego Melgarejo did the same, exceedingly frightened as he himself later recounted.

The next day the whole town was in an uproar over the efforts made by President Nestares and the chief magistrate, Pimentel, to discover who had killed the servant; but they could not find the culprit. A few days later those prankish maidens determined to make another sally and therefore sent the woman slave (who knew the whole story) to the house of young Melgarejo, the youth who had guided them on the previous night, telling him that on San Juan's Eve he must accompany them a second time. But the young man declined, fearing another accident like the previous one. However, since they wrote him a note ridiculing him as a woman and a coward, he was forced to reply that he would go with them; but he begged them repeatedly to desist from such dangerous and childish tricks, for sooner or later some irremediable evil might occur. But how can one's own choice be correct and how can one decide important matters without accepting advice? Humans making decisions are fallible; nor are things any more certain to turn out well if left to chance. Repentance is a fine thing, but when it is deferred so long through the refusal of good counsel that it and the discovery of error strike home to the spirit simultaneously, the greater is the grief, for then guilt is more deeply felt and the evil that has been done cannot be mended. This was the experience of those two maidens, because they had been guided solely by their own inclinations and would listen to the advice of no one.

When the Eve of San Juan arrived, Melgarejo was awaiting them at the door of their house and praying to God that they might never come out, so frightened was he—although better prepared than on the previous night, for he carried two pocket pistols in the belief that valor resided in them. It was a little past ten o'clock when Ana and Eustaquia appeared, wearing different clothing than before but very well armed; instead of swords they carried Damascus cutlasses and heavy shields, and they wore black hats, scarlet capes embroidered in silver, white hose, black shoes, short tunics of silver cloth (which barely covered their knees), and doublets of blue brocade, and under these, jackets and mail shirts. Thus attired they appeared before their guide, to whom they handed a sweet-sounding guitar so that he might sing with them in one or another of the streets, as was the custom in that part of the country.

Having passed through several streets, they reached the Plaza del Gato and sat down on the benches that were there (as if in a room of their own house); the charming Eustaquia tuned her instrument and sweetly sang songs of her own choosing, attracting with her delicate voice and skill a great many people who were strolling in the town until she thought it prudent to stop the music. Everyone wished to see the faces of the singers, expressing amazement at the sweet voices of those whom they supposed to be men (but the girls concealed their sex very well); and the crowd never ceased to praise their sweetness and skill, desiring them to play and sing again. But they departed and by strolling through other streets reached the Calle de la Pelota, which in those days was so famous.

They sat down in a doorway underneath a balcony to rest and, again taking up the instrument, were engaged in tuning its strings when four young men appeared at the corner. Seeing the persons who were sitting in the doorway, they approached and asked, "Who goes there?" Eustaquia answered, "Two gentlemen." The reply was: "Whoever you are, you have done very ill in coming to these doors, for there are young girls living in the house and you sully their reputations by hanging around because you are young, and unknown in the town." To this Eustaquia replied, "Indeed, it seems that you are the wardens of this house, for if not, you would not be so meddlesome; but we do you no offense, not even in thought, for we do not know whose house it is or who you are; and we have sat down here only to rest and to entertain ourselves with this instrument." The four responded (as Diego Melgarejo, who was present during all this, later described it) with some unintelligible words and then angrily told them, "Get away from here; you are young rascals and know how to cover your evil desires with excuses." To this Eustaquia and Ana replied, "Now we have hit upon the motive for your suspicions, and we tell you again that we have offended you in nothing; and if our words do not give you sufficient satisfaction, our weapons and our actions will make that satisfaction complete." On hearing this, the men again said to them, "Get away from here, scoundrels, before we take you on." The spirited girls replied, "Now we will see if your deeds are as good as your words," and so saying, Eustaquia handed the guitar to Diego, who already foresaw disaster.

 A valiant spirit is indeed a great thing: if it attacks first, the victory is won, for initiative and determination are held to be half the battle in acts of courage and repute; but cowardice and hesitation are not well regarded in any sort of person, nor do they do him any good. The young man took the instrument and retired some distance away without using his pistols; but Doña Ana, drawing hers, said, "Stop there, you roughnecks, or you will feel the force of this thunderbolt." Greatly angered, the four men crowded around her to grab the pistol, but she fired; and when the ball left the gun (since at that very moment two of the men had quickly stepped aside) it passed between them and lodged in the doors, making a great deal of noise. Doña Eustaquia also tried to cock her pistol and indeed succeeded in doing so, but it did not fire, and as the shield in her hands prevented her from lifting the hammer again, she stuck the pistol in her belt and unsheathed her cutlass (as Doña Ana had already done); they fiercely attacked the four men, who responded with their own swords and shields.

 They set upon each other from every direction, making such a din with their weapons that it seemed a hundred men were fighting; sparks of fire leaped from their swords, the fierce blows they were exchanging rang, and the voices of the men they were fighting resounded in the street. In the thick of the encounter one of the four said to Doña Ana, "Ah, villain, you have wounded me," and rushing at her he administered a brutal thrust with such force that it pierced her shield and wounded her in the chest, tearing through her clothing, jacket, and mail shirt, and wounding her just under the left breast; the girl fell to the ground. When the valiant Eustaquia saw this, she leaped to place herself in front of her sister and, brandishing her cutlass in all directions and very conscious of the danger they were in, nudged Doña Ana with her feet, saying to her in great anguish, "Get up, sister, for our honor is at stake." The injured girl rose to her feet like a lioness and, recognizing the man who had wounded her, said, "Monster, now I will revenge myself for that wound you have given me"; rushing at him fiercely she gave him such a mighty blow with her cutlass that she broke his shield and wounded him in the hand. He, not daring to wait for another, again joined his three companions as Doña Ana rejoined Doña Eustaquia and the girls fought on like wild things.

The valiant Eustaquia knocked down another of the four, for the stroke of her cutlass caught him on the upper part of his head and he fell to the ground half-stunned and badly wounded; he began to cry out for a confessor, and the servant who was guiding them began to shout, so that between his cries and those of the wounded man the whole neighborhood was aroused. A crowd of people emerged from the house (the same one that had been the motive for the bloody encounter) just as Doña Eustaquia aimed another cutlass stroke at the man on the ground, which would surely have killed him had not one of his companions, with a mighty effort, given the valiant lass a savage blow from behind. This made her turn on the man who had wounded her so basely, but he fell back as if to flee.

It was then that Doña Eustaquia heard someone say that a man had been killed, and calling to Doña Ana under the name of Don Juan, she quit the battle. The neighbors came rushing up with weapons; and when the girls realized that they ran the risk of being discovered, they hastened to the corner where young Melgarejo was awaiting them, calling to them and begging them to flee. The girls followed him, leaving the ensign Mendoza, a native of Madrid, dead behind them with his brains spilt and one Rufino, an Andalusian (for the other three men were of that nation), badly wounded. The girls were also severely wounded, so that by the time they reached the cemetery of San Francisco, Doña Ana could not take another step because of a wound she had in her thigh, not to mention the chest wound, which was very grave; struggling to overcome their weakness they reached the bridge and paused under one of its arches to stanch the blood from each other's wounds, for both were bleeding copiously.

They removed their armor and found that Doña Eustaquia had three wounds, one in the back, a small one in an arm, and another in a foot; the wound in her back was a serious one. Doña Ana, as I have said, had two, and both were dangerous; they bound them up tightly and, rearming themselves, continued on their way, for it was nearly dawn. Thanks to those trusty weapons they had not perished on the spot, though in addition, God was responsible for their great valor, for such bravery had never before been seen in Potosí in women of such tender age and gentle rearing. Finally they went to the Ribera (where the ore refineries are) and reached their house, with Doña Eustaquia and Melgarejo carrying Doña Ana because she could no longer walk. They reached the door, the slave opened it, and the young man told her to take care of the girls because they were badly wounded; and he went home swearing by all the saints that he would never accompany them more.

The next day our Melgarejo managed to inform himself of how they were and learned that they were very ill because their wounds had not been attended. Their father, Don Antonio (whom they had persuaded that they were ill of some other malady), brought them a doctor, but they refused to let him examine them on grounds of modesty and instead had recourse to a Sevillian lady who lived nearby and who went to see them under the guise of paying them a visit. Her they told of their wounds, but concealed the gravity of the injuries. It was God's will that she succeeded in curing their wounds, giving their father to understand that they had some other illness. They kept to their beds for almost two months, after which their health was completely restored.

Three months later the Negress returned to Melgarejo's house with a note in which the maidens made an appointment with him to go out once more, but the young man was unwilling to commit such a senseless act and responded in no uncertain terms that he did not wish to accompany them. They, unwilling to recognize that they were being unduly rash and that they could not always hope to get off so easily, determined to go out by themselves; but God frustrated their plans, for when they were ready to leave the house their father discovered them dressed in men's clothing and with their swords and pistols. The noble Portuguese very nearly fired the pistols at them without waiting to find out what such preparations could mean, but after beating them soundly he shut them up in their bedroom, meaning to punish them more severely that night. But God saved them from this danger (which might even have cost them their lives, for Don Antonio was a man of violent temper) even as He had saved them from others, perhaps to the end that later in their lives they would make amends by serving Him in perpetual chastity (as indeed they did). For the Lord uses many means to increase His glory and save those whom it is His pleasure to save, to bring light out of shadows, roses out of thorns, and life out of death. And what man would not be confident of his ability to conquer the weakness of his flesh by divine grace, seeing how it was conquered by these young women, surrounded (as we shall see later) by base men, like unto vipers and basilisks, and seeing how they passed through the midst of the flames and were not burned?

Therefore the two girls, finding themselves in this peril, placed their trust in God and found the strength and craft to escape. This they did with the aid of the slave woman, who, by tying a rope at the window of the bedroom, helped them to flee; carrying no weapons and wearing not men's clothing but only short skirts, they slid down the rope to the roof of a stable and thence to the street at about seven o'clock in the evening. From there, in the company of the Negress (who always remained exceedingly faithful), they went to the home of Doña Paula, the Sevillian lady who had tended their wounds. She took them in under promise of great secrecy, but could not extract a single word from them as to the reason for their leaving home.

That same night the girls sent the Negress, dressed in Indian costume, to the house of the young man who knew all that had happened; she asked him to write a message to the valley of Mataca, to a son of hers who lived there, telling him that his mother bade him come with four good mules and that the girls were sending the money to buy them; he wrote the letter and it was sent off immediately.

Don Antonio's anger and his efforts to find the missing girls were extraordinary, though to his honor it must be said that they were not public. But he could find not a trace of them, which increased his anger and even undermined and ruined his health.

Diego Melgarejo, the agent of all these doings, always talked with the slave when she came to his house in Indian dress. By order of Eustaquia and Ana she instructed the young man (giving him a sum of money) to buy in the market place two swords and sets of men's clothing, which he thereupon did. A week later the Negress's son arrived, bringing four stout mules provided with saddles, and when he reached the house where the girls were, he rested for a day. On the following night the girls, in men's clothing, and the Negress, in Indian dress, thanked Doña Paula for the help she had given them and departed for the city of La Plata with the Negro.

When they arrived in that city, still dressed in the same clothes, the beauty of those two ladies served as a letter of recommendation, since everyone who saw them was enthusiastic about them. Their own prudence of conduct helped to gain the good will of all, so that they had a very agreeable stay there. After a month's time it happened that a merchant was going to Lima on business, and they took this opportunity to go with him, leaving the Negress (now dressed in her ordinary clothes) in the house of a reverend canon and taking her son as their servant; they were still dressed in men's garments, for these hardy girls did not leave off wearing them for a long time.

Once they had arrived in Lima, and because they possessed many jewels and a large quantity of gold and silver (which they had taken from their father's house), their appearance was so handsome and dashing that they created a very favorable impression on everyone they met in the city. There was no one who did not aspire to their friendship, and so they were sought after and feted, everyone believing them to be young noblemen. And it is a remarkable thing to realize how perfectly accustomed they were to men's clothing and also to recognize their great moral restraint, for despite the many opportunities that were offered them they were not carried

69 ❧ *The Warrior Maidens*

away by the natural appetite of sensuality. But he who has God on his side and trusts in His divine majesty lives safely in the midst of danger, for all he undertakes is secure, even in the hands of his enemies.

And so, having passed two years in Lima, they went to Trujillo and visited other cities, after which they again returned to Lima; and there, in the fiestas and bullfights of that city, their appearance was exactly that of men. While they were in Lima they learned of the death of their father, who had died of grief; and in his will he stated that should his daughter Eustaquia reappear she would inherit his large fortune, but only in case she were still single, for if she were married she would lose it all.

Hence, five years after they had left Potosí and in the twentieth year of their age they returned to Chuquisaca accompanied by the faithful servant who had so successfully kept the secret of their disguise. Before entering that city they dressed in richly adorned women's clothing, which only enhanced their beauty. Then Eustaquia took possession of her inheritance, and both made arrangements to become brides of Christ in the convent of the nuns of Santa Mónica; but this did not come to pass, because the beautiful Doña Ana fell ill of an ailment that lasted many days, the result of a fall from a horse in the city of Lima when she was engaged in a bullfight, and for other causes which I do not relate because I am not certain of them.

After he returned to Potosí the Negro who had served them during their journey to Lima and their return told other piquant details to Don Diego Melgarejo, and he in his turn recounted them to me. In the town of Chayanta I also made the acquaintance of a certain Don Juan de Itulaín, who told me some things that had happened to those two valiant maidens when they were in Lima and of the friendship he had had with them there in the belief that they were really men. When he went to La Plata in the same year that those ladies left Lima, he learned that his friends had not been men. Never ceasing to marvel that he had seen with his own eyes the valor of those two females, one day he begged Doña Ana (even though she was ill) as well as Eustaquia to put on their men's garments, for they had kept them; since he asked it so insistently they donned them, and Don Juan Itulaín had portraits made of them in that garb. At the foot of one he caused to be inscribed, "The valiant Doña Eustaquia de Souza," and on the other, "The valiant Doña Ana de Urinza, Peruvian ladies of Potosí." Having learned of this, when I next journeyed from Chayanta to the city of La Plata, I went to this gentleman's house and saw those portraits; indeed, their beauty was beyond my powers of description, and I took the liveliest pleasure in seeing them, although at that time I did not have the slightest idea of writing this history, which would relate the story of those two ladies.

After living in La Plata a little more than two years, Doña Ana died of her ailment, and four months later Doña Eustaquia also died (of an affection of the chest), grieving for her beloved companion; and at the end of their days both declared that they died as virgins, for though both had been placed in perilous circumstances and had undergone terrible temptations, they had been fortified with divine favor and had overcome temptation and always preserved their chastity. Everything that they had was left to be judiciously divided among the poor, and they freed their faithful servant the Negress, also leaving her, together with her son, a sum of money sufficient for the rest of their lives and for their return to this city. Nor did they forget Diego Melgarejo; they sent for him and presented him with a thousand pesos and all their men's clothing.

1656 · On Rancor and Christian Charity

RANCOR and a lack of the charity that its inhabitants ought to have had for one another, seeing that all were Christians, had so far taken possession of the imperial city of Potosí that it was impossible to establish a blessed peace in which all might live in safety; and all this despite the efforts of judges and ecclesiastics, although it is true that the secular leaders were also guilty of national rivalries, either secretly aiding their partisans in fights or concealing their public scandals and misdeeds. If judges were the first to obey the laws, it would only be necessary for all to imitate them, as can be seen in a number of cases, for no magnet is more effective in influencing subjects to carry out any action—either for good or ill—than the example of their prince, lord, or judge.

Not a single day passed that various kinds of injuries were not inflicted by these factions. One Monday morning early in 1656 the bodies of three women, cruelly murdered by beating, and bearing other wounds, were discovered on the heights of Munaypata. Their relatives identified them and (since it was obvious that the naked bodies had been dragged some distance) followed the trail assiduously and found that it ended one street below the church of the Society of Jesus at a house inhabited by some Spaniards from the Montaña region of that realm. They entered the house, for it was there that the trail of blood and furrows in the earth began. The inhabitants of the house came out, denied the accusations made against them (for they were innocent), and replied in very angry terms. The relatives of the victims attacked them in a rage and killed one of them after inflicting numerous wounds; the other two would also have been killed had they not made their escape, though they were badly wounded.

It was soon learned that some other men, friends of theirs, had murdered the women. The Montañeses, Basques, and Navarrese thereupon set out to avenge the death unjustly inflicted on one of their number by the murdered women's relatives, and the Peruvians of this city rose in defense of their compatriots. There was a fierce encounter between the two groups in the Plazuela del Rayo, in which Juan de Figueroa, Eugenio de Portugal, and Don Alejandro Dávalos were killed, while on the other side a Biscayan named Don Rodrigo de Echevarría and a Montañés named Don Blas de Ortega died, along with two others whose names I do not know.

The riots and bloody feuds continued in this city with so many deaths that the year 1656 was held to be memorable in this regard. The bowling court opposite the Jesuit church (where the church and convent for orphan girls is located today) was memorable at that time for the great number of deaths and notorious events that took place there. On Monday of Holy Week two men were bowling:[13] one was Estéfano Curzio, an Italian by birth, a man of valor and greatly feared in the city, and the other was Pedro del Casal, a native of Potosí and a youth of twenty years of age. The two quarreled over a stroke badly played by the Italian, and he angrily seized the lad by the collar and kicked and beat him; the youth left the court, bruised and battered. People who were loitering about urged Estéfano to call the lad back and make it up to him, for since his parents were noble Andalusians they would naturally look after their son. This Estéfano refused to do. Indeed, he arrogantly responded that he would mete out the same treatment to them.

The lad, Pedro, having left the court, shortly returned with a sword and waited for his assailant to come out, as he soon did, and greeted him with insults. But the Italian, treating the whole matter as a joke, took his sword from his belt without unsheathing it and rushed at the youth with the intention of knocking him down. Pedro del Casal had time only to draw his sword, and as he turned to flee, the point accidentally entered the Italian's eye and he fell dead, for the sword had passed through to the nape of his neck. His death soon became known everywhere in the city, and three Neapolitans who lived there, friends of the dead man, began to bluster and swear vengeance on the youth and his father. An alliance was formed between the Andalusians and Peruvians of the city (not to give them always the name *Creoles*, which is a vulgar term) because the Neapolitans had allied themselves with the Basques and Catalans. There was a fight that night in Munaypata, and a Neapolitan and two Basques were killed, with many others on both sides wounded.

Two days after this misfortune it happened that two brothers named Silveiro, Peruvians of this city (nicknamed "the Shrimps"), were in the billiard hall of Juan Bello playing with Pedro de Orbea, a newly arrived Biscayan. Since our common enemy strives always to cause conflict, he made use in this case of a cock that had got into the gallery where the candles were placed for illumination. Some lads chased it out just as the Biscayan made a shot, thus winning his wager, and as the cock flew over the table it dropped some excrement there. One of the Silveiro brothers immediately said in jest, "Look, there is the real,"[14] pointing to the excrement. Since Orbea was shortsighted, he thought that it was indeed a coin and hastily stretched out his hand and dirtied it with what he thought was a real. Being a sensible lad, he laughed along with all the others who were there. But "El Azafranado"[15] (an arrogant though brave Biscayan who was present) was stung by his compatriot's attitude, took out his dagger in a rage, and attacked Silveiro, who very bravely parried the attack with his cue in such a way that, giving the Biscayan a blow on the head, he stretched him at his feet. This put everyone into an uproar, and unsheathing their swords they surged out into the street exchanging blows; there one of the Basques, Don Juan de Urriaga, was killed.

On the following day the Basques and Peruvians of this city fought again in the Calle de los Mercaderes, and Don Diego Alvarez gave Pedro Cajica two sword wounds that resulted in his death. Several days after these two deaths Basques and Peruvians had another encounter in the same street; the Basques were Don Juan de Urdinzu Arbeláez (who was later royal alférez[16] of this city), Francisco Belzu, Juan de Casanova, Don Diego Orospeyta, and Martín de Urigurguro; and the Creoles (or Peruvian natives) of this city were Francisco Castañeda, Captain José Vela, Francisco Carreño, and Don Isidoro de Leiva. These men killed Orospeyta and Urigurguro, and left Arbeláez badly wounded.

At the time there also lived in this imperial city one Pablo del Castillo, a native of the same, who because of his enormous size was nicknamed "Castillote."[17] So monstrous was his strength that he could lift a fully laden mule singlehanded. He was the son of Sebastián del Castillo, a Manchegan by birth, and during General Velarde's term of office in the city he committed many notorious crimes against its officials, who by order of the general not only made every effort to arrest him for his heinous deeds but tried to rid the earth of him by having him killed. After Velarde's departure, the corregidor Sarmiento and President Nestares published proclamations calling for his life, for he still continued his depredations. The reward promised to anyone who killed or captured him was five hundred pesos.

Greedy for gain, some women who were not natives of Potosí (three sisters who lived in Munaypata) lured him to their house by pretending to be in love with him, and when they had him safe one of them tried to go out to summon officers of the law. Castillote, observing how readily they had acceded and that they were whispering to each other, immediately smelled betrayal, and when he saw one of the women about to leave the room he got up from his seat and, seizing her by the arm, angrily asked where she was going. The woman was so perturbed that his suspicions were confirmed, and seizing her by the feet he began, with his enormous strength, to batter the others with her body. As they tried to escape the blows, he slammed the woman he was holding by her feet against the wall, dashing out her brains. Then he attacked the other two, throttling one of them until she died and wounding the other in the breast with a dagger, killing her also; and then he fled the house. The corregidor learned of the barbarous crimes on the following day and ordered a search for Castillote, but he was clever enough not to be caught.

One night in the month of October of that same year, when the president was having supper in his room at eleven o'clock, a young boy who was in his service came into the room, trembling with fear, and told him in great distress that there seemed to be a soul in torment at the door of the principal church, for it was emitting mournful cries. The president opened his windows in alarm and when he listened could hear those pitiful lamentations. He sent his servants to find out what it was, and though at first they were afraid to go, at length they went out and found a man writhing on the ground in mortal anguish. They asked him who he was and he answered, "I am

Francisco Trujillo, a shipper of the king's quicksilver, and, my friends, I was standing at the corner by the clock when that minister of Satan whom they call Castillote came up to me. Seeing that I was smoking, he asked me for a puff, but as I had come to the end of the cigar I begged off; and for no other reason than this he took out this beastly knife you see and drove it into my face."

The bystanders approached him and saw that the murderous blade had been plunged into his face up to the hilt, just below the corner of his eye. They took the wretched man to the hospital where, since it was impossible to remove the knife by any other means, a cord was tied to the hilt and it was drawn out by the efforts of two men. As soon as the president was informed of the case he gave orders that the wounded man should be assiduously cared for; and, Divine Mercy having decreed that he cheat death, he was eventually cured, to the great amazement of all who saw him.

Now, this event and the cure of so mortal a wound by God's mercy furnished the occasion for that wicked and monstrously cruel man to return to Him, for one night he came fully armed into the chamber of the president, who (having had no time to call his people) listened with horror to the following speech: "I, my lord, am Pablo del Castillo, against whose life so many proclamations have been issued by your lordship and other officers of justice. I recognize that in all the world there is no man as bad as I. My sins are innumerable, but if they are great, greater still is the compassion of God: His mercy calls me to a religious congregation so that I may do penance. I cannot do it in any community of this archbishopric, for there is no place in it where I have not offered a thousand offenses to its inhabitants. I am determined to go down to Cuzco in company with the Reverend Father Provincial of San Francisco, who is going to make the journey three days from now, for he, overlooking my unworthiness, has offered me the holy habit of the Franciscans. The only thing that makes me sorrowful at present is that I owe two hundred pesos to a poor priest, Maestro Don Pedro Villalobos; I stole the money from him because of my evil nature, and much harm has come to him from it. Your lordship's mercy is great, and so for the love of God I beg you to send for him and make him a gift of the pesos in my name."

When the president, who had been filled with fear when he

saw that terrible man before him, heard his good intention and plea, he promised to give the two hundred pesos to the priest. Castillote humbly and gratefully took his leave, and on the following day the president went to the convent of San Francisco. After having verified that the Reverend Father Provincial was going to take him to Cuzco and had offered him the holy habit, he gave Castillo a considerable sum of money to prepare for entering the order. And that was the end of the townspeople's anxiety, for all had been terrified of Castillote.

1657 · A Virgin's Revenge

In this imperial city there lived a noble Andalusian couple who had a very beautiful daughter, at this time only thirteen years of age. One day her parents (because they had been ill) went to the baths of Tarapaya to convalesce, and the girl stayed at home to take care of the house and the family. At that time the foreigners who lived in the Calle de los Mercaderes (near the Plaza del Regocijo, where they sold their goods) shamelessly flaunted their sensuality in both deed and word, boasting about things they had never done. Oh, what vilely barbarous tongues; oh, what a terribly infamous way for any man to behave! If you boast of what you have not done, how will you hide what you have done? How will you honor the woman who perhaps forgets her honor for your pleasure, for your pleas and promises, and pawns her chastity to satisfy your lascivious desires?

But to go on with our story, the merchants agreed among themselves to play a trick on women in the following manner: they would take their pleasure of one of them and next morning would say, "Go to the shop next door and you will be given whatever you want if you ask for it in my name." The woman would go there, and as all were wicked, they would say to her, "Come in, and we will give you every satisfaction." And so she would go in and, once inside, be raped by the merchants. This cruel game did not last long, for in the retaliation that followed, the merchants suffered great losses.

On this occasion, however, when the merchants had not yet been brought to account for their vices, it happened that our beautiful girl, capriciously but innocently having left her house to visit a sick friend (since her parents were not at home), discovered on the way back that she was near the Calle de los Mercaderes and went into the first shop she came to in order to buy a bit of silk. The evil merchant, oblivious of the offense to God and not caring that the girl was an innocent child, told her, "Señora, in the next shop they will give you what you are looking for." The trusting girl went there (it was the shop of a rich merchant) and asked for the silk she was seeking, saying that the owner of the shop next door had sent her there. Now, as we have said, all the merchants were involved in these crimes, and so the merchant thought that since his neighbor had sent her, she must be one of the women they used for this purpose. Hence he said to the child, "The silk is within, for I have none here. Let us go in, and I will give it to you." He shut the doors of the shop and went into his living quarters with the maiden, and as soon as he saw that he had her safe, locked the door. The unhappy girl cried out, but there was no one to help her, nor did it avail to tell him that she was a virgin and of noble family and that her parents were alive; nor was it of any use to defend herself with hands and teeth and all her strength, for the wretch raped her all the same.

When she realized that she had been deprived of her virgin state against her will, the girl, furious and desperate, gazed at the floor without saying a word while the merchant waited eagerly to see what she would say. At last she recovered herself and said to him with exquisite politeness, "How will you account to God and my honor for this offense?" To which the man responded, "As for God, I do not need to tell you what I will do, and as for yourself, I say that I can satisfy you in nothing, on the one hand because the merchant who sent you here knows who and what you are and on the other because not everything in the shop is mine." When the girl heard this wicked answer she hid her feelings as best she could and said to the merchant, "Well, the damage is done and there is no help for it. The only thing I ask of you is that, since it is my intention to place myself in your hands, you do not fail to help me; I will come back tonight and we will see what can be done." The merchant, overjoyed, replied that he was more than willing. The girl took her leave, and as she passed by the shop of the merchant who had sent her, she said to him, "I found what I was not looking for; I will repay you for your evil."

She arrived home and sent a young girl who had been brought up with her to prepare a number of cotton cords, tubes of gunpowder, and dried cactus fibers, saying that they must go to a certain man's house to avenge a wrong perpetrated on a woman friend of hers. When night came, she went

A Virgin's Revenge

to the girl's room to fetch her, and without rousing the servants, they went out to attend to the matter of the merchant.

She found him waiting for her in the shop; he took up a candle and went out of the house to light it, disguising his poverty (which was the reason he had no servants, although he made use of those of others) by telling her that he was a newcomer to Potosí. Meanwhile, according to plan the girls had the cords ready and the tubes lighted, and quickly hid them among the folds of the most expensive bolts of cloth, brocade, and Castilian stuffs. The merchant returned with the lighted candle and found them quietly waiting for him; the girl suggested that they go into the living quarters; the merchant obeyed, closing the shop, and they went in. The girl launched into a long and pleasant conversation, giving the fire time to damage the valuable goods, and after an hour had passed (which was the time the girls had agreed upon), she said to her companion, "We have forgotten our shawls and will not be able to go out tomorrow. Let us bring them here, and this gentleman will accompany us in both directions." This the merchant did, overruling the objections of a slave belonging to the first merchant (the one who had sent the girl to his shop), who warned him of the risk he was taking because of the evil he had done, for often a slave is a better and more God-fearing man than his own master.

The merchant went with the girls, and when he was near their house, the one he had raped told him to wait under a balcony that was there and not to go away until they returned. He obeyed. The girl entered the house and called one of her Negro slaves, to whom she said, "Take a stave and with it beat a man whom you will find under the balcony; and make sure you do this, for I know that he is seeking my favors and along with them the unhappiness of this whole house." The slave obeyed; he rushed out furiously into the street (for he, too, was virtuous and was greatly angered by the offense against God attempted by that evil man). Since the criminal was all unsuspecting, the slave approached and with the first blow stretched him on the ground, opening a great wound in his head; had not people come to help him, the Negro would surely have killed him, so overcome with rage was he.

The bystanders picked up the injured man, but he declined

to tell them who had attacked him, because he was well aware of the cause. They took him home; he bade farewell to those who had brought him, opened his shop, and (since he smelled smoke) brought a light, and much to his astonishment saw the great damage that had been done to his shop. He rushed shouting into the street, asking how it had been set on fire. People rushed to the place and discovered that the cords were still burning the cloth. It was then that he realized how the damage had been done. Unwilling to make any further outcry, he extinguished the flames, withdrew to treat his wounds, and in the morning discovered that his loss amounted to twelve thousand pesos in pieces of eight, for some of the bolts of cloth had been burned right through.

Nor did the other merchant, he who had been the cause of the girl's violation, go unpunished; for one night she sent the Negro (who had done her bidding with the results I have described) together with some others from the mint (who are very lawless Negroes) to kill the merchant and steal the merchandise from his shop. This they did, burning down the doors and carrying off fourteen thousand pesos in coin that they found there; and when the merchant heard the noise and came out to see what was happening, they abused and wounded him by pelting him with stones, with the result that he very nearly lost his life. It was never learned who the aggressors were, for they had gone about their work in disguise. The fourteen thousand pesos were brought to the girl's house, and with them (on her orders, though carried out by another's hand) was purchased the freedom of the six slaves who had taken part in the raid, and she kept the remaining eight thousand. A short time after this her parents died and she inherited all their fortune; when she married, she provided her own dowry as well as those of her two sisters, whose children are alive today.

1657 · The Wages of Sin

In this imperial city lived Doña Josefa Camargo, a native of Salta in Tucumán. She was a widow and was notorious in the city of Potosí for her cruel nature. Her dead husband had left her with a daughter named Doña Angela, a girl of exceptional beauty and virtue who, because she had been reared in Potosí, was greatly beloved by all good people in her earliest years. But it is well known that in the usual course of events a human soul is like the fragrance of those flowers that are born by day and die at night. Some flowers pour out their fragrance at dawn, but as the day progresses, their odor decreases, and when they are full-blown, their gift of scent is entirely lost. And so it was with that beautiful girl, for in her early years the fragrance of her virtue was pleasing to many; but in the bloom of her youth she fell away from virtue and was corrupted by unchaste vice. Nor is this anything new, for we see many persons who are very fervent in the first stages of virtue, and in a few days much cooler, and soon forgetful of all virtue. It is true that at first the ill-made bow shoots a few arrows, but with use it gradually loses its strength and lessens its vigor. So it was with Doña Angela; and there are many such bows, which are tightly strung at the outset but soon slacken, and lose their strength. There are many men—and women too—who begin virtuously. How they punish their flesh, mortify their passions, and take the sacraments often; then, alas, how quickly all is lost!

At last, like a flower that fades and loses its fragrance, this maiden, now lukewarm in virtue, began to seek the company of men without her terrible mother's knowledge, with the result that a certain captain named Don Pedro de Córdoba fell in love with her and courted her so expertly that, overcoming every difficulty, he soon achieved all he desired. The pair enjoyed the sensual pleasures of love for some time; but since in this wretched life it usually happens that any well-being is but the harbinger of disaster, Doña Angela came to grief:

a maidservant in whom she had confided informed her mother of everything that had taken place.

When the submissive daughter saw that her mother knew everything (for she had proof of it) and that concealment was useless, she came to her one day and, falling on her knees, tearfully offered her a dagger and bade her mother either to wash away with that weapon the stain she had placed on her honor or to grant her daughter pardon, since God (whom she had most offended) had moved her to confess and she placed her hopes in Him. Indeed, so persuasive were her arguments, together with her tears, that they would have melted stone; but they made no impression on the heart of a cruel and heedless mother. What the mother did was to leave her daughter's presence in a rage and go out of her house, although she soon returned in a calmer mood, hiding the poison of her anger and evil intent until the time should be ripe. The daughter tried by every means to please her, with no other result than the realization that her mother was concealing some wicked intention.

When Don Pedro learned that the mother of his beloved Angela knew everything, he sent a message asking her pardon and promising her the sum of fifteen thousand pesos to provide a dowry for her daughter, since he could not marry her himself owing to the presence of a certain impediment. But the mother made no reply to his offer. A few days later Don Pedro had occasion to go to the city of La Plata on necessary business and therefore parted from Doña Angela with great sorrow, promising to return in a short space of time. She implored him not to leave her in the company of her mother, for she feared some evil; her heart told her that this was so, for she saw that her mother could not look on her calmly, and she told the captain that it would be better to leave her in some house of retreat. He replied that if he left her elsewhere than in her own home, the loss of her honor would surely become public knowledge. With these arguments the beautiful and sorrowing Angela was appeased, and leaving her with the necessary means, her lover departed.

As soon as the mother learned that the captain was gone, she determined (urged to it by the devil) to wreak her terrible cruelty on her only daughter. On a certain feast day she sent her to confession (which was still the act of a Christian).

The daughter obeyed, not foreseeing what awaited her that night. That morning she confessed and received communion and returned to her home, passing the rest of the day in the company of her mother. When night came, the mother had the instruments ready with which to take her daughter's life. The unfortunate girl went to bed and fell asleep; but scarcely had she done so when her mother (who was still awake) called a brother of hers and two servants who, having been instructed in what they were to do, went to her bed and dragged her into the salon.

The daughter, realizing the punishment her mother intended to carry out, begged her with great humility and many tears to punish her like a merciful mother and not to give way to cruelty. The mother was enraged by this; she stripped her daughter naked and hung her up by the hair, and all began to flog her with heavy whips so cruelly that blood ran freely from her body. And when she was on the point of expiring from this brutal treatment, the cruel and inhuman mother thrust a red-hot iron into her private parts, showering obscenities upon her, and she died as a result of this barbarous cruelty. They then dressed her again and gave out that she had died suddenly; but it was not long before a member of the household sent the sad news to her highborn lover, who came posthaste. While he was on the way, Antonio Camargo (brother of the cruel Doña Josefa), foreseeing danger, persuaded her to flee with him. They gathered together everything they possessed, and one night all four of the murderers departed from the city.

On the following day Angela's lover arrived and went to the house of the corregidor with the information that had been sent to him. The corregidor, indignant at such an atrocity, went in search of the criminals, but they had gone into hiding. The grieving captain heard that they were traveling in the direction of Tarija; in swift pursuit he overtook them on the road and attacked the dead girl's uncle, who defended himself valiantly, and both were mortally wounded. Antonio Camargo went on to Tarija and died there a few days after his arrival. The captain, Don Pedro, returned to Potosí and also died there, for his wounds had not been properly attended to.

1657 · The Twelve Apostles and Magdalene

It was during the administration of General Don Francisco Sarmiento that the evil-doing and rash actions of twelve men who blasphemously and sacrilegiously took the name of "the Twelve Apostles and Magdalene" were at their height. Their notoriety was great, not only in Potosí but in all the provinces round about. This band was composed of men of various nations and stole not only property but also honor, violating maidens and married women alike, as well as committing a thousand other acts of insolence. Following their example, many other thieves and idle and sinful folk, both in the city and in its vicinity, were responsible for public insults, robberies, and thefts, for evil-doing of this kind is open to all, and such folk seize the opportunity and take advantage of the fact that the law is busy elsewhere and preoccupied with what is easiest to remedy.

Persons who saw these evil men and suffered from their depredations state that instead of being only twelve in number they were a gang of more than fifty, and that they were known to be persons from many nations who might well have called themselves nobles had they not clouded their honor with such evil. Potosí so greatly feared their depredations that all the householders stayed up at night, watching over their homes with weapons in hand; but despite such precautions these wicked men did great damage because they were so numerous. Those blasphemers who called themselves Apostles gave the name of Magdalene to one of their number; they dressed him in women's clothing, and he would precede them into the houses, sometimes pretending to be a woman whose husband was trying to kill her. The householders would open the door to help her, and then the accomplices would enter and loot the house.

In the month of October, 1657, the following incident took place involving those evil men. There lived in the Plazuela de

San Lorenzo one Doña Martina Díaz de Lucu, a noble and virtuous lady who at that time was a widow; she had two unmarried daughters, equally beautiful and virtuous. The special devotion of these maidens was for the blessed souls in purgatory, and they made offerings and did works of charity for their sakes. Owing to the servants' carelessness one night the door of their house was left open; and when the Apostles chanced upon it they went in, entering the house to pillage it. When the girls heard the noise they came out, and the thieves immediately seized them and began to wrangle over who had the most right to them. Both girls, seeing themselves in such imminent danger, called out, "Souls in purgatory, help us!" As soon as they invoked them, the thieves seemed to see thousands of men and fled in such haste that they tripped over each other. The girls then locked the doors and found in the patio a pouch containing two thousand pesos that the thieves had stolen elsewhere and, in their fright and haste, had left behind.

The affair became known on the following morning, and the neighbors said that they had seen innumerable men pursuing the thieves out of the house, wielding weapons and striking them as they fled. Doña Martina and her daughters were asked who they might be, and they replied that they had not seen any such men, but only the thieves fleeing. And so they realized that the blessed souls of purgatory, the objects of their devotion, had come to their aid. The good lady Doña Martina divided the money between her daughters and the blessed souls, ordering many masses to be said for them in gratitude.

In that same year there was another very amusing occurrence in connection with the so-called Twelve Apostles. In this imperial city there lived the bachelor Trotolo, a clever priest of a very witty turn of mind, for there can be no wit where there is no intelligence; and he was lively and spirited as well. One night, since he customarily went to bed very late, he was coming along the Calle de Copacabana when, emerging opposite the cemetery, he met them. That day he was wearing for the first time a new cloak of double taffeta and a cassock of rich cloth. When he saw that he was surrounded by the thieves he said to them very calmly, "Who are you?" They answered, "The Twelve Apostles." Again he questioned, "And what do you want?" "That cassock," they said, "your cloak, your hat, and the silver in your purse." To this the priest replied with admirable coolheadedness, "And do you want nothing more?" They said that they did not. "Well, if you want nothing more," replied the priest, "here is what you asked me for," and he began to take off his garments. "I want to give them to your lordships folded and neat," he said. Oh, how inspiring is necessity and how sharp is human sagacity when fate makes life, solace, or some other good dependent upon its exercise! The thieves waited very civilly, and after the good priest had made a bundle of his garments and fastened them with his sash, he said to them, "So your worships are the Twelve Apostles?" They answered, "We have already told you so." The priest replied, "Then let the Twelve Apostles follow Christ," and so saying, he ran down the street with indescribable swiftness, keeping tight hold of the bundle containing his clothes; although they ran headlong after him, they could not catch him. And so he escaped.

1658 · Honor Lost and Redeemed

THERE was a rich and noble widow, the owner of an ore-refining mill in this city, who had a daughter as beautiful as she was intelligent. This daughter, daily seeing the man who served as overseer of the mill, fell so madly in love with him that she submitted to him in everything. The remarkable feature of the girl's love was that she bestowed it on a man so ugly and fearsome in appearance as was this overseer; but when has love respected the conventions?

Although it is true that beauty is the foremost and principal motive that causes us to fall in love, it must be said that there are two kinds of beauty: one is of the soul and the other of the body. Clearly, beauty of soul exists and shows itself in honorableness, in intelligence, in good conduct, in liberality, and in good breeding; and all these elements are appropriate and can be present in an ugly man. When one looks for this sort of beauty and not that of the body, fervent and satisfying love often follows.

All these good qualities were combined in the person of the overseer (who was an Estremaduran), with the result that the young woman, in love with them and not the monstrous ugliness of his face and figure, gave herself to him under promise of marriage; and in a short time the unfortunate girl's belly began to declare her sin. Her condition rapidly became obvious, but there was no way or opportunity to fulfill the promise of marriage. The mother was terribly intolerant about such matters, and as soon as she learned of her daughter's pregnancy she cruelly and rashly called upon her one day to help her make the bed. The daughter obeyed, all unsuspecting of what might happen, and as they were lifting the mattresses the mother told her to bend over to hold them. This the poor creature did, and the cruel mother pushed the mattresses on her so violently that (since she was in the last months of her pregnancy) she fell face down, and in a moment both she and the unborn child were dead. Nor did that unnatural mother show any grief, but pretended to everyone that her daughter had died unexpectedly.

A death no less unhappy and pitiful was that which came a few days after this to another noble maiden, whose name was Damiana and whose parents were among the most respected inhabitants of this city. Now, this girl, forgetful of her obligations, unchastely set her eyes on a young servingman who had access to her house and who was not her equal in any sense. At last Damiana declared her intention to him, heedless of any possible obstacle. The young man thought it rather a good idea, although, since he was more cautious and foresighted, he told her that it should be by means of holy matrimony. Damiana agreed, and as she knew full well that her parents would not be pleased with the match, she decided to enlist the aid of the vicar, who went to call on her parents. It happened that they had gone with their daughter to the house of a relative, where everyone knew of the romance; as soon as her parents learned the truth from them, they left her shut up in that house and went back home to consult the vicar. He asked where their daughter was, and they spitefully told him that she was many leagues away from the city. After a great deal of quarreling the vicar returned home and the parents went back to the house where their daughter was being detained. As soon as he beheld his daughter, the father, in a transport of rage, stabbed her until the unhappy girl died a miserable death. That very night the parents gathered up all the belongings they could and left Potosí, never to return.

At this same time, during the administration of Corregidor Don Francisco Sarmiento de Mendoza, it developed that that gentleman's nephew had made carnal solicitations to a lady of prominence, one married to a gentleman of great natural endowments who was much admired in the city. He succeeded in his designs, for the rashness of some men is horrible and the frailty of all is great. This lady was in the habit of sharing her riches (which were very great) with the blessed souls in purgatory; in addition to having a large number of masses and other offerings performed for them, she also prayed very devoutly to our Lord for the alleviation of their torments.

Now, the lady having stained both her husband's honor and God's (which is the more important), the matter was not so secret that the husband did not eventually learn of it through a friend (or traitor, which is a more proper name for such a man). The offended husband was greatly perturbed and grieved exceedingly; he had her spied upon at all hours to satisfy himself about the terrible case and in particular to satisfy his informer, the man he had thought to be his friend, who was the author of all his anguish. This man advised him to pretend to go away for a whole day, assuring him that his wife, feeling herself secure, would let his enemy into the house and that he, the friend, would then let the husband know and he would have the lover in his power.

This the husband did, telling his wife that he was going out of town and would not return until the following day. He hid in another house, and the wife, taking advantage of his absence, sent for her lover. They spent the afternoon in conversation, and when night fell she offered him her table and bed. The officious enemy learned of all this and immediately sent for the husband. He came like a raging lion, armed with two deadly pistols, and beat upon the door. The maidservants informed their mistress that her husband was coming, and the poor lady was in such a state as can easily be imagined: powerless to do anything else, she clasped her hands together and called on the blessed souls in purgatory, imploring them to help her in this terrible danger—and in the same breath told the adulterer to hide under the bed. The wife sat down and very calmly awaited her husband's arrival. He entered in a rage, but suddenly, two steps inside the room, he stopped and took off his hat and then made salutations as if to a number of guests. (A remarkable occurrence!) Then he went to the writing desk and pretended to take out some papers, telling his wife that he had forgotten the thing he needed most and that this had been the reason he had ridden hard to return home. He took his leave as if of many persons, saying, "Farewell, ladies." His wife was completely astonished and had no idea what was the matter with him.

The husband, filled with rage and scorn, set off to confront his friend who had made him run such a risk. He demanded of him, "Villain, why did you say that my wife was with another man and had broken her vows and stained my honor? Why do you lie? I found the platform of her bed occupied by beautiful ladies!" So saying, he attacked his friend with intent to kill and would have done so had not the friend escaped; but he never appeared in the husband's sight again.

Next day the husband pretended that he had returned from some matter of business and after caressing his wife very lovingly, asked her, "Tell me, who were those ladies who were here last night? I assure you their beauty pleased me greatly, but I had no opportunity to meet them." Then the wife realized how mercifully God had dealt with her and that the souls to whom she was devoted must be the ladies her husband saw, for she had seen nothing. She answered that they were friends from another city who had come to visit her. The husband was greatly relieved, and ever after they lived in much harmony. After some time had passed, he told his wife of his suspicions and the intention that had brought him home that night. His wife reassured him, privately giving great thanks to God. And ever after she lived in a very different way from before, and her devotion to the blessed souls of purgatory increased.

1658 · The Salvation of Antonio Escorrón

At a time when the armed atrocities in Potosí were so great that officers of justice had general permission to take criminals from the churches where they had claimed sanctuary, it happened that Antonio Escorrón, a native of this city and a brave though impetuous youth, fought a duel and killed his adversary, a wealthy man with excellent connections in the city. The assassin fled to the convent of Santo Domingo, with the corregidor Sarmiento hard on his heels. This judge was severe on occasion and still more so when he was angered, though apart from this he was pleasant in speech, a prudent man, and an admirable jurist, for any matter that came into his hands was treated with notable discretion. He was also (when not carried away by anger) affable, modest, and well-bred. In adversity (for he had had some reverses) he was firm and courageous, and in prosperity not at all overbearing; but in addition to these qualities he had another, which was that he insisted upon being treated by everyone with extreme veneration. In nobility of blood no one in the city surpassed him, and his disposition, great stature, good manners, and fine appearance were superior to those of all the men who lived in these realms at that time. He was most fortunate in acquiring riches, for he possessed an infinite number; yet they hardly sufficed to last to the end of his life.

Antonio de Escorrón, knowing that the corregidor was pursuing him hotly and angrily, and realizing that his life was in danger should he be caught, rushed headlong into the church and gave himself up to the brother sacristan who happened to be there. This sacristan, acting very charitably (for he knew that the corregidor was coming in search of the aggressor), had time only to take him into the sacristy, where the corpse of the servant of God, Fray Vicente Bernedo, lay in a cedarwood urn. The sacristan took the corpse and quickly moved it to the crypt and put the criminal into the urn and closed it; he also shut the body of the holy man into a coffer and then went to the cloister, where he found the corregidor accompanied by many officers of the law. The angry officers left no place unsearched—the church, the cells, the kitchens, and the hiddenmost parts of the convent, for the dead man's relatives were urging them to be diligent.

The corregidor entered the sacristy, brushing aside the arguments of the brothers who were trying to dissuade him from going in. He demanded to know what was in the coffer, or urn, that was there, to which the brother sacristan tremblingly replied that it was the blessed corpse of the servant of God, Fray Vicente Bernedo. The corregidor said, "Open it, father, for I wish to do it reverence." The monk, seeing that he could do no less, opened the urn; the corregidor approached, and by the will of God and the miracle wrought by His servant, the criminal was transformed into the blessed corpse, and the corregidor bent forward and kissed its feet. The monks were mightily astonished and, casting glances at one another, gave thanks to God and praises to His servant. They shut the urn again, and the corregidor went to search for the criminal in other parts of the convent. He went into the crypt, where he necessarily had to look also, and asked them to open the coffer in which the blessed corpse actually rested.

At this point the reverend father prior, who was present with his whole community, said to the corregidor, "Sir, if I tell your worship of a marvelous occurrence that has just taken place, will you pardon the criminal?" The corregidor replied, "What occurrence could possibly cause me to pardon him?" The father prior repeated his question, saying that if the corregidor promised to pardon the criminal he would relate it to him; since he was so insistent, the corregidor told him that if such was the case he would not remove the criminal from the church. Thus reassured, the prior said, "Then your worship must know that in this coffer lies the corpse of the servant of God." The corregidor replied, "How can this be so if it is in the sacristy where I kissed its feet? How can it be both here and there?" "These are the miracles that God has wrought through His servant," said the father superior, "for the one to whom your worship did reverence in the sacristy is not the corpse of the servant of God, Fray Vicente, but the very criminal whom you were seeking and whom we hid in that urn, having previously transferred the corpse to this coffer; and so that your worship may be satisfied, look on it with your own eyes." He opened the coffer, and there was the blessed corpse.

The corregidor was greatly astonished, and giving thanks to our Lord, he told the prior that for his part he pardoned the criminal and that if his accusers would do the same he could certainly remain free. The news spread throughout the city and reached the dead man's relatives, who, seeing what God had wrought by means of His servant, forgave the death for which the criminal had been responsible. And he changed his life so much that in later years he became much better known for his virtues than he had previously been for his vices.

1658 · The Fearless Avenger

LET us return to the constant calamities suffered in Potosí by reason of national factions whose encounters neither persuasion nor force of law succeeded in halting. General Sarmiento ordered two natives of this city garroted because they had killed Captain Victoria and Don Rodrigo Chauri, both Basques, in a sword fight outside the city; many men were indignant at this, making complaints and stirring up feeling against the corregidor, and all the condemned men's friends and relatives were criminally intent on killing him. With this aim one day, knowing that the general was going to Tarapaya with some friends of his, they fired two shots at him from the heights of Munaypata as he passed along the road; and although the corregidor escaped, Don Antonio de León and Pedro de Albornoz were killed. The assassins fled and the general returned home, and the deaths caused by those men were made public.

Pedro de Albornoz had been married to the daughter of the sergeant Don Claudio de Vera, a native of this imperial city, who was much affected by his son-in-law's death and made plans to avenge it. On learning that two of the killers were on their way to Lipes, he went in pursuit of them and, coming upon them, shot both of them dead. He returned to this city, where he learned that two other accomplices had left the convent of San Juan de Dios, in which they had taken sanctuary. He followed them without their knowledge and, being abnormally strong and of great courage, took both of them and brought them to the jail, where they were executed by order of the corregidor for the offense they had committed against him; and thus the unhappy men paid for their crime.

Big fish always eat little fish, and that is why the gallows were made for the poor and defenseless (as these men were); and even though the rich deserve it, as many did at that time for thir monstrous crimes, they do not fear it: as the philosopher Anacharsis said, laws (at least here in Potosí) are like spiderwebs, where only the poor flies are caught, but birds of greater size at the first transgression carry away with them both web and weaver.

This Don Claudio, as I have already said, was a native of the city of Potosí. He was not large of stature, but his valor was great. He had been a prominent member of several gangs during the administrations of General Don Juan Vázquez de Acuña and General Don Juan Velarde, and had accounted for many deaths in hand-to-hand combat. He was the terror of his enemies. One night some friends of his, deciding to find out the extent of his courage, went to the bridge of San Sebastián, where on the wall hung the head of Chocata, who had been hanged by order of General Velarde and his head placed on the spot where his crime was committed. There it stayed for many years, striking fear into children, for as it was already hollow, the wind made it whistle and thus increased their fear. Many grown men, as well, dared not pass by the bridge at night because the Indians and Spaniards who lived nearby said that sad groans and frightful noises were heard in that spot.

Two of Don Claudio's friends, therefore, dressed all in white, awaited him by the bridge, and when he passed by at eleven o'clock at night they made a great noise in the place where the head was. Don Claudio stopped on the bridge and very coolly began to conjure it, begging it in the name of Jesus Christ to tell him who it was and what it wanted. Just then those two white shapes emerged from the vicinity of the mill wheel (dressed in robes similar to the habit of our Lady of Mercy, which is given to condemned criminals to wear) and silently attacked him with two Turkish cutlasses. But though they supposed that he would flee, he had not the least intention of doing so; instead, with tremendous courage, he quickly unsheathed his sword and, seeing that one of the men was already upon him, aimed so fierce a blow that he wounded him in the chest and pushed him off the bridge. Then the other revealed himself, begging Don Claudio for the love of God not to finish him off as well.

The neighbors came to see what the noise was about, and Don Claudio went and found the man who had fallen from the bridge; he was half-dead, not only from a grievous wound in his chest but from another, worse one in his head as a result of the fall. They took him home, and although it seemed for a time that he was recovering, it turned out not to be so, for in the end his desire to trick a valiant man cost him his life.

After a number of remarkable events and exploits in which Don Claudio de Vera spent the flower of his youth, he went as captain of a company with Don Benito Quiroga to the conquest of Paititi, which, not being graced by divine favor, was unsuccessful.[18] Don Claudio returned and took the habit in one of the convents of the city of La Plata and there retired to a quiet life.

1661 · Big Gaspar

When the sergeant major Roque del Salto was senior magistrate of the cabildo, in 1661, he had his celebrated encounter with Gaspar Díaz de Santos. This man was a native of Otavi, a town in the Mataca region eight leagues distant from this city. He became well known for his strength, great courage, and memorable deeds. Since he was a very tall man, he was commonly called "Big Gaspar" [Gasparote]. He took part in several wars and raids against the hostile Indians in the provinces of Tucumán, where he performed marvels; and as a captain on the frontier of Tomina, in a rebellion of heathen Indians, he defeated and killed them even though they were ten times as numerous as the Spaniards. He returned to Potosí during General Velarde's term of office and had some great fights with the men of various nations who lived in this city, killing many of them. The corregidor was unable to lay hands on him and finally ordered his men to shoot Big Gaspar on sight. Many tried to do so, but all were unsuccessful, for with his mighty broadsword, seven handspans long, he could scatter crowds of men. His strength was so great that he could take a quince in his fist and squeeze out the juice as if from a press; and more remarkable still, he could get under a horse and take its hind feet in one hand and its front feet in the other and lift both horse and rider on the nape of his neck. When riding horseback (if in a narrow street or in the country near a tree) he would dig in his spurs, loosen the reins, and in mid-gallop stretch out his arms and, seizing hold of the walls or the branches of the tree, stop the horse with his legs; he would even lift the horse off the ground with his legs.

But as for men of monstrous strength, not even the man I have just described nor the many others who have lived in this world could match in strength that monster of nature named Milo. Among other monstrous feats that are told of him, they say that he killed a full-grown bull with his naked fist and, having dedicated it to his god, ate it all that same day, leaving not a scrap behind and experiencing not the slightest diminution of appetite; and that when he was old, believing his strength to be the same as in his youth, he tried to split a tree trunk with his hands. But his strength failed him and his hand was caught in the cracks of the tree, and since no one was at hand to help him, he was devoured by wild beasts.

Now, Big Gaspar offered tremendous resistance to the forces of the law in this city and escaped from jail as often as he was arrested, sometimes summoning the jailer with some deception or trick, like throwing red pepper in his eyes as he passed and then taking his keys and setting free any prisoners who wanted to go with him. One day when General Velarde was pursuing him, he fled into the church of San Agustín and climbed into a niche where there was a statue of San Juan. The general searched for him everywhere and could not find him. By chance he lifted the veil covering the saint's image and seeing Big Gaspar there, was speechless with astonishment. But the criminal's audacity did not stop there; placing a finger on his lips, he signaled the general to remain silent. This he did and went away without saying a word. That night he sent Big Gaspar fifty pesos, telling him to make use of them to leave town at once, for if he caught him he would be hanged and quartered.

Big Gaspar departed, only to return as soon as General Velarde had retired from office and left the city. He continued to disturb the peace during the whole administration of General Don Francisco Sarmiento. One day this corregidor went looking for him with more than twenty men and found him in a little plaza behind the church of San Juan de Dios. All of them attacked Big Gaspar, who unsheathed his broadsword and scattered the whole company with his blows, felling some and wounding others. The corregidor ordered him to give himself up and promised him his life, but Big Gaspar rejected this offer with trivial excuses until at last, seeing himself hard pressed, he seized the corregidor by the waistband and carried him in one hand (for such was his monstrous strength) to the church of San Juan de Dios and, leaving him in the cemetery, took sanctuary in the church.

He escaped to Mataca, but since all the officers of the law for many leagues around Potosí wished to kill him for his crimes, the corregidor of Porco surrounded him in a country house. Gaspar defended himself with his broadsword and wounded more than nine men; the others fled, and he returned to Potosí. At that time the two magistrates of the cabildo were the aldermen Armendáriz and Don Pedro de Brizuela; they made a determined effort to capture him and for that purpose called together many men, whom they summoned in the king's name. They encountered their quarry one afternoon in the street beyond the Calle del Contraste, Armendáriz on one corner with twelve men and Brizuela on the other with still more. The invincible Gaspar Díaz de Santos, seeing himself in this predicament, drew his great broadsword and rushed upon them like a ferocious bull, sweeping all before him in his attack; though they surrounded him again he dispersed them once more and succeeded in reaching the church of San Francisco. There he turned and attacked them again and finally entered the church, leaving many wounded men behind.

As soon as General Don Gómez [the succeeding corregidor] arrived in Potosí he issued proclamations calling for Big Gaspar's life, but the latter defended himself without difficulty against all attempts to capture him. That year the judicial officer of the cabildo was (as I have said) the sergeant major Roque del Salto. He captured Big Gaspar one night when he was off guard and immediately sentenced him to death. The culprit appealed the sentence to the royal audiencia[19] of La Plata, but the judge refused to allow his appeal.

Since last efforts are usually very strong ones and desperate remedies are sought when peril is greatest, Big Gaspar, seeing no way out of his predicament, attempted to extricate himself from it through daring and trickery. Antonio de Hoces, a Spaniard, was at that time constable and turnkey of the jail and a close friend of Gaspar's. Late one night he called the Spaniard to the death cell, where he was already, as a condemned criminal, dressed in the habit of the Order of Mercy, and asked for the loan of Antonio's cape and sword because he wanted to leave the jail. His friend the turnkey was astonished at his request and tried to persuade him of the risk to them both, but Big Gaspar insisted that he lend him the cape and sword and open the doors, promising that he would surely return safely in a short space of time. His arguments were so persuasive that his friend did all that he asked, and

Gaspar, giving his solemn promise to return, left the jail and went straight to the house of Roque del Salto. He knocked on the door and told the servant to announce that Gaspar Díaz de Santos was there.

The justice—believing that the servant was mistaken and that the person who had come was Gaspar Martín de Vargas, secretary of the cabildo—had him come in and suddenly found himself confronted with Big Gaspar. He looked upon him with indescribable horror, for fear led him to believe that the terrible man had come to kill him. Greatly alarmed and gasping with fear, he proffered a seat; but Gaspar told him that he had no intention of harming him and, glancing at Doña Ana, his wife, who was in bed and as frightened as her husband, said to her, "My lady Doña Ana, will your worship please ask his honor to allow the appeal that I have requested of him before the king my master in his royal audiencia of La Plata?" Trembling, Doña Ana replied, "My son, I promise you on my honor that as soon as it is light you will be granted what you wish or henceforth I will give my husband pleasure in nothing. Further, it is not he who is responsible for your plight, but many other men who wish to see you dead." How flimsy are the excuses offered by fright and how unreasonable are fear and alarm, and how often are they shown to be humble and craven! Roque del Salto added to his wife's plea by saying that he pledged his word to issue the appeal without rebuttal; but Gaspar replied that he asked nothing of his honor.

The criminal returned to the jail, but before arriving there he entered a sweetshop and asked for a generous order of sweetmeats; then, wrapping them in his cape, he went to the jail. His friend Antonio de Hoces was already at the door, hastily removing his bed and belongings because he was convinced that Big Gaspar would not return; and so he rejoiced greatly to see him, especially when he laid eyes on the sweetmeats Gaspar had brought, for they were sufficient to sweeten the bitterness occasioned by his absence. Gaspar said to him, "My friend, take these sweets, open the doors, and make haste to put my habit and shackles on me. Return to your quarters, undress, and go to bed, because it is important to the successful conclusion of my stratagem." This he did, and no sooner had he closed the doors than Roque del Salto (who had had second thoughts) arrived at the jail accompanied by a crowd of people; he pounded on the doors and threatened the constable with death, assuming that it was he who had let the prisoner go. The jailer came out half-dressed and answered the official very calmly, saying, "Not a single prisoner is missing from the jail. Either your honor is out of his senses on this occasion or I do not understand what he is saying to me. Come in and see for yourself." The official went into the death cell and found Big Gaspar, loaded with chains and holding a holy crucifix in his hand, saying acts of contrition. Roque del Salto stood petrified with astonishment, believing without a doubt that Big Gaspar's spirit had gone to his house to ask for what he had promised. He returned home still overcome with horror, pondering the case, and in the morning admitted the appeal and sent it to Chuquisaca.

Our Gaspar Díaz, meanwhile, sent a trustworthy friend to discover secretly whether the sentence was to be confirmed, with orders that if this were so, he was to be informed of it. All was put into execution and meanwhile, realizing that nothing good would come of the affair in view of his reputation and crimes, Gaspar asked his friend the jailer to leave his turnkey's post on some reasonable pretext before the dispatches arrived. This he did, and another man was put in his place.

A few days later the friend returned in great haste and told Gaspar that his sentence had been confirmed, with the added stipulation that he be quartered. That same day Gaspar removed his shackles (which had been worthless since his previous escape, when he had filed them through) and at two o'clock in the afternoon called the new turnkey. The man entered his cell, and Gaspar, seizing him by the hair, brandished a spike from his irons and threatened him with death if he raised a cry to give the alarm. He took away the man's keys and invited all the prisoners to pay him a visit. All went to the death cell, where he asked them one after another why they were in prison: some said for murders they had committed, and those Gaspar told to leave the jail; others mentioned debt and various crimes, and he put them all out of the cell. Then he called in others, and when he asked them the same question, they said that they were in prison for robbery; these he told to go back inside. Finally he took more than twenty prisoners, some incarcerated for debt and some for murder, and marched out of the jail, herding them before him. Leaving them in the principal church, he went to his house, armed himself, and departed from Potosí in the direction of the kingdom of Chile. He took with him only his fierce broadsword, of which many persons who saw it report that the stains of human blood with which it was covered never came off, no matter what efforts were made to clean it. Gozcalco (and he is quoting Pliny) says: "I do not know whether one very remarkable thing is true, and that is that the sword or knife with which a man has been murdered can never be made clean again." Two days later the sentence of death and quartering arrived, and since the judges were aware of what I have recounted above, they were both disappointed and angry.

After two years had passed, Gaspar returned to Potosí from Chile, now old and sick, and within a few days suffered a mortal illness. He went to the hospital of San Juan de Dios and received all the sacraments. One day when the charitable monks were attending him, he suffered a terrible paroxysm; recovering consciousness (oh, frightful case!) with a tremendous groan, he cried out in a loud voice, "It is not I who have condemned you, but your sins, and for your sins the just and divine Judge." Greatly astonished, those who were caring for him asked the reason for those terrifying words, and he answered, "Among the offenses I have committed against God I am especially harassed by the sins I committed in taking the lives of twenty-six Christian souls on various occasions; ten of these have been condemned to hell, and now they are asking for my condemnation, saying that I was in part to blame for the fact that death overtook them in a state of sin. Alas for me!" Then he said, "Mercy, Lord! Souls in purgatory whose corporal life I took away, rise up against those cruel souls who are asking for my damnation!" And so saying, he entered the last agonies of death and soon expired.

1661 · Doña Magdalena

Doña Magdalena Téllez was born in this imperial city of Potosí of very noble parents, though the milk on which she was suckled was that of a Chiriguan Indian woman. Now, all the members of this tribe are proud and cruel, and it seems that Doña Magdalena imbibed the traits of her wet nurse, for from childhood she was known for her great arrogance. If we ponder this with care, we will see that the good character of slave and Indian women is most important in those places where they suckle the children of their masters, for vices are transmitted and transplanted in children and in milk with indescribable ease. Many (and I among them) have discussed this matter as one of the chief causes for the prevalence of vice in these parts, where mothers think themselves so ladylike that they do not deign to suckle their children, and give them to slaves and Indians to be nursed, whence (leaving aside other evils and harms) they should not be astonished to find that their children are often ungrateful and love them little and scarcely recognize them as their mothers. Heaven permits this punishment for the lack of love demonstrated by those mothers in denying their children that first nourishment from their breasts that so greatly fosters fidelity and love. Such mothers are nothing but the stepmothers of their children.

The little girl increased in beauty as in age, which indeed was remarkable, for among the many beautiful women who lived in the city at that time—natives of Potosí as well as those from other parts—she excelled like the sun among stars. Her harsh and arrogant character also increased: she lost proper respect for her mother and disobeyed her teachings, frequently quarreling with her. She was, therefore, already lost, for nothing can be expected of that young person, either man or woman, who lacks respect and veneration for his parents. There is a well-founded story that on one occasion when the girl went to the city of La Plata with her mother she had an argument with her in the plaza, and the perverse child slapped her mother; this was in the same spot where she was later exposed as a public spectacle by divine permission and her mother's curses (for this and other acts of disrespect), since the mother's only means of revenge (though a rash one) was to call on God to punish her daughter in this life.

Magdalena grew up and reached woman's estate, and her parents gave her in marriage to Don Alonso de Escobar, a noble and quiet gentleman of angelic disposition, a very poor match for the arrogance of his wife. She tried to kill him by making his life as disagreeable as possible: she denied him her company, her conversation, and her bed and board, and made him sleep outside on a cold balcony. This caused his death, and there are even some who say that she gave him poison in addition. Magdalena, well satisfied, became the widow of a good husband, though for her he had not been a husband at all.

And so she was exceedingly cruel, arrogant, and rich. Her servants went in mortal fear of her, and hence it was not without horror that Valentín de Arteaga, a Biscayan, used to tell of an amusing thing that happened to him on a certain occasion. He was squire to Doña Magdalena, with a wage of twelve pesos a week. One day the lady was preparing to go out to pay a visit and, looking herself over from head to foot, said to herself, "Magdalena, you are beautiful. Nature took care to present you and adorn you with many gifts. You are rich: you have more silver and gold than you need; jewels, pearls, precious stones, slaves—all these you have. Tell me, what do you lack?" Immediately Arteaga, who was listening to these remarks from outside the window, said, "Good sense, Magdalena." Scarcely had he uttered this than he dashed out into the street, Magdalena running after him with a cutlass in her hand and screaming a thousand curses. Since she was unable to catch him, she swore to have him killed though it should cost her whole fortune, and he found it prudent to move to Chuquisaca. When humans are rich in the things of this world they grow presumptuous and dream that they are gods; they lose their good judgment because of those riches and it is not surprising that they do and say extravagant things. But those who are just and humble with the treasure of God's love partake of His grace and become more godlike.

Omitting mention of a number of strange events that happened to this lady, we come to one that took place in the year 1660. It happened that both Doña Magdalena and Doña Ana de Roeles, wife of Don Juan Sanz de Barea, went to a feast-day mass and sermon in the Jesuit church one Monday in Lent, and the two ladies had a dispute over their seats. The result was an act of ill-breeding on Don Juan de Barea's part, for, completely wanting in the respect owed to the Church, he rose from his seat and, going up to Doña Magdalena, slapped her in the face. Everyone who was in the church raised a great outcry, some taking the part of one lady and some the other, with so much shouting and jostling that all the priests of that holy company had to rush in to prevent them from killing one another. When Doña Magdalena was at the height of her terrible rage and uttering screams inside the church, a certain woman came up to her and said, "Señora, it is God's mercy that you pay in this life for the death you dealt my niece." And it was true, for a year previously Doña Magdalena had killed a young girl out of jealousy by personally flogging her to death; although she had concealed the crime by some pretext, it had eventually become known, and on this occasion the woman publicly charged her with it.

Magdalena's brother, Don Juan Téllez, who was a spirited youth, happened to be in a shop near the church in conversation with other merchants. He was informed of what was happening and was urged to go to his sister's defense and kill Don Juan de Barea. But Téllez said very calmly to those who were urging him to do this, "Hold your peace and do not ask me to do anything of the sort, for it is heaven's will to crush my sister's arrogance." Doña Magdalena hated her brother for no other reason than the ferocity of her own cruel disposition. On a certain occasion when he had come to visit his brother-in-law Don Alonso de Escobar, this cruel lady's deceased husband, she launched a large flowerpot at him from a balcony that would certainly have killed him had it landed on him, being exceedingly heavy.

Don Fernando de Encalada, a noble gentleman, was married to Doña Magdalena's sister, and when he was informed that Don Juan Sanz de Barea had insulted his sister-in-law in that fashion, he took up his weapons; but as he was leaving the house on his errand of vengeance, his wife stopped him, saying that he must not lose his life over such cruel arrogance; and this shows how much the lady was abhorred, even by those of her own blood. Her enemies, who were numerous, had showered her with insults in the church; among them one Don Francisco de Merlo insulted her more vilely than the others, and had not the venerable fathers interceded he would have laid hands on her. This was because Merlo had once been in a stall in the market place when Doña Magdalena attacked him with a cutlass (because he had spoken some indecent words about her in private gossip) and had aimed such a savage blow at him that, had he not tumbled backward into the stall, it would have split his head in pieces. As a result of this the lady had been placed under house arrest and had had some harsh exchanges with the officers of the law.

There are no words to describe the fury and rage she felt toward her attacker after the incident in the Jesuit church, which owing to her arrogance she considered a monstrous outrage. With a deadly desire for vengeance Doña Magdalena had herself carried home in a sedan chair, and there, after going in and shutting the doors, she began in her rage to utter frightful cries and then to destroy all her valuables; she tore her costly tapestries, broke her handsome mirrors, and bit off the ropes of pearls she wore on her neck and arms. These and the other outrages she committed caused horror in all who saw them; madly swearing vengeance, she uttered imprecations on all mankind. When her rage had passed she sought revenge by every means, but this was difficult because Don Juan de Barea had a very large retinue. What schemes did she not devise, what modes of revenge did she not contemplate! But she could make up her mind to none. She dressed in men's clothing, went out by night with sword and buckler, and skulked about her enemy's house; sometimes she reached the door; at other times she stopped at the corner because she knew that Doña Ana returned late from her visits, but she never succeeded in finding the pair alone, because they always came with relatives or a large group of servants. She also tried to lay hands on her enemies' son, a small child at the time, intending to cut his throat and lay him at their very door; but none of her plans came to fruition.

At about that time the treasury official Pedro Arechúa, a noble Basque, wished to have an illicit affair with Doña Magdalena. When she learned of his desire she acceded to it on the condition that he take responsibility for avenging her and told him that if he promised to do as she wished, she would regularize their relationship with the bond of matrimony. All this her gallant promised to do, for the passion of love always makes men blind. Doña Magdalena's second marriage was celebrated with great pomp, though to the uneasiness of the whole city, for it was regretted by all because of her cruel disposition. After the ceremony she asked her new husband when he was going to fulfill the promise he had made to avenge her affront. But how could he do so in cold blood? Therefore he dissembled and tried to dissuade her from such an intent. But what could a relationship entered into for sinful reasons and in the expectation of evil bring in its train except the shedding of blood, murder, and lamentable tragedies?

The proud Magdalena, observing her husband's procrastination and realizing that he showed no signs of carrying out her revenge, gradually conceived a mortal enmity toward him, so that she now looked upon her husband as her greatest enemy. She was sad, pensive, and disturbed in mind. Her husband was sorry to see her in this state, since he loved her and did not suspect her abominable intent, and as a diversion he offered to take her to Pucara, sometimes called Miraflores, a place of recreation in the valley of Tarapaya, half a league distant from the lake.[20] When he observed that his wife seemed pleased with the idea, he arranged for their departure, providing her with every possible comfort. The day before they were to leave (which was the Friday of the Holy Ghost in April, 1661) he went to the Jesuit church. There he made his confession, and it is said on good authority that his confessor told him that he was destined to die at the hands of a woman. He was astonished, asking himself whose hands these might be, but thought that harm might come to him only at those of a jealous woman who had been his mistress before his marriage, for when he broke off his sinful relations with her she had threatened him fiercely; he did not realize that he had a still crueler enemy in the person of his wife. Troubled by this warning, he went to the church of San Juan de Dios, where he received communion with great devotion.

He returned home and on the following day departed for Miraflores with his wife. They stayed there for several days, and since Don Pedro observed that his wife's melancholy did not leave her, he suggested to her one afternoon that as a diversion they should go to the country to hunt partridges. Magdalena consented, and her husband took his hawks and dogs. They caught a few of the birds, and Don Pedro brought them to his wife, who was sitting in a little meadow. In her presence he opened two of the partridges and taking out their hearts gave them to his hawks (a sure omen of what was soon to happen to the gentleman himself). In doing so he removed from his finger a precious ring that his wife had given him. Observing all this very closely (the occasion seeming opportune for her to undertake her evil plan), she took the ring and hid it without her unsuspecting husband's knowledge. Unmindful of his loss, the good gentleman returned to the hunt without asking her for it. Magdalena told him to continue the hunt, that she would return to their lodging to wait for him and prepare for his rest and pleasure.

The husband thought well of this, and Magdalena went off to prepare the death she had planned for him. For the purpose she sent an Indian maidservant, a Christian girl, to offer a certain poison to her husband in a glass of water that she had prepared against his return. She waited for him, and he was not long in appearing. He arrived tired and in an amorous mood; his wife offered him the drink, and the maid handed it to him; but as she placed the glass in his hands (being loyal to her master) she made signs to him not to drink it.

The husband observed the signs made to him by the servant and, affecting carelessness, let the glass drop from his hand, pretending that he no longer wanted it. Magdalena hid her rage, but she was furious over the failure and said to her husband in a changed voice, "Indeed, it seems that you were not so careless elsewhere," and pretending to miss the ring she asked him where it was, and continued, "Perhaps you left it in a house where they treated you well." The husband, not knowing what had happened to the ring, was much distressed and replied that he had not gone to any house and that it must have fallen from his finger in the country. In this way Magdalena sought an excuse to quarrel and make herself unapproachable.

With the fall of night, still concealing her hellish intent, she told her husband to go to bed and rest while she prayed with her maids, for oftentimes evil folk cover their wicked deeds with the cloak of good ones. The husband went to sleep, and sleep betrayed him, for when Magdalena saw this she sent two of her Negro slave women to kill their master, telling them that she would give them their freedom and surely save them from the clutches of the law. In view of these assurances they did not refuse; one took up a heavy hammer and the other a large iron spike, which the devil had provided close at hand. All three, possessed of the evil one, approached the bed and opened the curtains, and one of the Negresses coolly gave the innocent Basque a savage hammer blow on his forehead and temples. He awoke in a death agony and though he tried to rise, he could not, for they struck him again and again. The husband said in a voice already feeble, "Magdalena, what have I done to you? Let me confess." But (oh, what a terrible woman!) she said only, "Strike him again, my girls, and finish him off!" And so they did. Not satisfied with this, Magdalena went up to her dead husband and opened his chest with a butcher's knife—and there are many who say that she cut his heart out and ate it, though others say that she merely wounded him in the heart without going to such savage extremes.

When her desperate fury was sated, she sat down to rest and sent her Negresses to the home of her overseer, Lucas de Campos, a noble youth who was married to one Doña Josefa, a most agreeable woman. I later made their acquaintance and they told me all the circumstances of the case. When the overseer came in response to her summons, she said to him, "Come in, Lucas, and you will see what I have done." He entered and saw that spectacle and, unable to conceal his feelings, said to her with a mixture of sorrow and anger, "Is it possible, my lady, that your heart was capable of such cruelty? Is it possible that you have so unjustly killed your husband, the companion God has given you?" But the woman choked off these and other arguments by telling him, "Well, Lucas, it is too late for that. Now you must help me. Go and get the most vicious mule you can find; we will tie the body to it ingeniously and say that the mule balked and broke my husband's head with his hooves, and thus we will conceal the wound in his chest. To do this, have the mule carry the body to those rocks yonder; and meanwhile bring me your wife, Josefa, to keep me company." Lucas obeyed and, having left the room, was trying to decide what to do when he heard Magdalena say to her maids, "As soon as Josefa comes we must kill her, and we will say that I caught her in adultery with my husband. Then we will give Lucas some of those poisonous powders, and that will be the best solution for this matter."

Well may the evil tremble, for they forget the memory of a just God: indeed, His memory serves as prosecutor in the circumstances of sin. The cruel man kills because he finds occasion and because he finds someone to help him in his crime and does not remember that he who kills can and must perish. He thinks that he is exempt from punishment, because he does not remember Him who is watching and will judge him. Magdalena found someone to help her take her husband's innocent life—those Negro slaves who were as disloyal and cruel as she—but did not remember that God was witnessing her crimes and that by His will her life would be forfeited in exchange for the one she had so unjustly taken.

Our Lord God, therefore, who sees everything, allowed Lucas to learn of the new betrayal and the abominable crime that the wicked woman was planning. He went to the place where his wife was, informed her of what was happening and of Magdalena's plans, and giving thanks to God for delivering them from that peril, he took Josefa away. Then mounting a mule, he reached Potosí at midnight.

When Lucas de Campos arrived in the city, he informed the officers of the law. All the Basques rose up in anger when they learned of their countryman's death and went in a rage to Tarapaya with the provincial justice. Arriving at eight o'clock in the morning, they found Doña Magdalena's house and its doors surrounded by guards, for Diego del Aguila, the judicial lieutenant of Tarapaya, had heard of the case at dawn and had decided to keep Doña Magdalena from escaping. The judges of Potosí entered the house and found Doña Magdalena seated on the bed platform surrounded by her Negro maidservants. She arose without a sign of fear, greeted them all, and said, "My lords, I know already why you have come. Open those curtains and you will see your countryman and my husband. My servant must have told you who is responsible for his state. I do not complain of his disloyalty to me, for God and the world will acclaim his loyalty to his master. I am Creole-born and thus your enemy. The Judge of heaven and earth has also sent you to punish me. Here is my neck for your satisfaction. But so that you will not think that I am faint of heart, I beg you to rest, for you must be tired; surely you will take some chocolate or other refreshment."

When the officers of the law saw how shamelessly she spoke and felt the sorrow that overwhelmed them at the sight of the bed platform and the wall behind the bed covered with blood (for on them were bloody handprints made by Magdalena with the hand she had used to open her husband's breast and had then wiped there), the judge said to her angrily, "We do not wish to rest; rather, give us your feet that we may put these irons on them. And may you die for the crimes you have committed, for it is not right for a cruel woman to live in the world." So saying, though she tried to resist, they placed two pairs of irons on her. The dead man's body was carried before them to Potosí, and soon the city was in an uproar as innumerable persons came out to see it.

With the murderess riding on a shabby old sidesaddle, the officers set out for the city. On the way several unsuccessful attempts were made to free her. Just before they reached the cemetery of the church of Tarapaya, Doña Magdalena received a message from the Very Reverend Padre Fray Juan de Osorio, of the Order of Preachers, telling her to fall from her mule as the group approached the cemetery and that he would offer her sanctuary in the church with the aid of six bold men who would be on the scene in disguise. But things did not turn out as planned, because as they approached the cemetery (the road passes close by it) the mule turned balky for no apparent reason and, despite Magdalena's efforts, backed off more than a hundred paces and passed the cemetery by. There were other attempts to free her, but none succeeded. The company arrived in the city with more than two hundred men guarding the prisoner. Magdalena, as I have said, was riding on a shabby sidesaddle, and her Negresses were with her; the girl who had showed loyalty to her master came riding on her mistress's fine saddle, demonstrating that fortune has many twists and turns.

They took Magdalena from the saddle at the doors of the jail, and she, dressed in mourning and wearing a veil, hung her head in shame. Just then—it was five in the afternoon—the procession bearing the body of her husband, whose funeral was to be held in the church of San Agustín, was crossing the plaza. The indignant judge, stopping Magdalena, said to her, "Lift that face of yours, cruel murderess." Striking her with his staff of office, he forced her to look up, and said (gesturing toward the dead man), "Are you satisfied with what you have done?" They placed her in the public jail, and the townspeople were moved to compassion, on the one hand, by the miserable death of her husband, and on the other, by Magdalena's wretched state; seeing that the one case could not be remedied, they tried to remedy the other. For this purpose Don Jerónimo Antonio Taboada, a knight of the Order of Santiago, Don Gaspar de Arcibia, and Don Pedro and Don Juan Téllez (Magdalena's stepbrothers) formed a council of Creole gentlemen and determined to remove her from the jail by force of arms. They informed her of this, but Magdalena, without ceding one whit of her arrogance, sent a message to her stepbrothers saying that she wanted no help at their hands and did not recognize them as sons of her father, along with other insults that defamed their good name. As the wise man said: "The man who murmurs against others and has an evil tongue is a poisonous serpent who destroys or at least smirches honor, as the serpent with its venomous fangs destroys life." This woman was always evil, not pardoning even her own brothers. And in addition to refusing her brothers' offer she also refused to accept any of the food sent her by the townspeople.

Since her worthy Creole neighbors knew that her case must end in a sentence and a frightful death, they pledged 200,000 pesos for her freedom, to be raised among them all, and even the Indian fruit-sellers offered their gold and silver brooches. But the judges, in particular General Don Gómez and the provincial judicial officer, refused, for they were bitter enemies of the Creole nation. Realizing that their efforts were worse than useless, the Creoles attempted to take up arms among themselves and free her. When the general learned of this, he informed the royal audiencia of La Plata, which immediately sent a large body of men to take her to that city, each man to receive a wage of six pesos of full weight, to be paid for by Magdalena. They took her from the jail of this city in a sedan chair to foil any attempt to free her, and thus they carried her to San Roque del Ttio. There they placed her on a mule, and scarcely had the animal taken a step than she fell from it in a most indecorous posture, causing injury to her beautiful face, an occurrence that also pained the sympathetic hearts of those who looked upon her.

When she entered the city of La Plata the citizens (and especially the compassionate women) came out when they heard of her arrival; and when they saw that she was beautiful—though already disfigured by her sufferings—and learned who she was, they wept bitterly for her misfortune. The case was heard before the most honorable justice Don José Calvo, and she was sentenced to die on the gallows, her noble estate availing nothing.

When the most illustrious and most reverend lord Don Fray Gaspar de Villaroel, archbishop of Charcas, saw the great peril in which Magdalena stood, he tried to ransom her with money. His lordship immediately offered twenty thousand pesos from his own funds and asked all charitable people to give a large amount as well so that a great sum of money might be gathered; and his lordship also offered to collect the amount offered by the city of Potosí, all of which would be delivered to the royal officials within the space of two months in exchange for her life. But the judges of the court refused absolutely to grant this. Then this gentle prince of the Church requested an audience, and when it had been granted, he went to the court. They gave him a suitable seat, though he at once stood up and, bareheaded, began to plead most eloquently for Magdalena's life in the name of charity. Sometimes the king's justice replied, "Father, hold your peace," and sometimes, "Father, it is not possible; there is no way to do what you ask." That merciful prince of the Church repeated his pleas, begging the chief justice to accept for His Majesty's expenditures the amount of money that had been promised for the woman's life. He implored him to temper his justice and leave room for mercy, and pointed out that it was hardly a question of her life, for she was already a dying woman, that the woman was already so crushed and trampled that she would never rise again, and other merciful and eloquent arguments, alleging all that he could in her favor. But all was in vain, and that just and charitable prince of the Church left the court deeply afflicted; but this did not prevent him from asking each of the judges yet again for her life; and they, seeing that he persisted in his entreaties, decided to send the case to the viceroy for review, which they did. And meanwhile we will recount what happened to Magdalena in her prison.

All possible attempts were made to free her, and none succeeded. Religious from various congregations entered to confess and console her; they dressed her in their habits, but when they put on the cowl to take her from the prison in that disguise, she cried out that she was choking, that they must take it off, which clearly showed that it was God's will that she should pay for her crimes. She also pretended to be mad and did so with such skill that it seemed to be sufficient to gain her freedom: she performed innumerable exaggerated antics and indecent acts, and spoke insane words. But one night the royal judge Don José Calvo was clever enough to have her watched through a crack in the door to see whether she performed those mad acts, some so obscene that they cannot be described, when she was alone. A maidservant was with her in the cell, and Magdalena, all unsuspecting, asked her, "Tell me, did I feign madness well, did I perform the proper actions? Will they think that I have truly lost my mind?" And the girl answered, "Yes indeed, my lady, they will surely believe it, for you have feigned it very well; continue to behave thus and it will serve to set you free." Now, since the constable at the door heard this, he went in saying, "So, Señora Magdalena, your madness was feigned? Be sure that there is no help for you now. Make your peace with God, for you must die."

When Magdalena saw that death was indeed approaching, she made earnest efforts to prepare herself for her passing. The inhabitants of that city felt pity for her and as a last resort tried to remove her from the prison. For this purpose they poured a large quantity of very strong vinegar on the parts of the houses adjoining the walls of her cell in order to soften and break them; but the walls became all the harder, and so this and other attempts failed. At last the sentence arrived from Lima, which added that she should be dragged to the foot of the gallows and hanged there publicly. As soon as the archbishop learned of this, he sent word to the two religious colleges that all the seminarians must wait at a certain corner she had to pass and that there they would snatch her from the arms of the law. The students, together with the clergy and monastics, procured a number of weapons and hid in various houses before which she must pass. But it was not God's will that she be saved, for the officers of the law became suspicious, and on the day when she was to be taken from the prison (a large bag in which to drag her ready at the door and the ecclesiastics lying in wait to rescue her) she was brought out dead, for they had already garroted her.

They hung her body in the plaza from three stakes, to the great sorrow of all who came to see her. They thought of her noble degree, her riches, and esteem, and then they saw her dangling from a rope, poorly and filthily dressed—she who had owned more than 200,000 pesos in gold, silver, jewels, pearls, slaves, fine clothing, and precious objects—and to see her there with one coarse red stocking and the other white, with an old, broken pair of men's shoes—she whose tiny feet had been shod in sweet-smelling cordovan leather and exquisite pattens, she who, when she passed through the streets of Potosí, had outshone the sun with her great beauty and high degree!—to see her there astonished and grieved the whole city. Who could have predicted that such fortunate beginnings would come to so disastrous an end? Who could have said that such favorable circumstances would breed irremediable misfortunes? Who could have foretold that from so many creature comforts and splendid feasts and pastimes, unforeseeable sorrows would arise? Truly there is no order in the good and evil things of this life: what seems like pleasure is often torment, and what causes sorrow can end in glory. These are judgments of the Lord Most High, and it is not right that our poor human understanding should presume to encompass them.

One of the Negresses was tortured with pincers and then hanged. The other had her punishment postponed because she was with child; she gave birth and after that was hanged. This pitiful tragedy was recited by poets in Castilian verse, and others sang it in Castilian mixed with the Indian tongue; and simply hearing it sung was enough to make the women who heard it fall to weeping.

1674 · Claudia the Witch

Let us now relate the strange exploits or diabolical deeds of a famous witch whose crimes were discovered in the year 1674, when they came to an end. But before recounting them I wish to declare the unhappiness and great evil that, among so many felicities, this kingdom of Peru experiences in possessing the coca herb (which is taken by those ministers of the devil for their abominable vices and execable evil-doing), although I will first set forth some of its good properties.[21]

In his *Chronicle of Peru* Pedro Cieza de León,[22] referring to the value placed on this herb in his time, writes: "In all parts of the Indies where I have traveled I have observed that the native Indians take great pleasure in holding in their mouths roots, branches, or herbs. And thus, in the district of Antioquia some are accustomed to use a small coca leaf and in the provinces of Arma other herbs; in the provinces of Quimbaya and Ancerma they employ small soft trees that are always very green, cutting twigs from them, which they hold between their teeth and never tire of chewing; in most of the Indian villages of Cali and Popayán they keep the small coca leaf I have already mentioned in their mouths and extract from small gourds a certain mixture or preparation that they make and put in their mouths and hold there; and they do the same with a kind of earth resembling lime. Everywhere in Peru," continues this author, "it was the custom, and is the custom today, to hold this coca in the mouth; and they keep it there from early morning until they go to bed without removing it. Inquiring of some Indians why they always have this herb in their mouths (which they do not eat or do anything with except to hold it between their teeth) they said that with it they feel little hunger and that it gives them great strength and vigor. I believe," he continues, "that there must be some cause for this, though it seems to me to be a vicious custom and appropriate for such folk as these Indians are.

"This coca is planted in the Andes from Huamanga to the Villa de Plata" (this is the city that was later named La Plata);

"it grows into small trees, and the Indians cultivate it and care for it assiduously so that it will produce the leaf they call coca, which resembles myrtle" (and, indeed, there is some resemblance, but the leaf is twice as large as that of myrtle and more slender), "and they dry it in the sun and then place it in long narrow baskets, each of which holds somewhat more than an arroba.[23] And this herb or coca was so much esteemed in Peru in 1548, 1549, 1550, and 1551 that there has never been any herb or root in the world, nor anything produced from a tree, that is cultivated and produced each year (apart from spices, which are a different matter) that is so highly valued as this; repartimientos were valued in those years—that is, most of those in Cuzco, the city of La Paz, and the Villa de Plata—at eighty thousand pesos of income and at sixty and at forty and at twenty, some more and others less than these figures, all from this coca. And the man to whom an Indian encomienda was given considered as its chief income the baskets of coca he gathered. In short, it was held to be as precious as grass in Trujillo.[24] This coca was carried to the mines of Potosí to be sold; and so many trees were planted and so many leaves of it gathered that it is now worth a great deal less than formerly, but it will never cease to be esteemed. There are some rich men in Spain who grew wealthy through the value of this coca, trading in it and reselling it and buying it from the Indians in their tiangues, or markets." Thus far the quotation from the aforesaid author.

As for what this chronicler says about having asked the Indians why they always kept the herb in their mouths and their reply that they did so because it made them feel little hunger and gave them great strength and vigor, this is true to the present day, to the point that no Indian will go into the mines or to any other labor, be it building houses or working in the fields, without taking it in his mouth, even if his life depends on it. Since at the present time this herb grows only in the Andes (in a spot commonly called Yungas, which is almost three hundred leagues distant from this imperial city), it is brought from there in great abundance to all these higher provinces, which never lack for it, especially this city with the excuse of the mines; a basket weighing one arroba, more or less, is worth seven or eight pesos, with some variations.

Among the Indians (and even the Spaniards by now) the

custom of not entering the mines without placing this herb in the mouth is so well established that there is a superstition that the richness of the metal will be lost if they do not do so. When I was only ten years of age, I was in the Vilacota mine (some fifty leagues distant from this city), and one day when I tried to enter the main shaft, the Indians stopped me, saying that I could not enter without taking that herb into my mouth. I was reluctant, but they insisted, until the Spanish miner informed me of the Indians' superstitious belief and that in consequence I must either refrain from going in or chew the herb. Eventually I took it in order to please the owner, who was sending me to keep watch over a storage chamber where there was a rich deposit of ore so that the Indians would not steal it. As soon as I placed two leaves in my mouth, my tongue seemed to grow so thick that there was no room for it in my mouth, and it burned and prickled so much that, unable to bear it, I told the miner that I could not enter the mine owing to the effects of the coca. He laughed at me and gave me a small piece of a doughy substance resembling a black lozenge, saying that it was called "sugar" and that if I took it along with the coca the bad effects that it had caused would disappear. I took it into my mouth believing that it was what he had said, and I swear that I have never tasted anything so bitter in my life, so much so that I spit out the so-called sugar together with the herb I had in my mouth and would have vomited up my entrails after them had not the symptoms passed off. I was then told that the Indians call that little lozenge "llipta" and that they make a mixture of ashes and roasted grains and bitter roots, and form it into lumps about eleven inches long and sell it in this form for the Indians to take along with the coca.[25] At last, after having washed out my mouth thoroughly, I took a piece of bread and went into the mine with this; nor was the wealth that God had put into the ore diminished thereby.

The Indians being accustomed to taking this herb into their mouths, there is no doubt that as long as they have it there they lose all desire to sleep, and since it is extremely warming, they say that when the weather is cold they do not feel it if they have the herb in their mouths. In addition, they also say that it increases their strength and that they feel neither hunger nor thirst; hence these Indians cannot work without it.

When the herb is ground and placed in boiling water and if a person then takes a few swallows, it opens the pores, warms the body, and shortens labor in women; and this coca herb has many other virtues besides. But human perversity has caused it to become a vice, so that the devil (that inventor of vices) has made a notable harvest of souls with it, for there are many women who have taken it—and still take it—for the sin of witchcraft, invoking the devil and using it to summon him for their evil deeds. There are some people who doubt the efficacy of witchcraft; this must be because they observe this vice almost exclusively in women who, for the most part, lack the capacity to reason and know how to do nothing but doing nothing. (I refer to foolish women, those who lack intelligence and the many who have fallen prey to vice.) Those who ignore this are vastly mistaken, so much so that the very things that make them doubt it are those that should convince them. For who could fall into such madness but one who was weak in intellect—namely, a woman?

Moreover, since the devil's chief intention is to corrupt our holy Catholic faith and since women are so prone to believe in evil, it is they whom the devil most frequently attacks by tempting them to this sin. We must also bear in mind that women's unquiet tongues often lead the devil to pursue them with this lure; for they are either unable or unwilling to keep their mouths shut, communicating with each other shamelessly and fearlessly, and thus the number of women who fall prey to this superstition is infinite and the offense offered to heaven by this enemy of ours is all the greater. And as I have been saying, in this kingdom of Peru this evil spirit has offered them the coca herb to invoke him and commit the sin of witchcraft; and when they do not take it to perform witchcraft, there are innumerable addicts who have been lost by taking it into their mouths (neither eating it nor drinking its juice), men as well as women. They soon end as beggars, all the alms they collect going merely to maintain this infernal vice.

With such ferocity has the devil seized on this coca herb that—there is no doubt about it—when it becomes an addiction it impairs or destroys the judgment of its users just as if they had drunk wine to excess and makes them see terrible visions; demons appear before their eyes in frightful forms. In this city of Potosí it is sold publicly by the Indians who work in the mines, and so the harm arising from its continued abundance cannot be corrected; but neither is that harm remediable in other large cities of this realm, where the use and sale of coca have been banned under penalties as severe as that of excommunication and yet it is secretly bought and sold and used for casting spells and other like evils.

Would that our lord the king had ordered this noxious herb pulled up by the roots wherever it is found, not permitting even the memory of it to remain, even though the proprietors and owners of those lands would protest that their private interests were damaged thereby; for it is worse to allow obstinate souls to perish because they have invoked and compacted with the devil to do such kinds of abomination as are caused by this coca. Great good would follow were it to be extirpated from this realm: the devil would be bereft of the great harvest of souls he reaps, God would be done a great service, and vast numbers of men and women would not perish (I refer to Spaniards, for no harm comes to the Indians from it). Let us choose one among innumerable examples, that of a woman who by taking this infernal herb caused all manner of evil in this city and in other places where she went, until God took away her life in the midst of her sins.

This woman was born in one of the cities of Tucumán. Her parents were Spaniards, her name was Doña Claudia, and her aspect was pleasing both in face and body. So great a witch was she in this realm of Peru that Erinto, Circe, and Medea were not her equal. Among the Indians, pagans as well as believers, in a number of Indian villages where she went in Tucumán, Tarija, and Chichas she froze the clouds whenever she wished, covering the face of the sun with them, and on other occasions she made the most stormy sky serene; she brought men from faraway lands and formed beautiful gardens with beautiful women in them, with which she drove men mad by making them love those visions; and there was a certain corregidor in Porco to whom she showed his home city of Madrid in a mirror because he wished to see it.

After she had come to Potosí, a certain lady went one day to her house (having heard of Doña Claudia's reputation) to ask her help against the royal auditor Andrés Sáenz Bretón, saying that he was pursuing her for her favors, which was displeasing to her. Claudia heard her petition, consoled her, and promised to find a solution for her problem that very night. She took coca and retired to rest in another room where there was an old woman more than seventy years of age, so ugly and fearsome to look upon that anyone who saw her had no trouble in imagining what the devil would be like. This old woman was a procuress and flitted about after midnight on her errands; it was known of her also that in Lima, where she was born, she had given suck to children in her youth, for she was a hired wet nurse, and that in her old age she sucked children (but in a different place), doing them irremediable harm. Claudia had brought the old woman to her house to assist her in the deceits employed by sinners such as she. Then Claudia came out of the room and told the lady to go home and to have no fear that the gentleman would continue to pursue her. She also told her that she would transform that repulsive old woman into the person of the lady and that the auditor would sleep with her, and in the morning she would return the old woman to her own body and that this would suffice to make him hate the lady. All took place as she had predicted, for the old woman slept with the auditor that night and it seemed to him that she was that elegant lady whom he adored; and in the morning he found himself in bed with the old woman, who nauseated him so much that he never gave the lady another thought, for he could not forget the transformation of the horrible old woman, whom he expelled from his house with all possible haste.

One day a young gentleman who had heard of Claudia's spells went to her house and, offering her a rich jewel, rashly begged her to find a way to make a certain maiden, as beautiful as she was noble and with whom he was madly in love, respond to his libidinous desires, for although he had made them known to her, there was no prospect of her granting them. The evil Claudia promised that he would attain his desire if only he would bring her some article that the girl had worn or had on her feet. The base youth laid hands on a shoe through one of her maids and took it to the witch. But while he was about the business of acquiring it (a matter of three days), God disposed that the girl should escape evil, for she was attacked by a chill and then a mortal fever, and within twelve days she was dead.

It is not that I believe in (rather, I deny) the power of

witchcraft, but its spells perturb the judgment and strangle and obfuscate the spirit, and all spells are sooner or later poisons that destroy life; but to believe that they affect free choice or rational will is a piece of nonsense unworthy of being set down in writing, much less of being believed.

When Don Diego Muñoz de Cuéllar y Umbría, a knight of the Order of Santiago, was senior magistrate of the cabildo in this city, some thieves stole the whole stock of a merchant, worth more than twenty thousand pesos in money and goods. That night the above-mentioned gentleman was out on patrol, and seeing from a distance that they were thieves who had just committed a robbery (for they were carrying the stolen goods on their backs), he set off after them. They fled into the house of the famous sorceress, Claudia, and entering her room, the thieves, fifteen men in all, brought in everything they had stolen and begged for her aid. The woman at once placed fifteen coca leaves in her mouth and quickly told them to huddle in one corner of the room close to the pile of loot that they had thrown down there.

The officer soon entered, for he had come in pursuit of those men, and in a flash the thieves were transformed by the force of the witch's spell into dogs and cats, and the stolen goods into a pile of meat, whereupon the animals began to snarl and bite each other. The woman, pretending to scream with fear, leaped out of bed and began to beat them with a stick to eject them from the room and complained that those animals were fighting to steal the meat from her. The officer, when he saw that the thieves were not in the room even though he had seen them enter it, departed in great confusion, and the witch undid the spell that had changed the thieves' appearance, although, like the "cats" they were, they continued to scratch.[26] No longer in the shape of dogs and cats but in great contentment, the thieves divided their booty, giving a large part of it to Claudia, whose art had made the transformation.

In this same year a certain woman came to see the witch and told her that she had arranged a marriage for her daughter with a man lately come to Potosí, that the girl was certainly not a virgin, and that because her husband-to-be was under the impression that she was, he had asked for her hand in marriage. She asked Claudia to remedy through her magic art her daughter's carelessness in not having preserved her virginity. The accursed female consoled the mother and assured her that the daughter would not lose her matrimonial chance on that account. And, indeed, through devilish means the girl found herself closed up tight again, to the point that the husband confided to his friends that he had had difficulty in consummating the marriage on the wedding night, so virgin was his bride. This caused much laughter among those who knew about the girl's earlier love affair.

Don Pedro de Ayamonte, an Andalusian from the city of Utrera, arrived in Potosí that same year with a large amount of Castilian clothing (for he was an important shipper of such articles) and, unaware of Claudia's evil practices, soon became engaged in an illicit affair with her. One day he began to complain in her presence of the lack of bread in this city, for there had been little rain that year and the harvest was meager. Then (since Spaniards are fond of saying that in their country mosquitoes are as large as elephants and other such absurdities) he told her that in his native town of Utrera the loaves of bread were so big that they weighed two hundred ounces apiece, to which Claudia replied, "That is not true, Don Pedro, for I have been in Utrera and seen them, and they are not of the size you say." The Andalusian took offense at being contradicted and told her very angrily that what he had said was true, that they were even larger than he had said, and that she could not have seen them. Claudia continued to contradict him and swore that she had been in Utrera and said that it was but a few leagues distant from Seville; she then gave this and that particular of the town, how it enjoyed a calm and temperate climate and how, as a result, it produced a vast abundance of wheat, wine, and oil; she said that he should not tire himself in trying to persuade her that the loaves of bread were so large and that for proof of this he should come for the midday meal (this was in the morning) and he would see and eat those loaves at her table. Don Pedro agreed to this; he went away, and before his return the witch took the coca and invoked the devil. She spoke with him, and in a few short hours he brought her the loaves; when Don Pedro saw and ate them (for they were indeed real loaves) he found that they were the very loaves of his home city. He was astonished by this occurrence, but at the time did not realize by whose agency they had been brought. Now these are the

"Utrera loaves" so celebrated in Potosí; the phrase became a byword when loaves of bread were small.

Not only was this woman evil in herself, but she also infected other women, who did not fail to follow in her footsteps. There is much weakness and want of understanding in many of this sex, for they are always curious about things that do not concern them (a defect inherited from the first woman) and easily betray themselves to the serpent. The witch trained them, therefore, in such a way that they imitated her in most of her evil deeds. During this same year, when four of her pupils were gathered together, a young man who was a harp player entered, and since he discovered them in that house taking coca (which they had on a silver platter as though they needed such niceties to sully their souls), the women were disturbed to see that he had found them engaged in so infernal an exercise. But to ensure that the young man would not reveal their secret, they begged him to join them in taking the herb.

The poor musician made his excuses on the ground that it would be harmful, since he had never taken the drug before, and said that all he could do for them was to play the harp. One of them rose and, going into a small alcove within the room, took out a glass of wine and offered it to the young man to drink. He did so, and at once his judgment was so unbalanced that, though at the time it was but seven o'clock in the evening, he wandered through the streets of the town and did not arrive home until midnight; his wife, who had gone to the door because she was worried about her husband's late arrival, found him there on all fours, believing himself to be an animal. She took him inside, and after several days he recovered the power of speech (which he had lost completely), and though he was unable to describe what ailed him, it was clear from his words that witchcraft was the cause.

At last the tears and efforts of his wife aroused compassion, for one day a Franciscan monk came to see her and told her that a woman would come that night in disguise to cure the sick man and that they were not to ask who she was but to do whatever she ordered. The plan was put into effect, and the woman came with her face covered; she brought a glass containing a liquor, added herbs, and, giving it to the sick man to drink, she went away without having spoken more than a few words to ask for what she needed, even then disguising her voice. The sick man recovered, but a little more than a year later he died suddenly, as a result either of this illness or of some other complaint.

In short, the like of this witch Claudia (the only Spanish woman who followed this trade) was never seen in this realm. According to the subsequent report of a maidservant she had brought from Tucumán, she could make the living see the dead persons whom they had asked her to show them in an infant's fingernail; and in a basin of water she painted for those ignorant folk, lacking in Christian faith, who used the services of this sorceress, whatever good or bad events they desired to know and see. This maidservant also recounted how three times every month they would go far away from this city (or so she believed, for the witch had taken her on one of these trips, although she did not know whether in body and soul or only in fancy) to a great field where many folk from different parts of the world were gathered, both male and female witches; and there other things took place that were so filthy and repugnant that she dared not, and indeed could not, describe them; she reported that the herbs with which her mistress Claudia anointed herself were extremely cold and that with them she conjured up a very black and horrible demon and that she extracted from those herbs the juice with which she made the mixture; and that the coca herb was exceedingly hot, as the demon had said, and was as pleasant to her as the profit she made from it.

At last came the end of the witch Claudia's life (she being forty-five years of age in 1674, in the month of November), which surprised her in the utmost obstinacy. God granted her no more time (in that last moment) than to call a priest of the sacred Society of Jesus and ask him to take certain lumps of wax and other infernal instruments from a drawer; and she said that if he would remove certain pins and wrappings from them, five priests on whom she had cast spells would be cured; two of them were in this city, one in La Plata, one in Los Reyes, and another in Mexico. Though she had cast spells on many men and women, she said, she did not know how at this late date to undo what she had done, for her life was coming to an end. While saying this she lost consciousness, and although the Jesuit father urged her to confess fully and beg God for mercy, he could not make her do so, nor did she return to herself; rather, she called out with a terrible cry to the servant to bring her coca (for this was all she was capable of saying), and when the servant refused to do so, she rose furiously from her bed, seized a basket that was in an alcove, and taking out a handful of the herb, thrust it into her mouth; raving, she fell dead before the eyes of the priest, who could do nothing to help her.

These and other irremediable injuries have been brought about by the vice of coca in this realm. May God permit it to be rooted out wherever it is found, so that not so many souls be lost and not so much harm be done to persons and to property!

1676 · The Brief Engagement of Francisca Irueña

A lady by the name of Doña Feliciana Carrillo took up residence in Potosí; a native of the city of Los Reyes, she brought with her a very beautiful daughter named Doña Francisca Mirueña, who had been born in the city of Oruro, where Doña Feliciana had been married; from this marriage, which had lasted but three years, she had only the one daughter. Soon after she became a widow the lady moved to Potosí with her whole household and, as I have said, established herself there. This had taken place in 1674. Two years later the daughter, Doña Francisca, attained the age of fourteen years; nature had truly endowed her with rare beauty. Both mother and daughter were in correspondence with Captain Don Luis de Villasirga, a gentleman belonging to the Order of Santiago, who was in Los Reyes. In the city of Oruro this gentleman and Doña Feliciana had reached an understanding that as soon as her daughter was old enough they would be married, for they were equals on every count and Don Luis was deeply in love with the girl's beauty and good qualities. So impatient was he (for which no one was responsible, since the only impediment was her tender age) that he tried to pass the period of waiting by traveling to different cities. It is a most useful remedy in such cases to avail oneself of variety and diversion, for although it does not bring affairs to a speedier conclusion, it at least makes the wait more tolerable and seemingly shorter. Among the servants employed by this gentleman was one Pedro de Triesta, of the kingdoms of Spain. He was a young and handsome lad, and, without Doña Francisca's knowing it, had been utterly lost in idolizing her beauty ever since the time when all of them had been together in Oruro.

After this beautiful girl had passed her fourteenth birthday (which was the date that had been agreed upon), both ladies wrote to Lima to tell the captain that they were awaiting his arrival so that the marriage could take place, and Don Luis replied that he desired nothing better and that within the month he would be on the road, bringing his large fortune with him. The evil Pedro de Triesta knew all this, and since his love had reached such a pitch that it allowed him not a moment's peace, he decided not to die of it without setting forth and attempting a stratagem as difficult as it was rash. But of what undertakings is love not capable, and what extraordinary things does it not inspire in those who follow its banner?

Pedro de Triesta, therefore, stole ten thousand pesos from his master, slipped out of Lima, and set out for Potosí without anyone's learning his destination. He arrived safely in Oruro and from there, forging his master's signature, wrote a love letter to Doña Francisca. He told her that he could not bear so much delay and had hastened there from Lima, and that within four days, should a favorable response from her overtake him on the road, he would be in her arms—the arms of one whom he felt to be already his wife. He begged her particularly not to give her mother any hint of his journey or his arrival, because he still had to return to Oruro to wait for the rest of his clothing and other property that was in Arequipa, so as to be able to make a grand entrance. In addition to this he implored her as his beloved wife to arrange for them to see each other alone on the night of his arrival as secretly as possible; he promised not to pass the limits of chastity, expressing the wish merely to see her and embrace her tenderly and return to Cuzco that same night. This was the susbstance of the letter, but it was written in such honeyed terms that it would have had the same effect on any woman as it had on the unfortunate Doña Francisca, who believed that her beloved Don Luis was showing his great love for her.

As soon as the girl saw her lover's own signature (as she took it to be) and the amorous terms of the letter, she was inflamed with passion in the expectation that that gentleman was to be her husband, and she acceded to everything that the servant, Pedro de Triesta, requested. She spoke with the messenger who had brought the letter more openly than she ought to have done; for when women of position and young girls disregard honor and give rein to their tongues, breaking through all reticences and thereby giving public notice of the secrets buried in their hearts, they are certain to find themselves in a very delicate position. The girl wrote a reply saying that on the night specified she would await him in all secrecy, after ten o'clock in the evening, in a room some distance away from her bedroom, thus showing how quickly and powerfully love had influenced her. (In Oruro she and Don Luis had pledged themselves chastely, but being a younger girl then, she had offered the gentleman merely the affection that she felt for him.) By good luck the servant was succeeding in his lustful design.

And so, when the month of August arrived, Pedro de Triesta also arrived in the valley of Tarapaya, and from there sent word of his coming to Doña Francisca. Still deceived, the girl was beside herself with joy and arranged for the hour and method of his secret entry into the house. To do so she made use of a maidservant who was to obtain the keys to the street door and who, after the household had retired for the night, would open the door and bring Doña Francisca's suitor to the appointed room. A message was sent to the impostor whom Doña Francisca thought to be Don Luis de Villasirga, her future husband. Pedro, who had already arrived in this city, was so crafty that, having fixed the hour of ten o'clock at night for his entry into the house, he came two hours later, so that the girl (now in despair of his coming) had undressed and gone to bed in that room, in a bed prepared for her by the servant, for she could not return to her own bedroom without her mother's hearing her. This is precisely what the evil Pedro de Triesta had anticipated—that he would find her in bed—the better to carry out his criminal intent.

At last he entered the house, and on the way to the room where Doña Francisca was he told the maidservant (giving her several pesos) to go back to her room and that he would tell her when it was time for him to leave, for the maid's room was close by. The maidservant obeyed him in everything, since Don Luis was unknown to her and Pedro had come well dressed in rich clothing. She merely informed her mistress that her lover was at the door and returned to her room. Pedro, with his hat pulled down over his face, closed the door and approached the frightened girl, who had quickly covered herself, leaving only her eyes showing. "My lady," he said to her, "do not be frightened when you hear what I have to tell you. Know that I am Pedro de Triesta, an equal of your master Don Luis de Villasirga and not his servant as I am thought to be; for nobles do not serve private persons," and so saying he uncovered his face by doffing his hat and continued, "and especially in these Indies. My limited means obliged me to serve him. I have helped him to acquire two hundred thousand pesos, and I myself have acquired twenty thousand; these pesos are yours; they are at my lodging, and once they are brought here you may make free use of them. I have been your servant ever since I first knew you in Oruro, and in the future I intend to serve you with all my strength. I implore you, my lady, to return my love, which is so great that had it not been sustained by my hopes I could never have survived without your presence. Do not hope to take Don Luis as your husband" (oh, what a traitor, a thousand times ungrateful to your master!), "for you should know that everything he has written concerning his arrival is false, for he is engaged in a love affair with a woman below his station, whom he intends to marry. Take me, instead of Don Luis, as your husband, without waiting around for someone whose merits are greater than mine. It is to beg this favor of you that I have come. My only crime has been to forge the signature of Don Luis; but even that was a lover's stratagem, for I believe that otherwise I would not have had the joy of seeing you."

The traitor actually went this far in his lies, born of his audacity in abusing the great trust and excessive affection in which he was held by Don Luis, who on a number of occasions had spoken to Pedro of his love for Doña Francisca, praising her beauty so enthusiastically that he had lit flames of lust in this false friend and worse servant that were hotter than real fire. The girl listened to this string of lies from the traitor's mouth, and as soon as he had finished his tale she uncovered her radiantly beautiful face, crimson with the natural shame his words had aroused (or, which is more likely, with the anger she felt), and said to him: "I do not doubt that Don Luis may have deceived me with another woman unworthy of his person, for he is a man and capable of doing what many others do; but I rather incline to consider everything that you have told me as a lie, and it all smells to me of treason; and though you say that I should hesitate to take Don Luis for my husband, I do not want to know any other man, even though he were a king. How much more ought I to mistrust you who, being his servant (though you deny it), give me to understand by your speech that you are base in every respect." When Pedro de Triesta heard this he replied, overcome with anger, "All may be as you say, but since the opportunity has come into my hands I am determined not to let it go, and so, with or without your consent, I mean to have my way with you."

The girl rose from her bed in a rage, but when she tried to open the doors the wretch held her back, and seizing a dagger informed her that he would cut her to pieces if she cried out and did not permit him to do his will. Then, completely undone, she fell to the floor, and that evil man took her in his arms and returned her to her bed, where he took his pleasure of her; and then, tying her hand and foot, he left the room and went to that of the maid, quietly asking her to open the street doors of the house. She did so, and the traitor returned to his lodging and the maid to her mistress's room, where, seeing the state the poor girl was in, she nearly went out of her mind.

Doña Francisca, the unhappy victim of the rape, did not even wait for the servant to untie her, but at once told her to follow that man as secretly as she could and take careful note of where he was lodging. This she did so skillfully that, without Pedro's knowledge, she saw him enter one of the houses in the Chingana district,[27] where he stayed behind closed doors. She returned to her mistress, whom she found in floods of tears; but when Doña Francisca learned of the good success her servant had had she became calmer for a time and began to plan vengeance.

The servant untied her, and since day was just breaking she was able to return to her bedroom without her mother's hearing her. Then she wrote a message to Lucas Alvarez, who was an elderly man and a native of this city, a person with a lofty sense of honor. Though well along in years, he was still a man of great courage (which courage in his youth had been remarkable). He was related to Doña Francisca on her father's side. She described the whole affair to him in writing and, placing satisfaction for the crime in his hands, sent her maidservant to give him the message and show him the house that she had seen Pedro de Triesta enter, begging her to be quick so that he would not escape. When Lucas Alvarez read the message, since age had not cooled the ardors of his youth, he immediately set off in search of the traitor, armed only with sword and dagger. Once he was sure of the house he wisely determined to behave in such a way as to take proper satisfaction without arousing scandal, and therefore made discreet inquiries as to what the man was going to do.

Great undertakings demand that one's own prudence prevail over the malice of others. Spirit must keep a tight rein on thoughts, so that not the slightest chink or outlet is left for emotions to influence actions. Eyes speak, and the body's movements are commonly indicators of the business at hand. He who does not put his whole mind to the task speaks unaware what he ought to hide within his breast. One must act in such a way that one's appearance does not allow the tyrant, the traitor, or the criminal to guess what one is thinking. In any undertaking the man who protects himself by hiding his intentions, though only one, is worth two.

Acting prudently in every respect, Lucas Alvarez soon learned that Pedro de Triesta was to leave this city that very night to go to Tucumán, and that for this purpose he had acquired a spirited Chilean horse in hopes that the animal would quickly carry him many leagues away from the city. Once provided with this information, he returned home and procured another swift horse and the necessary weapons, for the traitor had also provided himself with arms; sending a message to the unhappy Doña Francisca, he consoled her and gave her hope that she would soon be avenged. She sent him a message of gratitude through her maidservant, who also took him two hundred pesos for his equipment and three gold rings set with very valuable stones. Lucas Alvarez refused to accept more than one ring, which he placed on his finger, saying that it sufficed to give him courage and that he accepted it for that reason and no other.

Through further inquiries Lucas Alvarez received new information that afternoon, to the effect that Pedro de Triesta, in the company of a friend and countryman of his and a mulatto manservant from Lima—all three armed—planned to leave the city at ten o'clock at night, intending not to halt until they reached Toropalca, which is a town of Christian Indians in the province of Porco and eighteen leagues distant from Potosí. And so, at the same hour, which was about five o'clock, the doughty Lucas Alvarez mounted a mule and bade one of his nephews follow him in great secrecy with the horse and weapons; once in open country they joined forces and traveled so fast that before dawn they had arrived without much effort at a spot two leagues from Toropalca, where Lucas rested the horse so that it would be ready for battle.

At about midday Pedro de Triesta, Alonso de Prada (his countryman), and the servant reached the spot; their mounts were very tired because they had been ridden too hard. Lucas Alvarez, astride his horse and armed with superb weapons, a heavy shield and a long, stout lance (which he knew very well how to handle, for he had employed it in his youth against the terrible Araucanians in the wars of Chile), rode out to meet Triesta and Prada. The latter was riding a skinny, tired nag, and Triesta's Chilean horse was also exhausted, even though it was of a strong and fiery temper. Lucas Alvarez told him angrily that he had come to avenge the insult committed by Triesta against Captain Don Luis de Villasirga and against Doña Francisca Mirueña; and then, calling him traitorous, wretched, ungrateful, and perfidious, challenged him to fight lance to lance—for Triesta had a lance also, although it was very short.

Pedro de Triesta was astonished to find himself so quickly challenged by someone who knew of his wicked deed, but as he had been a cavalryman in several companies in Spain, it was no novelty for him to engage in a bloody skirmish with the old man. He could not exonerate himself, nor did he even try, for Lucas Alvarez had repeated to his face all the infamies he had committed, insisting many times that should his arm lack valor to punish such evil deeds, the heavens would shower thunderbolts on him in vengeance. At this juncture Triesta's mulatto servant aimed and fired the musket that he was carrying at Lucas Alvarez, meaning to end the confrontation by killing him. But God (Who was watching over this affair) guided the shot in such a way that it merely grazed the armor he was wearing. With the sudden noise the mulatto's mule reared and, twisting and kicking, tossed him some distance away, whereupon Lucas Alvarez's nephew rushed at him and administered two serious wounds and many blows, so that he was unable to move from the spot.

Meanwhile Triesta and his countryman, Prada, attacked Alvarez from horseback, the one with his short lance and the other with his sword; when Alvarez took Triesta's lance thrust on his shield, the lance broke and the point went through to his heavy jacket, where it was halted. Triesta could not pull the lance out of the shield, and when Lucas Alvarez realized his predicament and saw that Alonso de Prada was raining sword blows on him, he let go his shield to engage the other adversary; very skillfully turning his horse to set his lance at the ready, he fiercely charged Prada, who fell mortally wounded to the ground along with his horse. Then the nephew fell upon the wounded man, but seeing that he was incapable of coming to his countryman's aid, left him and returned to pick up Alvarez's shield, which Triesta had thrown on the ground after pulling out his lance; just as he laid hands on it he was wounded in the right arm by Triesta, so that he was rendered incapable of going to his uncle's aid.

Alvarez and Triesta, now fighting alone, attacked each other with terrible ferocity. The blow that Alvarez had received was very great, for it had broken through all his armor and left him wounded in the chest; and Triesta's was even worse, for he was wounded in the left arm under the shoulder, and the point of the lance had also penetrated his chest, breaking through his steel armor, his jacket, and his jerkin, and wounding him seriously in the breast. With this blow Alvarez's lance broke, and he turned his horse to draw his sword; when he turned to attack Triesta, he found that the other was already upon him, wounding him a second time with his short lance in the right thigh. Triesta's horse was an extremely good one, and had it not been tired there is no doubt the fight would have gone ill for Lucas Alvarez, for his mount had no other advantage than that of being well rested; and yet with all this his adversary had tired the horse considerably, for it had to advance and retreat each time that its master attacked.

They had now been fighting for an hour, and Pedro de Triesta was growing desperate because if the battle continued, his powerful horse would be too exhausted to move; and although he wished to finish the battle on foot, Alvarez did not give him the opportunity, owing to his age. At last Triesta saw that the fight was not going to end, and he turned his horse and went to the spot where the mulatto was stretched out on the ground, attempting to bind up his wounds. When Lucas Alvarez saw his adversary departing, he thought that he was going to give up the fight and went after him, demanding that he make an end of it; suddenly Triesta turned on Alvarez and flew at him like an arrow. At this point the mulatto got up quickly, for they were very close to him, and when Triesta's horse saw this it suddenly stopped and reared. What does not conspire to bring calamity to a traitor? Since exemplary punishment of the guilty is by divine leave, their arrogance itself sets them on the last stage of their perdition. The rearing of the horse gave Alvarez time to quickly spur his own mount, and on reaching Triesta he dealt him a frightful sword thrust. The blade went in under his left arm, and he fell from his horse mortally wounded. Then Alvarez dismounted and went after the wounded man, but seeing that he was unconscious, withheld further attack. He remounted his horse and, applying pressure to his nephew's wound, told him to take the mule and go where he could be looked after. At this juncture Triesta's servant began to utter cries and pitiful groans, saying that his master was dead. Alonso de Prada (who was also in bad shape from his wounds) then approached the dying man. Observing that he was coming to his senses somewhat and was asking them for a confessor, Prada mounted his horse and started for Toropalca. Before he had gone a quarter of a league he met the priest of that parish, who was taking the sacraments to an Indian; he brought him to Pedro de Triesta's side, and they were administered to him. Two hours later he died, showing signs of great repentance for his sins. The priest had the body sent to his parish, where a good funeral was given him. The mulatto servant also died of his wounds there, and Alonso de Prada was on the point of following him; but at last he recovered and, taking the money and everything else the dead man had had with him, went to Los Lipes after paying the funeral expenses.

Such was the result of Doña Francisca's having relied on the valiant Lucas Alvarez—in a few hours the wrongdoers were punished and killed, an end which their actions richly deserved, because it is madness for a man who consistently does evil to expect anything good.

Lucas Alvarez and his nephew reached a little Indian village that was nearby, and there their wounds were dressed; that same night they returned to this city, and on the following day told Doña Francisca the whole story. The lady, very glad to have been avenged, thanked them sincerely and then told it all to her mother, who was so astonished that she did not know what to do. Doña Francisca then dispatched a message to Captain Don Luis de Villasirga, sending him the letter of the dead Triesta, his servant, and recounting everything that had happened without departing one jot from the truth. She also begged him to return to Lima and marry another, for she felt that she was now unworthy of his honor. When the gentleman received this message (which reached him in Arequipa), he was moved to pity by the case and sent a letter consoling her and offering her his hand; but Doña Francisca refused and again implored him to return to Lima. This he did, and she remained in this city, grieving over her misfortune. Ten years later she departed this life, having occupied those years in works of merit, receiving the sacraments often and carrying out many works of charity among the poor.

1677 · Sebastián and His Golden Spurs

IN April, 1677, Sebastián del Canto y Cerro, a poor man burdened with debts and with a wife and children, and despairing because he had no means of supporting them, determined to go one night (which was Easter eve) to the Mountain and enter one of the rich mines unbeknownst to its owner in order to extract some ore with which to satisfy his needs. The ancients were quite right in giving necessity the name "golden spurs," for the harsh impediment of poverty (as Alciatus calls it) clips the wings and hampers the progress of necessity; and since its spur is so indispensable it is no wonder that men overcome all obstacles and place their lives in manifest danger because of it.

This poor man, then, put his plan into effect and at about eight o'clock that night, relying on the little knowledge he had of the paths within those very large workings, entered them through a hole far distant from the mouth of the mine, for he knew that it was guarded. Having descended into the mine with great difficulty, he began to walk through it (not knowing where he was) in search of some vein or cutting where ore could be extracted; having walked for a long time, he came to a certain chamber where he stumbled over an obstruction and in his fall put out his candle. Poor Sebastián was left in that terrible labyrinth filled with terror, for he had unwisely failed to bring tinder, steel, or flint to make a light, a precaution that every Spaniard takes when he enters these deep mines for just such an eventuality. This also happened to me and Bartolomé Cotamito, mining supervisor for the chief of mines Antonio López de Quiroga, in the great shaft also called Cotamito in the old workings of the Discovery Lode.

I had asked this miner to accompany me and show me some of the mines in this shaft, in particular the one through which the water had passed in 1701 when a large part of the water that had covered these workings was drained off. Bartolomé Cotamito, that good man, acceded to my request, telling me to take great care with my feet, hands, and eyes, for all these are necessary to traverse the mines of this Mountain. We entered the shaft by a long and broad staircase hewn out of the rock, and then we traversed a number of cuttings so laboriously that I cursed my curiosity. Sometimes we had to climb straight down and at others to make use of hands and feet to climb up to other passages and scaffoldings, which he negotiated very skilfully, while I was so frightened that it seemed each step was going to be my last. There were passages so narrow that we had to crawl through them, always taking care not to extinguish the light I carried.

Soon we came to a bridge formed in mid-air of the stout wooden stakes used to make scaffoldings and ladders that are used in the deep mines to get from one place to another; the miner insisted that I cross it (merely to frighten me, as he afterward confessed). In reality, all the walking we had done and the trouble we had been to previously had been a path strewn with flowers in comparison with what we were now expected to traverse. That terrible bridge was about twenty-five yards long, with the stakes set into the walls on either side and about three handspans apart; beneath was a subterranean lake, so far below the stakes that it was barely visible. I told the miner that it would be difficult for me to cross over those stakes because I was afraid of falling, and not only would I lose my life but there would never be any way of recovering my body. "That is true," replied the miner, "but since you have come so far without showing signs of fear or weakness, I do not doubt that you will pass over those stakes very successfully, though I warn you that the tenth stake counting from this one is split down the middle, and hence you must step only on the ends, which are wedged into the walls on either side." As you may imagine, this was little comfort for a person who was convinced that he was going to end his life there, even without the new danger that had just been described to him. But whose vanity would not have been piqued, especially as the miner had begun by flattering me?

I therefore commended myself very earnestly to God and began to follow him. We were on equal terms, for neither was more familiar with the ladder than the other; then, only four stakes from solid ground, the miner's candle went out.

He stopped and asked me to hasten my steps so that I could give him light from the candle I was carrying, with which to light his own. This I did, and as I leaped to safety the movement caused my own light to go out and both of us were left in that terrible darkness. The miner was greatly mortified because, since both of us had carried lights, he had not taken the precaution of bringing a means of making fire. He told me that there was nothing to do but wait till night, when surely his assistant would pass by on his way to a cutting some distance from that place. He was much concerned and I was in despair, for it was only nine o'clock in the morning (according to our best calculations), and at this rate the miner would not arrive until eight o'clock at night. By the time he finally came, it seemed to me as if I had been there for more than two days. We relighted our candles and got out through another entrance, a long way from the one we had come in by, owing to the long detour we had taken, and full of dangerous passages.

Since I myself have experienced the anguish of having had my light extinguished, I can appreciate the feelings that overcame Sebastián del Canto, whom we left filled with terror and affliction, when, as he stumbled and fell, the candle he was carrying went out and left him with no hope of rescue such as we had, for the poor man neither knew where he was nor could suppose that anyone would pass by the place. Seeing himself in that terrible predicament and with the thought that his wife and children were waiting for him to alleviate their hunger and that he himself might well perish from hunger in that place, he felt grief so great that he was on the point of giving up the ghost. Now, Sebastián was very devoted to the Holy Christ of the parish of San Pedro (one of the most admirably fashioned images in the city and one that has performed many miracles), for since he lived near the church, he visited it often and prayed daily to the divine Lord to favor him in all his needs. Great was the need in which he now found himself, and so he earnestly pleaded for help and with a great effort began to grope his way through that terrible darkness to see if he could not find some path that would lead him to an open space, to an entrance, or to some place where he would find miners working. But he only succeeded in becoming more confused in that labyrinth, and so, despairing of ever getting out or finding human help in that desperate plight, seeing himself frustrated, and overcome with terror and hunger—for he had now been lost for three days—he fell on his knees and began to offer his life to God, resigning himself to His divine will.

Meanwhile his wife and children, knowing full well that poor Sebastián had gone to the Mountain with the intention of taking ore from some mine to assuage his need and seeing that by the second day he had not returned, guessed what had happened and began to bewail their misfortune. Just as all things that are greatly desired seem long in coming, though the delay be ever so small, so things that are feared seem to come quickly, though the delay be ever so great. Grief-stricken and certain of misfortune, they went to the church of San Pedro and fell at the feet of that miraculous image of Christ crucified and with copious tears implored it to cause their husband and father to appear, for they now had no one to support them.

The tears of Sebastián and of his wife and children were so efficacious that the Lord of Mercies was moved to succor them in their plight. He appeared to the unfortunate Sebastián in the same form as His sacred image in the chapel of the church of San Pedro, at some little distance from him and bathed in such radiance from the rays of light that streamed from Him that it seemed as if the sun itself had entered whole into that narrow place, but even brighter than the sun because it was the divine Christ our Lord. He made signs to Sebastián to follow Him and Sebastián complied; he soon found himself in the mouth, or opening, he had come in by. Nor did divine favor cease here, for he also found at the entrance, in a niche that was there, a good supply of very rich ore that could not have been in that place by any natural agency, but must have been put there supernaturally by God. Sebastián took it and, loading it on his back, started for home; after he had walked a few steps he met some friends of his who were coming to look for him, having heard from others that he had gone to the mines and had not reappeared. Sebastián asked them what day it was, and when they told him that it was Wednesday, he marveled greatly at having been favored by our Lord; he had been lost inside the mine for a little less than four days, for he had entered it on Saturday night at about eight o'clock and it was now ten o'clock in the morning of Wednesday.

They all came down from the Mountain, and before returning home Sebastián entered the church of San Pedro. Kneeling before that miraculous image of Christ our Lord, he fervently offered thanks for His divine mercy and then, accompanied by his friends, returned to his home, where he found many other friends consoling his wife and children in their misfortune. But seeing him enter alive (they were already mourning him as dead), all rejoiced and exchanged tender embraces. He told everyone who was present of the miracle, and all gave thanks to our Lord. With the ore he had found Sebastián satisfied his present needs and had enough with the rest to provide a modest living, for Divine Providence had solved all his problems.

1677 · A False Alarm

ONE day at the end of February, 1677, at five o'clock in the afternoon, a terrible alarm sounded in this imperial city, but the fright that it caused to all was more serious than the damage that was done. The situation was that, the rains having been very abundant that year, the city's inhabitants were concerned about the lakes, which ever since the memorable flood of Lake Caricari had not ceased to cause fear and apprehension.[28] It was, as I have said, five o'clock in the afternoon when suddenly the whole city was in a turmoil, with the tolling of bells calling for public prayer, children crying, women lamenting, and men in terror, and everyone saying that the dam had burst.

No words can describe the terrible fear that laid hold of great and small. The most modest and dignified men ran through the streets bareheaded and dressed as the alarm had surprised them; the most respectable women had no thought for their bare heads or whether their skirts decently covered them; those who were ill, if their condition was serious, begged to be carried from the houses, wrapped in blankets; and if they were able to walk, leaped out of bed and ran through the streets in their nightshirts, some to the slopes and hills of Munaypata and others to the heights of La Cantería and other places of safety.

The panic was so severe that two men who were carrying a sick woman between them wrapped in a blanket, hearing everyone repeat that the floodwaters were coming (though no one saw them) and realizing that they were hampered by the woman's weight, unwound her blanket and sheet in order to flee more swiftly and, seizing her by the hands, forced her to run all the way to the Mountain; her exhaustion was such that, though her illness was not grave, she died that night through the foolish action of those two men.

A certain noble lady of this city, whose temper was fierce and whose character reckless, happened at the moment the alarm was given to be cruelly and barbarously punishing one of her five daughters. Now, punishment of children is very necessary, for the parent who indulges a child when it is behaving badly is raising up a slave who may one day break his heart; but punishment must not be so severe that it turns to cruelty. The child loves the father as long as he does not realize that when his father dies he will inherit the estate: when he knows that, he soon forgets the existence he has been given and thinks only of the inheritance he has not yet received. This is the reason for the little love he has for his father once he has ceased to be a child, and whether or not he is the son or daughter of natural evil, he will often lose proper respect for his parents.

That mother had stripped her daughter naked and had her hanging by her hands with fetters on her feet and was giving her a cruel and fierce beating; this she did because the child had gone alone to hear mass at the church of San Francisco when her mother was out of the house, not to mention other acts of disobedience that had irritated the mother greatly. The lady's four other daughters, observing what they felt to be cruelty, in addition to many other things that their mother had done to them, were tempted by the devil to seize sharp knives and other steel weapons that lay at hand; taking sides against their mother, they determined to kill her, and they would surely have done so had not the alarm of the floodwaters been given at that very moment.

As soon as the mother realized what the tumult in the city meant, she left her daughter hanging there and quickly went to her room to fetch a shawl in order to flee. Then she called her four other daughters, and when they realized that she was about to lock them in a room and save herself, they turned the tables on her and fled, leaving the mother shut inside and taking the key with them. Then they hastened to the room where their mistreated sister was hanging, untied her, took off the fetters, and quickly getting dressed, fled with her to the Mountain. Meanwhile their mother, screaming at the top of her voice and cursing them roundly from her prison, showed her horrible character by invoking demons as she begged her daughters to let her out; but they repaid her cruelty in her own coin and fled, leaving her imprisoned.

After the panic was over, they went to the parish priest of San Juan, who was a relative of theirs, and begged him to help them, recounting all that had happened. The good priest took pity on those maidens, for he was aware of their mother's cruelty. Because it was now eight o'clock at night and raining pitchforks, he kept them in his house, assuring them that in the morning he would take them home and plead with their mother not to harm them, and that if her indignation had increased as a result of having been shut up and having passed such a bad night, he would inform the vicar and have them placed in a house of retreat at his own expense. Thus calmed, they supped and went to bed that night.

As soon as it was dawn they all went to their mother's house; on opening the room they found her dead, with her hair torn out and scratches on her arms and face, an indication of the ferocity and rage of her spirit, for she had not spared even herself the effects of her terrible passion and ferocious cruelty. Nor were the daughters blameless (apart from the act of parricide they had attempted); their disobedience had occasioned such despair that during the two years their mother had been a widow she had been able to control them only by harsh treatment. In the end their reputations suffered from the affair, though they were left more than moderately rich thanks to a large inheritance, a circumstance that made them regret their mother's death not at all.

1678 · The Making of Ambrosio de Soto

IN February, 1678, Ambrosio de Soto, a native of Mérida in Estremadura, arrived in this imperial city. Ill nourished and worse clothed, he began to beg for alms two days after his arrival in Potosí, asking that they be given for the love of God to maintain and provide dowries for four daughters whom he had left in his homeland. Alms were given to him generously and willingly, as is most customary in Potosí (and in this the city can offer an example to the whole world), for since it is the adopted fatherland of many, all who come here from far away to beg return to their homes with a great deal of money. In this charitable city no license is required to beg, either for the native poor or for those who come from outside, and still less to ask alms for building temples in different regions or realms, or repairing ruined churches, or providing dowries for maidens, or for any works of piety whatsoever. The city aids everyone generously, thinking not of the person to whom the alms are given but of Him in whose name they are asked, namely, God's.

For this reason many idlers, drones, and men incapable of work, in order to enjoy the privileges of poverty, dedicate themselves to begging for alms under various pretexts, traveling many hundreds of leagues with the certainty that they will return to their countries very comfortably off. (It is the poor who have the privileges of hidalgos, since they cannot be imprisoned for debt and do not pay commoners' or excise taxes, and in addition have other exemptions such as not needing to keep a manservant to spy on them while serving or betray them at the neighbor's house by telling, besides what has really happened, whatever he maliciously imagines or ignorantly suspects to have happened.) Now, wickedness finds a way to enter all human affairs, and so it is that more than one man has collected a large quantity of alms in this city under the guise of virtue and has employed them in very grave offenses against God. Our Ambrosio de Soto was not one of these, for in view of the fact that God's divine majesty as well as men aided him in the need he described, it must have been genuine. But let us go on with our story.

One day when he went out to beg he collected only eight pesos and returned to his lodging in despair at the little he had received and completely exhausted by the long distance he had walked. While he was resting, his landlord (his lodging was in one of the houses beyond the bridge of San Francisco in the Calle de la Amargura) approached him and said that he wished Ambrosio, since he had returned from begging at ten o'clock in the morning, would serve as overseer in the work of rebuilding a room that had collapsed, while he, the owner, went on an errand outside the city; and that he would give him a hundred pesos and meals for his labor. The poor Estremaduran accepted this arrangement joyfully, promising the owner that since he had offered him food and paid him so liberally he would not leave the house for a moment but would supervise the work very assiduously.

After all the necessary preparations had been made, the owner of the house went off on his journey and our Ambrosio set to work. The masons dug the foundations, and at a depth of a little more than a yard they reported that they thought there must be some masonry belonging to a vault beneath, to judge from the sound made by the blows of their pickaxes. This put the overseer on his guard, and guessing what it might be (or perhaps his heart gave him a premonition of good fortune), he ordered the masons to stop working in that place and to excavate for the foundations elsewhere. He did this more to keep them busy for the rest of the day, so that he could search the spot at night, than for any need to move the foundations.

With this intention, as soon as the masons had left for the night and accompanied only by a boy he had kept to help him, Ambrosio took a pickaxe and began to break through the roof of that vault. After very little effort he discovered an underground room, and the two descended into it and found, on a great stone in the middle of the room, two women's skeletons dressed in rich clothing and shod in pattens embroidered with gold and pearls (which had not deteriorated because they were not in the earth), giving the impression that they must have been important persons. In the rest of that room were many other bones, and on a peg, or nail, fastened to the wall our Estremaduran found something that amply repaid the trouble he had taken: a gold chain, twelve strings of pearls, and nine necklaces of precious diamonds. This seemed little enough to poor Ambrosio, for since his poverty was very great he wanted never to experience it again; in pursuance of this desire he began to turn over and search the bones and shift the stones from one place to another, a task that resulted in the discovery of five thousand pesos' worth of gold ingots. These he found in a box, or coffer, with certain letters in which expressions of love and jealousy were mingled. The signature on some of the letters was Don Pedro and on others Don Antonio, and the names of the women were Leonor and Damiana; according to the date of one of these letters they had been written in the city of La Plata fifty-four years previously.

It is unnecessary for pen to describe Ambrosio de Soto's joy, for anyone can imagine it. In the belief that God was looking after him and aiding him in his need, he told no one of the fortune he had found but kept it all for himself, revealing only his discovery of the bones, to which the brotherhood of the Mother of God of Mercy gave Christian burial. A few months later Ambrosio de Soto returned to Spain and from there wrote to the owner of the houses where he had found such a fortune (for indeed his discovery merited that name, especially when it had been made by a poor man) telling him that he had used it to provide a dowry for two of his daughters and expected to do the same for two others that he had.

1682 · A Servant of God

THE Reverend Padre Fray Juan José Ortiz, a religious of our father San Agustín, died in this city in 1682. He was a great servant of God, and among his admirable virtues that of charity toward the poor was particularly resplendent. Having given his whole estate (which was large) as alms to the poor, he went penniless to the monastery of San Agustín and requested the holy habit, which because of his great virtue and other merits was given him at once. He undertook and completed his studies and was ordained. Although he had been a good man when he lived in the world, as a priest he was much better, for in his new estate he continued that signal charity and acquired nothing that he did not give to the poor, who came to his cell to tell him of their desperate needs; and for their relief this servant of God would go and beg from the charitable rich folk of the city.

One day when this good friar was standing at the gate of the cemetery of his church, he saw a very beautiful girl, scarcely more than a child, pass by. As soon as she saw this blessed man she appeared to be greatly embarrassed, and thus His Divine Majesty made possible the remedying of her troubles. Padre Ortiz, realizing the cause of her perturbation, approached the girl and said, with the modesty appropriate to his cloth, "My daughter, why are you hastening to your perdition?" The unfortunate girl, still more distressed, heaved a great sigh and, covering her face, replied, "Father, I do not wish to go against the truth, for the manner of your question makes me believe that God has revealed to your worship that I am on my way to give myself to a man, a rich merchant in that street yonder. For many days he has solicited my love, promising complete security for myself, my beloved mother (who is a poor cripple confined to her bed), and two other little girls, my sisters, all of whom my father left to perish when God took him from this earth two years ago." Having said this, she began to weep softly and continued, "I, Father, am an unfortunate girl who, even though I should wish to marry, can find no one to love me because he would have to support my mother and sisters; and I cannot offer a penny of dowry. Although it is an offense against God, many men have tempted me to this course despite the burden of my family, and since there is no help for it, Father, all must be lost."

The good servant of God was moved with compassion and begged her earnestly to return home, telling her that on the very next day he would come to see her and make arrangements to alleviate her need. "And for now," he said, "take these two pesos, which have just been given me to say a mass tomorrow, and go home, for the public nature of this place gives no opportunity to speak further. I only beg you in the name of Jesus Christ our Lord and His most holy Mother not to carry out this offense to His divine majesty and the perdition of your soul, but use these pesos to live on until I come to see you tomorrow." "Father," replied the girl, "your worship may be sure that from here I will go straight to my house without giving offense to God, for He has offered me the means to live for four or five days and has promised to help me in my need. May our Lord repay you, for He has spared me from this evil."

The girl returned home rejoicing, giving thanks to God for looking upon her with eyes of mercy, and the blessed friar, wrapping himself in his cloak, went that very afternoon to the house of Doña Francisca Ayala, wife of the royal herald Don Juan de Urdinzu Arbeláez. Putting to her the girl's need and peril, he begged the lady for alms to prevent the evil that he feared. The lady's charity was great, and I mention her display of it on this occasion to remind the princes and the rich and powerful folk of this world to be liberal with the poor (as this lady was) and not to fail to give alms out of fear that they will some day need what they have given. The treasures of God can never be exhausted for those who share what they have in charity with the needy. This lady and her husband, the royal herald, never lacked for these treasures, nor did the many others who contributed so liberally to the needs of the poor. Rather, their riches multiplied a hundredfold: thus our Lord provides for those who in this life are good stewards of Christ and are mindful of the poor (since He commended them to our care) and do not gather riches to possess them like idols but to lay up treasures in heaven.

This noble lady, therefore, with her great charity took pity on the maiden's poverty and, thanking the good friar for having prevented her downfall, at once gave him two thousand pesos, promising that in the future she would always concern herself to help the girl. The holy man blessed her for her liberality, had the two thousand pesos brought to his cell, and as soon as it was day, said mass and went rejoicing to the maiden's home. His appearance there was a great consolation to both the girl and her mother, who also were grateful to him for having prevented the sin she had been about to commit. He spoke such praises of chastity that the poor girl's heart was touched and she straightway vowed to preserve hers, as she did all her life long.

The servant of God gave them the two thousand pesos, and with them (by setting up in business with a handball court) they had enough money to spend their lives very decently, and the virtuous maiden was even able to provide a dowry for one of her sisters, who lives with her husband today in very comfortable circumstances. Oh, how great a good it is to serve God and prevent offenses against Him, thereby attaining both temporal and eternal bliss! Perhaps if this poor girl had sold herself for momentary gain, her perdition would also have been eternal. O charity, O alms, from what evils are you capable of delivering us! Forever blessed may be he who, because his charity was great, prevented so lamentable a loss, and blessed may she be also who so generously aided the maiden in her need.

The good Padre Ortiz's extreme charity was shown not only in supplying the needs of all who asked him for relief but was extended even to the dead, for he used to bury in all charity the bodies of little children that poor parents placed at the church door. So great was his zeal in this work of charity that he caused a sumptuous vault to be built at his own expense—that which lies under the choir of the church of our father San Agustín, with its coffers of gilded cedar, and all very beautiful. The charity of this servant of God became known throughout the city, and all the poor brought their dead children to this church in larger and larger numbers, for in Potosí innumerable infants die by the end of their first year. This blessed man would emerge from his cell and take them up, and if the body was that of a little girl, he would dress her with her crown and palm, and if a boy, a beautiful cross; then he would dispose the body in an immaculately clean coffin that he kept there and would invite the other members of the community to go with him to bury it. He would carry it around the cloister, performing the obsequies to the sound of soft music, before placing it in the vault. On the Feast of All Souls he built a magnificent catafalque in their honor, all covered with white cloth, and sang a mass for them.

When the priests of the mother church saw that all the dead infants were being taken to San Agustín, they told the reverend prior of the community not to permit Padre Ortiz to go on with those burials, because he was taking them away from the mother church: the inhabitants of the quarter, pleading poverty, were refusing to pay for burials there. The servant of God replied that he was mindful only of the parents' grief and hence was constrained to practice charity with them.[29] Nevertheless, those priests insisted that he accept no more such bodies and that they should bury the infants of poor parents in their church. The friars of San Agustín promised to comply, but it was impossible to persuade the inhabitants of the quarter not to take the little bodies to San Agustín. Consequently there were so many that there was nothing else to do but send them to the mother church; and by twos and fours they were sent there every day. At first the priests there buried them willingly, but seeing that the numbers continued, they became impatient and begged the servant of God to continue his work of charity. He rejoiced greatly at this news and continued the work until old age, when, the year 1682 being the last of his life, a serious illness befell him. Its effects grew worse; he received the holy sacraments and before his death declared that he had buried eleven thousand infants' bodies and that their blessed souls were present. To the reverend prior and the other religious he said, "See, my brothers, these choirs of angels, these blessed souls who are with me and wait for my soul to leave my body, to present it to our Lord for my charity in burying their bodies. And so I beg of you, my dearest brothers, to continue the same work in which I have been occupied until now." With this and other expressions of admirable charity he delivered up his soul to the Creator.

1688 · The Reformation of Don Francisco Aguirre

THE mercy of God shines wonderfully upon the sinner and with its divine aid returns him to a state of grace. Such was the case of the venerable Don Francisco Aguirre, who was a priest. This priest was a native of the city of Cuzco (though some say that he was born in a town near there) and the son of a noble Basque family. He came to this city of Potosí as chaplain to Don Francisco Godoy, the chief justice. At the time of his arrival in the city Don Francisco Aguirre was a dashing youth with a handsome face and other excellent attributes, and rich also in worldly goods, for he soon amassed a fortune in this city. Hence he became one of the city's gallants, and the degree of his irreverence was such that, heedless of the decorum demanded by his calling, he dressed under his priestly garments in rich silver and gold cloth, and his outer clothing was of rich stuffs, plush and velvets, with doublets embroidered in silk, gold, and pearls and giving off rich odors—he was all one great scent, so that folk knew from some distance away that Don Francisco Aguirre was approaching.

Being in the flower of his youth and the height of his ostentation, he greatly neglected the love of God, to the point that he no longer thought of that most merciful Father and loved only an elegant lady of this city. Her he not only loved but idolized, and from the beginning there grew up between him and this lady so great an attraction and so strong a love that it took a miracle to separate them before their burning passion consumed them utterly.

Our divine Lord, therefore, in His infinite mercy wished to deny him the instrument that was leading him to the abyss, and He accomplished it by causing a mortal illness to befall the lady, whose life was suddenly placed in jeopardy. Don Francisco was overcome with grief; since he loved the lady to excess and possessed great riches, there was no doctor or medicine in this city that he did not bring to her bedside, but all efforts were in vain. Her illness continued without hope of human cure until at last Don Francisco, seeing that she was dying, went one day to the parish church of San Lorenzo (in his sinful state an act of irreverence) and, kneeling before the image of Christ our Lord crucified (which is venerated in one of the chapels of that church), humbly begged Christ to restore that woman's health; and while he was praying most fervently (a rare thing for him) the holy Christ addressed him in the following words: "Francisco, when your soul is cured her body will be cured."

The priest knelt there filled with terror and confusion; he cast himself at the feet of that divine Lord who was offering health for his soul and bitterly bewailed his sins; he cried to heaven, lacerated his face and breast, begged for mercy, swore to make amends, and left that sacred place a very different man from the one who had gone in. Returning home (and never resuming his relations with that woman, who quickly recovered from her illness), he locked in a room all the jewels and other valuable possessions that he had acquired during the time he had led a dissipated life, though most of his fortune had been squandered on vanities.

Virtues (as Pope Pius II remarked in his *Apothegms and Maxims*) made priests wealthy when they were poor, and vices will surely make them poor if they do not know how to be rich. Once this priest of God had rid himself of his riches (which had been responsible for all the evil in his soul), he was left rich in virtue; and during the fifteen years that he kept those valuables and jewels locked in that room he never once opened it until, at the end of that time, he took them out to distribute to the poor, many of whom were greatly relieved thereby. As soon as he had locked the room he retired to a small and humble lodging in an outlying quarter of this city. He emerged from it only to go to the church of San Lorenzo and to the church of Jerusalén, which was near his lodging. His life changed so radically that, though formerly he had occasioned scandal, now his virtues were the astonishment of Potosí. While in prayer, he underwent remarkable ecstasies, saw visions, and received divine consolation.

Many years after he had experienced conversion and taken up his abode in that humble lodging (though splendid because inhabited by this servant of God), a monastery for the clerics of San Felipe Neri was constructed in, or rather just behind, the church of Jerusalén; and on the urging of the community he went to live in one of its cells. There his sanctity brought him the reward of still greater familiarity with Most Holy Mary, and there he had many other holy visions: once when he was saying his holy rosary, the Most Holy Virgin, being visible in his presence, told the beads into his hands. It was there that at last, after having lived most holily, he achieved the tranquility of heaven, in 1688. The aforesaid church of Jerusalén is the urn and repository of his ashes, where about fourteen months ago I had the good fortune to see his tomb when it was restored to the place it had occupied before this church was rebuilt.

The monastery of San Felipe Neri did not endure, for after eight priests and five others who were lay brothers had taken up residence there, an order came from the most illustrious Doctor Don Bartolomé González Póveda, archbishop of Charcas, that this new monastery be abandoned because there were no funds to maintain it, a circumstance greatly regretted in the city because all knew of the great charity displayed by these religious in the care of the dying. However, three or four priests were left to continue this good work and to administer the sacrament of penance to the poor of all sorts. They were also left in charge of the church where that holy image of Our Lady of Jerusalén, of which we have had so much to say, is venerated.

To return to the passing of that servant of God Don Francisco Aguirre, I will state that many fragments of his clothing—vied for by the multitude of men and women who came to view his venerable corpse during the three days it lay in state—when applied to numerous sick persons, cured them of their ills; this, God did to honor His servant. Padre Pedro López Pallares of the most illustrious Society of Jesus, a man notable both for virtue and for learning who had been the confessor of this servant of God, preached about his admirable life during various days set apart for this purpose and wrote an account of that life with his own hand.

1688 · The Trials of Doña Teresa

THERE lived in this imperial city a noble married couple whose names I do not mention out of respect for their station. One of the five children of their marriage was the beautiful Doña Teresa, whom I have met and spoken with and whose features (when she was young and still a maiden) were as follows: her face like white marble; her hair the proper mean, for it was neither as dark as night nor as golden as the sun; green eyes, with lashes so long that they seemed to serve them as a canopy, and so luxuriant that they seemed like a fence protecting her eyes or like an ebony frame and embellishment to her face; her brows also luxuriant, broad, and so close together that there was no separation between them; her nose so perfect that it was not a whit too small or too large; her cheeks and brow adorned with charming ringlets, which, falling over her face, grudgingly allowed a little crimson to show in an expanse of snowy whiteness; her mouth small and adorned with small, white, and even teeth; her hands, bust, and waist all in graceful proportion; a winning charm in her manner and grace in her walk; her voice (which is often an additional embellishment of beauty) soft, sweet, and resonant; and her intelligence clear, keen, and extremely prudent.

Now, what man, seeing this beautiful creature at only fifteen years of age, could have failed to fall in love with her? Who would not have succumbed to so high an order of beauty —unless he lacked the finer instincts or was willing to run the risk of being considered insensible? There is every excuse for the two gentlemen who succeeded in gaining admission to her home, one a married resident of Potosí and wealthy quicksilver refiner, the other an outsider from the realms of Spain who held the title of count of Olmos (the fact that I reveal it does not matter, for everyone in the city was acquainted with his excellent character and he did nothing in this affair unworthy of his rank). Both gentlemen fell in love with Doña

Teresa, each unbeknownst to the other, and very soon made their desires known to her.

The parents of this girl were excessively harsh to their children and other members of their household; their daughter Teresa had been raised with such restraint and strictness that on many Sundays and feast days they did not even take her to hear mass. Now, freedom is one of the most precious gifts conferred by Heaven on human beings: the treasures enclosed in the earth or hidden in the sea are not to be compared with it; men can and must risk life itself for freedom, as for honor, and, conversely, the greatest misfortune that can befall mankind is captivity. I say this because the beautiful girl was provided with all possible riches and comforts, but since she lacked freedom (that freedom, I mean, which would not have exceeded the bounds of her natural chastity and modesty, for her parents never allowed her to go to festivities of any kind, either religious or secular), she became so desperate that she considered herself the most unhappy girl in the world.

The two suitors having declared their desires to the girl almost simultaneously, she inclined somewhat more to the quicksilver refiner, not because he was more deserving than the other noble foreigner (who was the aforesaid count of Olmos) but because the refiner (being married) managed to persuade her parents to let Teresa serve as companion to his wife. Now, the lady in question was unaware of her husband's dishonorable intent, and since she was virtuous, Teresa's parents did not wish to deprive their daughter of such excellent company; and so no festivity took place without the refiner's asking her parents for her so that they all might attend (though the opportunity to enjoy his lustful desires never presented itself).

Nor did the count of Olmos leave any stone unturned to achieve his heart's desire, and to improve his chances he moved from the house in which he lived to another almost opposite Doña Teresa's. Since it had a balcony over the door, the count was able to watch the girl unobserved when she entered or left the house. There he stayed for several days, and though his love was all the more inflamed by these glimpses of her, he had no occasion to speak to her because of her parents' vigilance. And since no misfortune in the world could have come to this gentleman that would have left him in greater confusion and tribulation, larger efforts than he was capable of were necessary to overcome it. As a result of his dilemma his heart and physical strength failed him, and he became like a man of stone, so that he neither heard nor responded to what was said to him. His wits were almost gone, and nothing he said or did made sense, for love (that terrible tyrant) displayed all its power against this lover. Like those who go about in a stupor because they have been frightened by visions or phantasms, so did he, until the beautiful Teresa learned of it and, finding an opportunity, spoke to him tenderly. The two agreed that for one hour at dawn and two hours after about ten o'clock at night she would stand at a small window almost opposite the balcony where the count was wont to stand and that they would speak together without the knowledge of her parents, their servants, or the inhabitants of the street.

And thus two months passed without an opportunity to achieve what their impassioned words were aiming at, until one night, by common agreement, it was arranged that Teresa would slide from the window down some knotted sheets and into the count's arms and would then enter his room to enjoy the desired consummation. But things did not turn out as they expected: just as the girl—already made doubtful by her lack of strength in fastening one end of the sheets to the window sill—tremblingly put herself over the sill (encouraged by amorous words from the count), the sheet came untied and she fell to the ground in the arms of her lover. Despite the fact that her fall had been broken, she suffered a severe blow to her head, back, and hips (for, so as not to hinder her descent, she was dressed only in shift and petticoat), and lay there like one dead, unmoving and unconscious.

The count, overcome with grief, had barely the spirit to lift her in his arms and bring her into the vestibule of his house, where he found it necessary to reveal the circumstances to his servants despite the fact that the girl had implored her lover not to let any of them know. But how could anything but these and other misfortunes come to one who was about to commit offenses against God? The count was in a state of apprehension because daylight was fast approaching; however, his great grief was somewhat assuaged when he observed that Teresa was coming to her senses. Moaning pitifully, she was less concerned with the pain of her injuries than the realization that when dawn came her parents would discover her absence, and all would be lost. The count, seeing her inexplicable distress and no longer mindful of his earlier libidinous desires, sought only the most expeditious means of returning her to the room from which she had so precipitately fallen. They discussed several ways of doing this, and though many were found to be impossible, at last it was accomplished by having one of the servants clamber up a knotty beam that by chance was in the house. Entering through the window, he tied one end of the sheet to the sill, and Teresa climbed up the same beam with the help of them all, so that she was spared the fear she had of her parents but not the effects of the fall, from which she suffered for many days.

Meanwhile, the girl's father had found it necessary to go to a mine in Lipes to bring back a shipment of silver marks. This was a good opportunity for her suitors, both of whom continued to press their claims, the refiner fruitlessly and the count with good hopes. When the refiner observed the excuses that Doña Teresa gave for not going to fiestas and the lukewarmness of her response to him, he began to suspect the possible cause of this new development. Although he was reluctant to discount the demonstrations of affection she had made to him previously, he soon began to understand full well the wretched habit some women have of responding to all who court them and accepting the words of all who speak to them. So successful were his efforts that he soon learned that she was occupied in another love affair, though he never discovered that his rival was the count. Whereupon, being enraged because Teresa had rejected him and inflamed with jealousy (for jealousy is always a concomitant of love), in addition to having a nature that was very malicious and ill-tempered, he revealed to the mother the cause of her daughter's anxieties, though concealing his own evil intentions; naturally he did not reveal them, because his sin was greater than that of his rival.

When the mother heard the news she was thunderstruck. Without disclosing to her daughter the terrible rage she had conceived against her, she called an Indian maidservant who served Teresa in her bedroom and secretly carried her away to her sister's house, where, by dint of a beating and other intimidations, she made the servant confess that on two occasions a man had entered Teresa's bedroom, very well dressed and with his face concealed, and that the two had conversed there, albeit with no indecency beyond the fact that when he left he had embraced her repeatedly. Having learned this, the mother returned home even angrier than before and turned into violence all the soft treatment she had previously used with her daughter, demonstrating that many persons who are gentle at first later become excessively harsh.

The presence of her husband was unnecessary, for the lady was made of sterner stuff than he. Taking her daughter to the meanest part of the house (a hencoop in an unused stableyard), she beat Teresa so cruelly that the blood ran. So many blows did she inflict to make Teresa name her accomplice that the girl was on the point of death, but she did not comply; rather, she denied everything. She wept bitterly for her misfortunes and begged her mother to desist from punishing her, with a voice as sad as that of the swan who celebrates his approaching death by singing. But nothing sufficed to soften the mother's cruel heart, although at last, not out of compassion for Teresa's battered body but out of sheer fatigue, she was forced to stop, leaving her daughter almost dead. In addition to so excessive a punishment and the wretched condition of the place where it was carried out and where Teresa was confined was the fact of being cut off from communication with her family and in a place so dark that light entered for barely two hours a day (at about six o'clock in the morning a little sunlight came through a small window high in the wall).

And there Teresa was a prisoner for three months, during the coldest season of the year (May, June, and July). Her life was more wretched and unhappy than she could ever have imagined, and it was a wonder she did not perish there, with the great cold and every conceivable discomfort and misery. Her dreadful mother did not permit anyone to see her except one of her brothers, a small boy who went in twice a week to clean the place, but for only a short period each time; and the mother stayed by the door while the boy was inside and then locked it again and took away the key.

The heartbroken maiden, finding herself in such a plight, was more than once tempted to put an end to her life: let this be a warning to parents not to treat their daughters so harshly or punish them cruelly after their love has been discovered, but to keep an eye on them before it begins. The truth is that

Teresa had been well guarded, but to excess; and in order to have some outlet she had initially turned her affections toward the refiner who was responsible for her present plight. If the mother had already ascertained that her daughter was still a virgin, yet punished her so cruelly because she learned that the girl had let a man into her bedroom, why should she now cast her into despair? Teresa wished to communicate her terrible plight to the count, but the difficulty of doing so dashed her hopes and thus she never tried to find a way.

The count, ignorant of all that had happened, was much grieved not to see her and made every effort to discover why the mistress of his heart did not appear. But two months later the little brother who was the only person to see her in her prison came to the count's house. The count asked about her, and the little boy, encouraged to speak by his cajolery, told of his sister's plight and the miserable existence she was leading. The count was astonished by the boy's tale, and giving him four pesos to keep the secret, he also handed him a note to give to his sister when he saw her. This note he wrote on the spot, asking Teresa the best way to set her free.

One day, then, when the mother opened the door of her prison so that her brother could come in to clean it (for meals were simply put under the door without a word to her), she entered and said to her daughter, "I wrote to your father to inform him of the evil you have done in discrediting our honor, and I have now received his reply, in which he says that he is coming home only to drink your blood. Take notice, therefore, that you will leave here only to be carried to your tomb," and so saying she went out again. Meanwhile the little boy was able to give her the note, and merely to touch it was an antidote to the venom in her mother's words. Since woman's frail nature is less capable of resistance, the mother was well aware of her daughter's despair, and knowing this she augmented the punishment with threats of even crueler blows and indecencies to be visited on her body.

Consoled by the note, Teresa went to the door, where a little light filtered through its chinks, and managed to read it. She gave thanks to God for it and waited until her little brother came again, two days later, and quickly told him to ask the person who had given him the note for another sheet of paper and something to write with. This the boy did, but he was then obliged to wait several more days, for the place (a stable-yard) in which her frightful prison was located was locked, and the key was held by her mother.

At last the day arrived when her brother came to see her, and he gave his sister the paper and ink. When the sun shone through the little window she could see to write to the count, asking him for a steel file to saw through the lock on the door of the room and informing him that when she had escaped she would climb a low wall that was there and then down to a flat rooftop. From there she would climb the roof, which was not very high at that place, and he must then toss from his balcony a strong rope tied into a bundle so that she might take it and, making one end fast to a nearby beam, throw the other end back to him; and since the distance was not great, with the aid of that rope she would reach his balcony and place herself in his hands.

Men are very foolish not to believe that it is more difficult for women to confess their love than to feel it, and this is so because the hardest thing for a woman is to abandon her sense of shame and speak her love for the first time. It is true, however, that there are many women who love very truly and, overcoming their natural sense of shame, manage to speak openly, for love respects no customs, nor is it devious. In this case her need and the desperate plight she was in, quite as much as her love for the count, had made Doña Teresa bold, for again she had placed herself in peril for his sake. Good fortune comes to men from many different directions, and what is most certain is the least aspired to: just at the point when the count was least confident of attaining what he desired, his good fortune entered through his very own balcony.

Teresa gave the note to her brother, who despite his small store of years was knowing enough for the purpose—and especially to keep the secret, which was the most important part of the whole business. On receiving the note, the count put the plan into execution, some four days before the arrival of Teresa's father, who was hastening home to punish her anew. To saw through the lock was the work of many hours for the beautiful girl, but she did it by the assigned hour and all went well until she reached the roof opposite the balcony, where the count and one of his servants were awaiting her. As soon as she reached the top of the roof they tossed her the rolled-up rope; she grasped it and made it fast around the beam and threw back the other end so that both could be fastened to the balcony. Once this was done she had only to climb down the slope of the roof and pull herself along between the two ropes until she reached the balcony. But as she slid down the roof (perhaps recalling her previous fall), her courage failed completely and she began to protest that she could not do it and to moan sadly. Master and servant, taking pity on her, decided that the servant must pass hand over hand along the rope until he could reach Teresa and help her across. This was done, and the servant made it safely along the rope (which was made of thick, strong hemp) and, encouraging her to cross it, began to do so himself; she went first and the servant behind.

As they were moving along the rope two things happened that might have caused serious injury had Teresa fallen from the great height. The first was that as the two of them swung down from the roof, the edge of the balcony (which was of wood and somewhat worm-eaten) gave a great crack and would have split and let them fall had not the count held on to it with both hands. The other was that halfway across the street the girl's arms became so tired that when the servant noticed it he had to hang from the ropes and seize Teresa by her hair and the front of her shift; and although the two hung there motionless for the space of a Credo, at last she recovered her strength and continued until she reached the balcony, where the count received her with the greatest affection. They then untied one end of the hempen rope and, pulling on the other, hastily drew it in, thereby removing the evidence that the beautiful Teresa had escaped by that route. She spent the rest of that night in the arms of her lover, who did not behave with as much restraint as he had on the first, second, and third occasions, especially because this time Teresa was quite willing. She was no longer fearful, for she had already lost her home and was under great obligation to that gentleman.

Her mother did not notice her absence until the following day when, as she went to place food under the door, she observed that the previous day's meal was still there. She rushed to the door in a panic, and since the lock had been filed through, it opened easily. Going in, she found her daughter gone, a circumstance that nearly drove her out of her mind. She made as many inquiries as she could to find out how the girl had escaped and where she was, but all her efforts were fruitless. Three days later the father arrived, and when he learned what had happened he was on the point of knifing his wife in his passion to have his daughter back—not out of pity for the girl but because he wished to kill her with his own hands.

Doña Teresa spent two months hiding in the count of Olmos's house, and her parents considered her as lost to them (since they had made so many unsuccessful attempts to find her). Then the beautiful Teresa decided to go to the city of Cochabamba, where an aunt lived, for it was also time for the count to leave for the city of Los Reyes. She assumed a disguise and set forth for Cochabamba, where she eventually found a noble youth who wished to wed her. After their marriage they lived in that city for two years, during which time Teresa's mother died, repentant for what she had done and grieving because neither her daughter nor her little son had reappeared. (Teresa had prudently taken him with her when she departed from Potosí so that once she was gone he could not tell what he knew.) At last Doña Teresa returned to this city with her husband, where they lived for ten more years in great peace and tranquility, and at the end of that time Teresa departed this life, leaving four sons and a daughter who bore her name, a girl as beautiful as her dead mother had been. And she is alive today, her beauty increasing as she grows older.

PAGEANTRY

1599 · The King Is Dead

In the month of April, 1599, the lamentable news reached this imperial city of the death of the king, Don Felipe II, a monarch who had always looked after its affairs with great concern and had been most generous in favoring it with grand privileges. In the previous year of 1598, after the betrothal of the prince Felipe III to Doña Margarita of Austria, and the infanta Isabel (sister of the prince) to Alberto, archduke of Austria, the king had retired to the Escorial, wearied of his labors, to prepare himself for his last days and do penance for some of his youthful excesses. He imposed upon himself the use of the scourge, wielding it with his own hands and with great severity, and living like a monk. For twelve years before his departure from this life he drank no wine and practiced many mortifications in his diet. He endured very severe illnesses with great patience, even allowing one of the fingers of his right hand to be cut off. In the miseries of this life all men are equal, and sometimes the most disgusting maladies are visited upon the most refined among us; but among the many painful illnesses that afflicted him the pain of his sins was greatest of all.

Utterly resigned to God's will, he delivered up his soul to Him on Sunday, September 13, 1598, being seventy-one years of age. He was a great man and a most prudent king, as can be seen in his famous history; his life was a constant battle against heretics, and he was often heard to say that if his own son were a heretic he himself would furnish the faggots for his burning. His virtues were worthy of admiration, and for that God favored him on all occasions; good works (as Cayetano so accurately said) can be called weapons (unlike sins, which cannot be called weapons but, rather, works of darkness), for virtuous actions performed in the light of divine grace are weapons both offensive and defensive for him who does them. Sins, on the other hand, because they outrage and wound the soul of him who commits them, are not weapons but works of darkness; and, since in addition to not being weapons they stand for frailty, they endow one's enemies with still greater strength.

As I have said, the news reached this imperial city in the month of April, 1599. And although the death of the emperor, his father, had been deeply regretted, the death of the city's greatly beloved and most benign monarch was felt even more keenly. The tolling of bells began to sound forth from all the church towers, even harsh bronze seeming to express the grief of all. It was not necessary to have town criers proclaim mourning to the populace, for on the day following the fatal news most of the city's inhabitants appeared in that sad garb, and very soon nearly everyone—Spaniards and Indians alike—assumed the same dress.

Four master carpenters were chosen to build a fine mausoleum to be constructed in the principal church, and on their request they were allotted twenty-six days to finish it with all perfection. It turned out to be a most beautiful, rich, stately, and sumptuous edifice, to all appearances made of purple and white jasper. The moldings and capitals were all of gilded marble; the columns were Ionic, with the lower third fluted. The fluting of the columns was gilded, and the railings, bands, and balusters were all elegantly ornamented with gold. The figures on it were gracefully and beautifully painted, and it was swathed in fine stuffs and brocade. This beautiful structure was about sixty-eight feet high and contained eighty columns. It was surmounted by a representation of the great Mountain of Potosí, on whose slopes (on the side facing the main door of the church) was a skilfully executed sculpture of the rich city of Potosí in the form of a grave and beautiful maiden with an imperial crown of the finest gold encrusted with many diamonds. Her draperies were of black and white cloth with exquisite embroidery of rubies, emeralds, zircons, topazes, and pearls. In all the arches (with admirable painting and well-arranged symbols) were represented the triumphs won in all quarters of the world by the royal arms, with many flags placed on the cornices and capitals bearing Latin and Spanish verses describing the metaphors and figures. During the whole construction of this elegant piece of work the tolling of the bells never ceased either by day or by night, for all the holy communities and parish priests went every day, in order of seniority, to the principal church to celebrate the royal obsequies.

When construction was finished, the twenty-fourth day of May was appointed for the climax of the royal solemnities. On the evening of the preceding day the procession set out from the royal exchequer in the following order. First went two hundred Indians (of those who are known as the king's yanaconas)[1] wrapped in black wool blankets and wearing baize hoods of the same color. They were followed by five hundred of the Indian inhabitants of the city, owners of mines and ore mills, artisans of various trades, and those who held official posts in the city; these wore mourning capes and hats with turned-down brims. After these came four companies of Indians in black woolen shirts and very high-crowned black caps; they carried bows and arrows at their backs and trailed their lances and flags on the ground. Then came the caciques,[2] those of this city as well as those of other towns who had come for the ceremonies, all dressed in mourning after the Spanish style except for their heads, on which they wore llautus[3] of the kind formerly used by the Incas. After these came the mita Indians (those who work in the mines and ore refineries and hence are tributaries of the king), all dressed in black baize shirts and woolen mantles that they dragged on the ground, holding one corner in their left hands, and on their heads they wore black caps. They were followed by the Spaniards, preceded by Captain Diego Grande, one of the local captains, with his company of harquebusiers dressed in black taffeta and carrying their weapons reversed, with their drumheads loosened and their flags trailing. Then came a crowd of the poor who were not natives of Potosí and who because of their poverty had been provided with mourning capes and black hats by the illustrious cabildo. They were followed by the artisans, and after them came the merchants, all dressed in mourning. After these came Captain Escudero with his company of musketeers dressed in dark silk with black bands. Then came all the nobility dressed in long mourning garments with black collars. They were followed by the royal officials and officers of the mint (sixty persons in all, together with the minters and silver merchants) dressed in long baize garments that trailed behind them, each train held by two pages in black, and their heads covered (over hats with downturned brims) by baize hoods reaching to their chests. Then came the company of Captain Alonso de Grado (the third of the official companies) dressed in tawny cloth with trimmings of black taffeta and with their muskets and harquebuses reversed and their flags trailing. Then came the guild of quicksilver refiners trailing mourning garb of the same kind as the royal officials and officers of the mint. The members of the clergy were already in their seats. On that day, as on all the other days since the arrival of the news, twelve hundred masses had been offered in the principal church for the deceased sovereign. The preacher for these final obsequies was the provincial of the Jesuits, who happened to be in the city. When this royal ceremony had ended with all solemnity, the whole procession returned to the royal exchequer, whence it had set out, and the members of each group returned to their homes. Previous authors and other interested persons who have described these obsequies state that their cost was 130,000 pesos in pieces of eight.

1600 · Long Live the King

In June, 1600, news reached Potosí that the king, Felipe III, had been married the previous year to Her Serene Highness Doña Margarita of Austria, daughter of the archduke Carlos and his wife María, and that his peaceful reign had begun with felicity and the satisfaction of his vassals. The inhabitants of Potosí were delighted with this news, and nobles and commoners, Spaniards and Indians, in mutual accord, determined to show their satisfaction that God had given them so benign and merciful a king by holding royal fiestas, which, displaying all manner of rejoicing, were to last for twenty days.

Before the fiestas began there were serious differences of opinion between the illustrious cabildo and the guild of quicksilver refiners, for the latter gentlemen did not wish to cooperate in what the cabildo was proposing, namely, that the fiestas should be postponed until the arrival of the new corregidor, who had set forth from the city of Lima but was ailing in Cuzco, which was the reason he had tarried so long in that city. The quicksilver refiners as well as some other citizens argued that, judging from the new corregidor's reputation, he was more inclined toward troublemaking and greed for riches than to the peace and joy of his subjects, and they had no doubt that his arrival would occasion new factional strife and troubles. The opinion of the refiners and other inhabitants prevailed, and so the illustrious cabildo had to accede to their wishes.

The fiestas began on the eighteenth of June with a showy and sumptuous masque[4] by the famous miners of the Mountain, in which there were admirable figures, very costly floats,[5] splendid costumes, marvelous embroideries, precious stones and pearls of inestimable value, spirited horses, and splendid trappings. The last float (which was extremely large and rich, and was drawn by twelve white horses) represented the rich Mountain of Potosí, all made of fine silver, and at its feet was the imperial city in the form of a grave and beautiful maiden wearing a dress of silver cloth covered with diamonds, emeralds, zircons, amethysts, and rubies, and kneeling before a portrait of His Majesty Felipe III, which was placed on a sumptuous throne under a canopy; it was surrounded by children dressed as angels, who sang songs complimenting him on the beginning of his reign. The figure representing the city held in her right hand a representation of the Mountain of Potosí in silver, and in her left, some bars of the same metal, both of which she offered to the portrait of His Majesty.

On the following night rich and noble Indians presented another very splendid and colorful masque, in which all the nations of Peru appeared in their native costumes, along with other figures, some ugly and some pleasing, but all very much worth seeing. All the incas of Peru came riding in richly decorated carriages of state, and in the last (which was made of silver and drawn by fifty savages dressed in the skins of different animals) under sumptuous canopies rode the three great monarchs who had been kings of both Spain and Peru: the emperor Carlos I, his son Felipe II, and his grandson Felipe III. Seated below these and dressed in their native costumes, which are very fine, were the Inca kings known to the Spaniards after their arrival in Peru: the powerful though unhappy Cusi Huáscar, his brother the tyrant Atahuallpa, Mancco Ccápac II, Sayri Túpac, Cusi Tito, and Túpac Amaru, who was the last; the latter three had received holy baptism.

The fiestas continued with enormous expenditures on the part of all the guilds. There were six days of stage plays, four being devoted to the allegorical kind called *invenciones*, six bullfights with fierce bulls, and various drills by the cavalry, sometimes masked and sometimes not. Evenings were enlivened with receptions and balls, illuminations in the streets and plazas, and a large number of costly fireworks displays. During every day of these royal fiestas the four companies of soldiers saluted the dawn with all their harquebuses and muskets. Horse races were held, and the sweet music of many instruments resounded everywhere in the city, performed by Spaniards as well as Indians. On the next-to-last day of these fiestas there was a tournament in which competitive field games were played, on one side the nobles and royal officials and on the other the quicksilver refiners, with such fine costumes, rich carriages, fancies, jewels, precious stones and pearls, that all the outsiders who happened to be in the city were virtually speechless with admiration.

On the final day as a fitting end to the rejoicing there was a great and magnificent joust, in which thirty gentlemen took part on each side. One side was composed of the gentlemen refiners and the other of royal officials and some members of the local nobility, and each side tried to outdo the other in feats of arms and in costly garb as well as in the fighting, in swordplay, and in encounters with the lance. Captain Pedro Méndez, Don Antonio de Acosta, Don Juan Pasquier, Bartolomé de Dueñas, and Juan Sobrino (all of whom described the grandeur of this fiesta in great detail) say that Don Fernando Arzáns, a representative of the guild of quicksilver refiners and the defender of the tournament,[6] wore a costume so rich that it was valued at eighty thousand pesos, for it was all embroidered with the richest pearls, zircons, rubies, and sapphires, and was adorned with thirty emeralds of unusual size and also twelve diamonds of great value. All the other gentlemen were dressed with equal sumptuousness, but, so as not to waste time, I will not describe their costumes in as much detail as did these authors. The shock of arms in these jousts was so terrible that many took falls and more than twenty men were injured and five died; that is why this spectacle is described as being not as dangerous as real combat but too dangerous to be taken lightly.

Ten days after the end of these fiestas General Don Alvaro Patiño arrived in this city as its corregidor and chief justice, and chief officer of the mines; he was the seventh of its officially appointed corregidors.[7] It was learned that he was very angry with the gentlemen refiners and other inhabitants because they had refused to postpone the royal fiesta until he arrived; hence, only the illustrious cabildo and a few ecclesiastics went out to meet him. After his reception only the cabildo held bullfights for him.

On the second day of the fights one Martín de Igarzábal, a Basque, was on a balcony in the plaza along with Nicolás Enríquez, a youth born in this city of Spanish ancestry. Because Nicolás passed a box of sweets to a lady who was on a nearby balcony the Biscayan became so angry and jealous that, without stopping to consider what he was doing (and as he was a large and very strong man), he seized the youth in his arms and threw him off the balcony. The force of amorous desire (a powerful witchery that lulls reason and the liveliest intellect to sleep) is so great that there seems to be no defense against it: sometimes it encounters innocence and sweeps it away, and it can pervert the sharpest and most prudent conscience and force it to relinquish the uprightness of its judgments.

The youth fell to the ground, so stunned that all believed him to be dead from the combined effects of the blow and his fall. The plaza was soon in an uproar, and in a moment the news reached Juan Enríquez (of the kingdoms of Spain), the youth's father, who was outside the plaza but not far away; when he saw his son in that condition he unsheathed his sword and rushed like a madman to the balcony. Igarzábal hid in a bed (though he would have been better advised to defend himself; but all happens by God's permission). The enraged father found his quarry and without allowing him time to make a move or receive the aid of anyone, killed him with many sword thrusts.

The uproar spread. The corregidor's servants came running up with other officers of the law and also Juan Enríquez's friends, who were Andalusians and Estremadurans. The Basques, who had already gathered at the Empedradillo, began to shout, "Kill the culprit!" Both groups entered the house, and a cruel battle began, in which Don Mendo Patiño, the corregidor's brother, was killed, as well as two of his servants who had rashly moved to pull their knives on the Andalusians. Sancho Ocoz and three other Basques were also killed. And this (says Captain Pedro Méndez) happened in so short a space of time that by the time the corregidor had left the balcony of the cabildo and entered the house (less than a hundred paces away) it was too late to do anything. The Andalusians, Estremadurans, and Portuguese joined forces and put up a bloody resistance to the corregidor, the Basques, and the Castilians in the plaza. There were deaths on both sides and more than thirty were wounded.

This occurrence was so confused and so regrettable that the aforesaid author Pedro Méndez, an eyewitness, states that he had never seen its like in Potosí (among the many fights that had taken place there); he says that since almost everyone in the city was in the plaza watching the bulls from balconies, stands, and scaffoldings, the women (seeing their husbands and relatives engaged in that cruel battle) threw themselves shrieking to the ground, many injuring themselves in the process, and rushed to interpose their bodies between those of the men who were fighting. Some of the women fell, others were wounded, and yet others got the steel blades entangled in their skirts; and men and children behaved in very much the same way. The same author relates that some malicious characters, when the fight was at its grimmest, loosed a fierce bull into the fray. With great swiftness and ferocity, the animal tossed some on his horns and knocked others down, wreaking a great deal of havoc. He attacked a woman who was in the thick of the fight and, catching her by the skirts (which then became entangled in his horns), dragged her around part of the plaza, leaving her badly injured and almost torn limb from limb. The men did not stop their fighting and stabbing, ten embroiled here, four there, and two elsewhere. The corregidor fled to save his own life, and the members and followers of the two factions finally tired of fighting and went home. But from that day onward deaths, wounds, and bloody quarrels continued; and for many years no one in Potosí enjoyed that supreme good which is peace.

1687 · The Fear of God

TEMBLORS, or earthquakes, ordinarily take place in maritime lands; thus it is observable in Europe and in these Indies that towns far from the sea feel the effects of this misfortune less frequently, and those that are seaports or on beaches or the coast, or are near such geographical features, suffer more from this calamity. However, proximity to these features is not necessary for divine justice to be called to our attention, for in the valleys of Pitantora, in the city of La Plata, and even in this imperial city earthquakes have occurred, although here in the city they have scarcely been perceived; but in La Plata and Pitantora they have been severe, even though those places are far distant from the sea. It has been a marvelous thing in this realm and very notable that earthquakes (when they are severe and famous) extend all the way from Chile to Quito, a distance of more than five hundred leagues. They have occurred again and again on the coast of Chile, doing enormous damage to the towns, and likewise in the city of Los Reyes. They have also occurred repeatedly in Arequipa, Cuzco, and Chuquiabo, and have wrought similar destruction.

In the year 1687, on the twentieth of October, at four in the morning, the city of Los Reyes was destroyed by one of these frightful earthquakes; and since bad tidings usually travel more swiftly than good, the destruction was very soon known in this city. By the end of November the particulars of injuries and lamentable occurrences became known in such detail that Potosí, fearing the wrath of the Lord, tried like a second Nineveh to perform great acts of penitence in order to mitigate it.

The ecclesiastical arm, as the most perfect in everything, tried to turn aside God's anger by doing great acts of penitence both publicly and in private. To move the people to do the same, the first act of the vicar and priests of the principal church was to order a pious procession in which five hundred children, barefoot and with their heads covered with ashes, led the way, followed by the citizenry of the whole town in the same condition and performing the most bizarre penitences: some dragging large and heavy chains, others naked and covered only by hair shirts, some whipping themselves till the blood ran, others with their hands tied behind them and with great iron gags and locks in their mouths, some with heavy crosses on their shoulders, and others with their arms extended and with heavy, knotty logs tied to them. The image of the glorious apostle San Pedro, that of Christ our Lord of the Column, and that of His most holy Mother were carried on litters. The procession passed through all the principal streets of the city, imploring God for mercy.

On the second day all the inhabitants began to make good confessions in order to place themselves in the grace of God; and they did well, for prayer, alms, and fasting, along with all the other works of piety and penitence, if performed in a state of mortal sin benefit neither the living nor the dead. But those who are in mortal sin should not because of this desist from doing all the good works they can (fasts, prayers, alms, penances, and other pious and religious works), for even though such works merit neither grace nor glory and do not avail either for those sinners or for others, they will serve to help the sinner attain from God not only temporal goods, health, honor, life, riches, etc., but also spiritual favors so that he may emerge more quickly from sin. Thus those sinners may be deserving for themselves and make recompense both for themselves and for the dead. In addition to this they can implore or attain grace for the dead through such works, even though they are not in a state of grace, for to receive favor from our Lord depends not on the quality and merits of him who asks it (though this plays a part) but on His infinite generosity and mercy.

In the afternoon of the day following the procession I have described, and after a most moving sermon, a procession set out from the church of Santo Domingo carrying the image of this great patriarch on a litter together with the miraculous image of our Lady of the Rosary. Innumerable Indian women went before with crowns of thorns on their heads and heavy crosses on their shoulders, and children followed reciting the holy rosary in chorus. They were followed by the artisans and tradesmen, all reciting the rosary with great devotion, who were followed by the nobility, the quicksilver refiners, and the officers of law and justice, also reciting the most holy rosary in chorus. After them came the holy community of this preaching order, displaying the secret mortifications with which they had lacerated their bodies (to the point that they could scarcely take a step) and reciting the rosary in loud voices. After the holy image of our Lady, came the illustrious cabildo with its noble presiding officer, who was the prime mover of such functions and never failed to attend them all; nor did this constant effort cool the fervor of his devotion. This procession was also followed in great numbers by the wives of the most prominent citizens as well as other women, all decently attired, which in Potosí was not the least of the procession's high merits, for customarily the female sex tends to dress immodestly.

On the third day, as soon as dawn had come and the doors of the church of San Francisco were opened and people knew that the Holy Christ of the True Cross was on its litter prepared for the procession, great numbers of men and women crowded into the church and, falling at the feet of the image, began to pray for mercy. Giving no thought to bodily sustenance, most of them stayed all day to attend the multitude of masses, sermons, and other exercises in which the holy nuns occupied the day until five o'clock in the afternoon, when the procession left the church accompanied by more than thirty thousand persons of both sexes and every nation and condition. The number of those who walked in it, using the scourge and doing great and various acts of penitence, was more than five thousand. Women walked in humble garb, barefoot and with other mortifications. The religious walked wearing gags, with heavy crosses on their shoulders, and shoeless. In short, this procession was one of the most devout and bloody that took place in these attempts to make amends to our Lord.

On the fourth day there was another, as devout and penitent as its predecessor, that of San Agustín, in which procession the holy friars of that monastery, all wearing gags, with crosses on their shoulders and ashes on their heads, took out the Holy Christ of Burgos and our Lady of Solitude. The laity imitated them and added other severe acts of penitence that were considered excessive by many.

On the fifth day the Mercedarian friars had their procession, accompanied by vast numbers of the people and the nobility in the same order as in the preceding ones. The holy friars went barefoot, with their heads covered with ashes and crowns of thorns, and heavy crosses on their shoulders. In this procession appeared the image of our Lord of the Column—the same image that once spoke to the priest in charge of it, obliging him to absolve a certain sinner who had confessed to him but whom he had refused; ever since that time the image had remained with its finger pointed as it had been in making that sign to the priest. The image of our Lady of Solitude was also in the procession, as well as that of the patriarch San Pedro Nolasco dressed as a penitent with a scourge in his hand like the other patriarchs in the previous processions.

As this devout and penitent procession moved along by way of the customary streets and churches, the Mercedarian friars arrived at the Jesuit church so exhausted that they could scarcely take another step; yet, making a supreme effort, they did their best to finish the procession, moving to compassion all who saw them. In particular the charitable fathers of that sacred company, filled with compassion, begged them to put down their crosses, saying that if they tried to walk farther their penance would be excessive. Although the friars refused, their only thought being to proceed, and said that God would give them strength to carry the crosses to their monastery, they at last allowed themselves to be persuaded by the pleas of the Jesuit fathers, who forcibly lifted the crosses from their shoulders; and the procession went on without them.

On the sixth day it was the turn of the Jesuit fathers to have their procession, in which the whole city took part in the following order: first went innumerable Indians of both sexes with crosses on their shoulders and ashes and crowns of thorns on their heads. They were followed by two religious associations of Indian women, one attached to this sacred company and the other to the Benedictine order, with their hands tied behind them and ashes and crowns on their heads. They were followed by more than five hundred children, some completely naked but most dressed in white tunics, barefoot and barelegged, with ashes and crowns on their heads, some bearing crosses on their shoulders and others with their hands tied behind them, chained together so that all who saw them were moved to compassion. (Since in Potosí children are always very warmly dressed owing to the extreme cold in winter, many children fell ill as a result of being undressed for these processions and four of the more sickly died.)

After this group of children came two rows of most of the men in the city, rich and poor, gentlemen and commoners alike; when men beg God for mercy there must be no division for vanity's sake, since we are all sinners, and perhaps the rich were greater sinners than the poor. Moreover, in this life charity bids us pray for each other, knowing as we do that all are equally sinners and in need of salvation. It may well happen that a man imprisoned for debt can intercede (because of his friendship with the judge) for another who is not a prisoner and a poor invalid can intercede with the doctor for another, even though he has neither strength nor resources to help him.

Between these two rows walked a large number of men of various stations in life, with covered faces and performing harsh and bizarre acts of penitence: some lashing themselves with savage whips; others wounding themselves with metal-tipped scourges; some whose bodies were tightly wrapped in ropes of straw and bristle; many dragging terribly heavy chains, barefoot, and lashing themselves cruelly; others with their arms extended in the form of a cross and tied to a heavy beam borne on the nape of their necks; and others walking with their hands tied behind their backs, gags in their mouths, and prickly haircloth on their bodies, with ropes around their necks pulled by Negroes and other low people. The holy images that took part in this procession were those of the great patriarch San Ignacio, the Apostle to the Indies, San Francisco Javier, the Holy Christ of Mercies, and the Mother of God of Solitude. The heads of the Jesuit fathers were covered with ashes, and they wore crowns of long thorns and carried heavy crosses on their shoulders. The most holy image of the Mother of God was accompanied by innumerable women of all stations in life, humbly dressed, some barefoot, others wearing heavy haircloth and other mortifications, and likewise with ashes covering their heads.

When this procession had arrived at the church of Nuestra Señora de las Mercedes and the Mercedarian friars saw that the Jesuit fathers were as exhausted as they had been on the previous day (when they had reached the Jesuit church and the Jesuits had helped them by mercifully lifting the crosses from their shoulders), they wished to repay this act of charity. With arguments owing more to emotion than to logic they begged them to unburden themselves of the weight of those crosses, for the distance remaining before they could rest was considerable and their exhaustion even greater; but since the burning charity of those fathers gave them greater spirit and strength as their exertion and fatigue increased, they begged the friars to leave them alone, for they could not renounce the obligation to follow in the footsteps of Jesus. Both groups engaged in pious arguments until the Mercedarian friars allowed themselves to be convinced by the Jesuits' pleas, and so that neither group would feel itself offended the Mercedarians agreed to help carry the Jesuits' crosses, and thus the procession continued, arousing the tenderest feelings in all who observed the scene.

On the seventh day the hospitalers of the great father of the poor, San Juan de Dios, held their procession and the whole city accompanied it in the same order as before.

On the eighth and last day of these divine penances another procession set out from the principal church. In all respects it was large and very penitent, for—in addition to five hundred children dressed only in white tunics and barefoot, and others totally naked and with crowns of thorns on their heads, their hands tied behind them, and dragging fetters and irons—there were all the priests of the Indian parishes (fifteen in number), with crosses on their shoulders, ashes and crowns of thorns on their heads, and ropes around their necks, barefoot and with their cassocks unbelted. Each one walked at the head of his parishioners, who were also carrying crosses and had ashes and thorns on their heads. What especially moved the spectators of this procession was the sight of about eighty girls of tender age from the orphanage, dressed only in short tunics, barefoot and barelegged, with their hair in disarray and covering their faces, with crowns of thorns and ashes on their heads, and their hands tied behind them. The vicar, the three priests of the mother church, and all the clergy walked in the same condition as the other priests. The count of Canillas and his illustrious cabildo, knights of the military orders, quicksilver refiners, and other nobles were all barefoot and barelegged, and had ashes on their heads. The noble countess, the general's consort, also walked barefoot and barelegged in the procession, without any adornment and with ashes on her head; and the important ladies of the town were similarly arrayed.

In short, these and many other penances both public and private were performed in this imperial city without reservation of age, social class, or sex; for all feared the wrath of God. And although His Divine Majesty had discharged His anger on the city of Los Reyes (more than four hundred leagues distant from Potosí), the Lord showed that He also had a scourge prepared for Potosí, which was made known at the nearby lake of Tarapaya; and this (though at the time its cause was unknown) happened at dawn and at the very hour when the earthquake destroyed Los Reyes. Many men and women were at the sluice of the lake and preparing to bathe in it when suddenly the water sank more than seventy feet and then rushed back furiously, raising enormous waves. All those present fled in terror, unable to imagine the cause. Later, when they recalled the day and hour, they realized that it was the very same as that of the destruction of Los Reyes.

During the period of these penances and processions the deserving poor were given alms amounting to ten thousand pesos, and many other works of piety were performed to appease the anger aroused in our Lord by men's sins.

1716 · The Triumphal Visit of a Viceroy

ON the sixth Sunday in Lent of this year an official message arrived in Potosí from the city of La Plata addressed to Don Francisco Gambarte, one of the senior officers of the cabildo and chief justice of the city (because the corregidor, General Don Francisco Tirado, was in La Plata, having gone there in response to secret information he had received), advising him that Don José Sarmiento de Sotomayor, count of Portillo, had come as ambassador from the city of Los Reyes with an order of our lord the king appointing to the office of viceroy of these realms the most illustrious, most reverend, and most excellent Don Fray Diego Morcillo Rubio de Auñón, archbishop of La Plata.

It was learned that as soon as the lord archbishop had received the embassy of the count of Portillo he had appointed as captain of his guard and as his chief advisor Don Francisco de Sagardia, a judge of the royal audiencia of La Plata, and had distributed other appointments; he had also made known his intention of visiting this city, a piece of news that caused a great deal of agitation, for all were upset by the fact that Holy Week was about to begin. On the evening of the day the news was received, in addition to a general pealing of bells, great bonfires were built in streets and plazas, and white wax candles were lit in windows and on balconies, together with other marks of rejoicing not inappropriate to the season. The city at once determined to send two ambassadors to His Excellency to convey its congratulations. Those selected for this office were the city councillors Don Diego de Ibarbarú and Don Juan Alvarez, and they began to prepare at once, sparing no expense in providing suitably luxurious costumes for themselves and livery for their retinue. In the middle of Holy Week (finding it necessary to travel even at that season) they departed for the city of La Plata, where they were received with all pomp and honor as ambassadors of so famous a city; and they demonstrated Potosí's magnificence by a lavish scattering of silver wherever they went. Festivities were held for them and His Excellency received them with every evidence of delight and honor, even coming to the doors of his palace to give welcome and usher them in.

The two senior members of the cabildo, Don Francisco Gambarte and Don Pedro Navarro, arranged for his sojourn in this imperial city with all possible luxury and without regard to expense, which was enormous both in this city and in Tarapaya when His Excellency passed through there. The corregidor, General Don Francisco Tirado, managed to escape these expenditures. Very shrewdly, before official news of the royal order had arrived but when its contents were already known to him, he had abruptly abandoned the Holy Week festivities in Potosí and gone to La Plata, where he fastened himself to His Excellency as to a benefactor, although it was his obligation to stay and receive him in Potosí as is the custom of all corregidors; and this duty was done by the corregidors of Yotala, of Pitantora, of Porco, and all the other cities from Potosí on down. But let us agree that everyone most willingly cultivates the land that he expects will bear him fruit, and this corregidor was not unmindful of the fact that by going to La Plata he could improve his position considerably, whereas if he had remained in Potosí he would only have experienced a diminution of his wealth.

O ambition, how bad a guide you are, for you overwhelm with errors any man who follows you! Greed invents all sorts of ingenious tricks; ambition gives strange embellishments to an idea; and even though grave harm is done to others thereby, the desire to rise in life is blind to everything except the furtherance of its own ambitions. A man who has acquired great wealth through excessive greed, taking advantage of the sweat of the poor, might better have met his obligations.

Somewhat unsatisfactory preparations for the viceroy's visit having been made—for this magnificent city was unable to discharge its obligations as it would have wished in so short a space of time—the most illustrious and most excellent lord Fray Don Diego arrived on Saturday, the twenty-fifth of April, at three o'clock in the afternoon, with a large retinue that included the judges of the audiencia Don Gregorio Núñez, Don Baltasar de Salamanca y Lerma, Don Francisco de Sagardia, and Don Juan Bravo; also, the count of

Portillo, Don Juan de Ocampo (the secretary of dispatches nominated by His Excellency), and many other gentlemen and the corregidors of various provinces together with the venerable clergy, many doctors and masters, and the parish priests of a number of towns.

Because of the affection that it had shown him on previous occasions, the viceroy loved this imperial city, which in the pleasure of having him as its viceroy forgot the unpleasantnesses associated with his past religious inspections. And so he was at pains to appear pleased with everything. Although private persons had begun to make collections everywhere in the city for the expenses of the visit and money was already being gathered in, the illustrious cabildo, like a wise father and prudent head of the republic, gave orders that such collections must cease, taking into consideration the hardship to artisans and other poor folk; and thus all the expenses of the visit were borne by the two senior members of the cabildo, some of the wealthier guilds, and the cabildo itself.

Two triumphal arches had been constructed with incredible speed though with great difficulty owing to the short space of time available, for since there was no paint to simulate jasper and marble, gold and colors, they were draped in precious stuffs, costly embroideries, and rich silks. The first and more magnificent of these was one street beyond the parish church of San Martín, outside the eastern limits of the city, on the road that leads to the upper provinces. Its construction and the orders of its columns were composite, for all four of the architectural orders were represented (Corinthian, Ionic, Doric, and Tuscan), although the four principal columns were Solomonic.

The structure had three arches (the center arch wider than those at the sides) and three tiers, of which the principal tier was large, the second of moderate size, and the third small; its over-all height was twenty-five yards and its width ten. The top tier was surmounted by a handsome throne in the form of a cedarwood pedestal all carved and with curious moldings, shining with the gold that covered it; on the throne stood a life-sized figure of Fame, very beautiful of face, with a banner in her hand and dressed in a shining tunic strewn with flowers and girdled with a richly embroidered sash.

Above the capitals, which were of gilded cedar and mirrors, rose the arches, curiously adorned with silks of various colors and trimmed with rich cloth and ribbons, and the cornices (decorated with satins and mirrors in gilded frames), above which there was room for a number of large statues set into the four corners, some enameled and others dressed in fine cloth and brocades; these signified His Excellency's moral virtues.

Over the first tier was a spacious gallery containing very elaborate mirrors, gilded frames, and a variety of other opulent ornaments; in the four corners of the principal cornice (on lofty pedestals covered with rich cloths and adornments) were four tall and elegant pyramids decked with silverwork and with pennons flying from their summits.

The second tier rose above this first one; it had well-proportioned arches whose columns were of the Ionic order, and from the semicircular ceiling of this second tier hung a large image of an angel who seemed to descend from the beautiful gallery above to see His Excellency pass by.

The third tier, although its columns were Corinthian, had blind arches and cornices adorned with rich stuffs and other ornaments.

Both sides of the first tier were covered with cedarwood and draped with rich silks both inside and out, as were the steps, pedestals, cornices of the columns, friezes, beams, architraves, railings, bands, and balusters, all covered with a variety of rich stuffs cut to measure, with vases wrapped with ribbons, mirrors in gilded frames, and other quaint decorations; between the cornices were spaces for inscriptions showing the symbols, devices, and emblems appropriate to His Excellency.

Under the first tier of the arch, in the middle of a canopy that could be seen under its roof, was a folded cloud, and just as His Excellency entered the arch it opened, and disclosed a tiara dropping a good distance through the air, that stopped and hung at the height of his head, as if to signify that only this was lacking to ennoble his brow; and at the same moment a veritable shower of beaten gold and silver descended from all four sides of the corridor above.

On one side (at the right) of one of the side arches were the chair and cushion for His Excellency to rest upon, and on the other, standing on a little stage on which they were to act out a welcome to him, were two children dressed to represent urbanity and generosity, virtues very characteristic of this imperial city.

From the triumphal arch an ingenious wooden walkway with stands and balconies lining it on either side led to the church of San Martín; the beautiful faces and clothing of those of the feminine sex (that embellishment of the world) who occupied them served to adorn this passageway. From the parish church of San Martín there stretched 120 arches of wrought silver (hand-worked, as they say here), each with two columns and a pointed arch, placed at intervals and leading to the house where the viceroy was lodged. These were the work of the Indian fruitsellers and market-women who wished to welcome His Excellency by this means; and as all were covered with so great a variety of silver objects, ribbons, and rich stuffs, they formed a very pleasant vista.

The other triumphal arch had been constructed on the corner of the Calle del Contraste (which is also one of the corners of the Plaza del Regocijo and the one that led to the home of Don Francisco Gambarte, who was the viceroy's host on this occasion). Its columns were of the Doric order, and among them were distributed a number of very well-painted images of saints in gilded frames, and the capitals and upper cornices were covered with mirrors, gilded foliage, flowers, sprays, and silver bows.

At the request of the cabildo, His Excellency had stayed until noon in the hospice where, before his official entrance, the illustrious guild of quicksilver refiners, the priests of the city, and the nobles had come to greet him. Meanwhile, by three o'clock in the afternoon a squadron of three hundred men was waiting, composed of nobles from various nations of Europe and of Peruvians and their sons; with news that His Excellency was approaching, they drew up ranks and assumed their formation. Their captain (there was only one company, owing to lack of time to arrange for others) was Don Fernando de Almanza, who had been appointed governor of Tucumán. His brother-in-law Don Bernardo Fernández Ponce de León (both were natives of Buenos Aires) was designated his lieutenant; General Don Silvestre de Brinas, of the Order of Santiago, was sergeant major; and Don Antonio Díaz Jordán was field marshal. To a man they were mounted on fine steeds.

As soon as His Excellency began to move down the Calle de Cantería the squadron, spreading out into the field of San Martín, offered a volley and then marched beneath the first triumphal arch, where the illustrious cabildo and other officials were waiting under a canopy of very rich pearl-colored cloth lined with silk, as befitted so distinguished a visitor. Equally luxurious were the canopy's adornments and poles, which were made of fine silver; and its value can well be imagined, for when it was presented to His Excellency in the house where he was staying, he sent the poles to the church of San Juan in this city and kept the canopy to send home to Spain.

The gentlemen members of the illustrious cabildo who had been designated to carry the canopy were attired in court dress in addition to the gorgeous clothing and headgear of their office; as all this was new to the city, it made a very favorable impression, especially on the common people, for they were glad to see that the local nobility lacked neither correctness nor experience in such matters.

With this noble retinue His Excellency proceeded to the center of the arch, where he descended from his mule and, seated on his cushioned chair, was invested with golden spurs. Meanwhile (the murmurings of the restless crowd having momentarily been hushed) sweet music began, offering welcome to His Excellency. And when the music had ended, Urbanity and Generosity (represented, as I have said, by two children) in the city's name celebrated his happy arrival with very elegant verses, comparing His Excellency to those peerless leaders Moses and Joshua. The music rose again in the midst and at the end of their discourse, and both music and verse were wonderfully sweet and graceful. They had been composed with matchless skill by the Reverend Padre Maestro Fray Juan de la Torre, prior of San Agustín, who also wrote, at the city's request, the entire program for the archbishop's entrance, reception, and celebrations in the city of Los Reyes. Would that my unworthy pen were endowed with even a part of his consummate skill as I write my own description of these events!

When the music had ended, the illustrious cabildo presented to His Excellency a richly caparisoned Chilean horse, with stirrups of fine silver washed with gold and shoes of the same (all of which had been specially made for this occasion at enormous expense). He mounted, and with the senior member of the cabildo and the royal standard-bearer walking by his stirrups and two magistrates at his reins (they in court dress with their jewels of office and gold chains, and the illustrious senators in splendid clothing), and accompanied by the mace-bearers and the canopy, His Excellency began his procession. The streets were blooming with members of the fair sex who crowded balconies, windows, and the stands built for the occasion. So many honorable matrons, chaste maidens, and ladies celebrated for their beauty, all richly and gorgeously dressed, had never been seen before. Nor had the city ever seen so many jewels and precious stones or such a profusion of pearls to augment the beauty of their faces. Smiling and graceful, all offered a thousand welcomes to His Excellency, supplanting the function of Flora and the beauty of Diana in the eyes of all who looked upon them and the hearts of those who loved; others, like the dawn when it covers plants and flowers with grateful dew, sprinkled the noble retinue with sweet-smelling waters that seemed to come from the angels, for those who sprinkled them were angelic indeed. This is no exaggeration of the richness and beauty there displayed, for although the Spaniards have made away with an enormous amount of wealth and have given it to the French,[8] yet enough is left to maintain the grandeur of this city; and as for beauty, apart from that of its native daughters, here the fair sex of all America and even of Europe represents the cream of every condition of womankind: only in this there may be one great danger, for if man is the essence of earthiness, woman is the epitome of heaven, and if divine commandments and laws are not adhered to, both sexes will suffer eternal damnation.[9]

The distance from the triumphal arch to the principal church is very long, yet all the balconies, windows, doors, and street crossings were filled with vast numbers of people, and the walls on either side were hung from top to bottom with rich and varied hangings of satin, velvet, and innumerable other silk tapestries, rich stuffs, damasks, beautifully painted pictures representing landscapes, and portraits; but the women surpassed all with their beauty, fine clothing, coiffures, jewels, and pearls.

His Excellency reached the principal church, where he

was received by the clergy with their vicar and priests and members of all the city's religious communities, and the choir sang the Te Deum laudamus. The bells hanging in the city's churches, with their soprano, tenor, and contralto voices in discordant harmony, rang out the Te Deum in their respective registers, all echoed by the sound of kettledrums, snaredrums, hornpipes, trumpets, and innumerable other instruments played by the Indians; and the noise made by the soldiers and the roar of the crowd added to the din.

At this juncture the noble infantry company was drawn up smartly in the Plaza del Regocijo, thanks to the skill of their sergeant major General Brinas; all were dressed in costly uniforms of the richest cloth, tissues, and brocades of various colors, with rich decorations of fringes and silver and gold lace. They wore jewels on their breasts and on their hats; gold chains, rings, brooches, and feathers shone everywhere on their clothing; never before had there been seen, either in beautiful gardens, in flowering fields, in imaginary painted scenes, or in crowded palaces masculine beauty as ornately adorned and with such gallant countenances.

His Most Illustrious Excellency, the viceroy, after offering thanks to our Lord, left the church and descended its steps to the plaza. He again mounted his horse and continued under the canopy toward the Calle del Contraste, crossing the plaza in review of the squadron. Taking salutes, he reached the home of Don Francisco Gambarte, and there he was lodged. The house (built by Don Francisco's famous grandfather, the field marshal Antonio López de Quiroga, during the time of his greatest prosperity) was so richly and appropriately adorned, so spacious and magnificent, that it was worthy of lodging our king and lord Felipe V himself, whom God preserve.

The squadron remained in the plaza, where with considerable skill and without embarrassing mishap it executed four charges in close order drill, with pikes now raised on high and now lowered, as if in a real battle, all very showy and greatly admired by matrons, maidens, and ladies as well as the rest of the people; for the fair sex occupied balconies and windows here also, and other spectators the whole plaza, as well as the walls of the cemeteries.

The banquets and other festivities held for His Excellency by the two senior members of the cabildo were exceedingly costly and magnificent. His Illustrious Excellency was well aware of this, for when during his approach to the city he was requested to stay more than a week, he replied: "Potosí has been very generous to me already, and I will remember its liberality, but this time I prefer not to stay long, so as not to inconvenience my hosts further." The great of this world remember benefits and store them in their hearts and thus keep them always present in memory, understanding how to judge affection and appreciate its effects; princes are grateful even if what is given them is owed to them by Nature, which is often so poor a paymaster.

On the morning of the following day, which was Sunday the twenty-sixth, Don Martín de Echavarría, a knight of Santiago and a rich refiner, presented His Excellency with a thousand marks of virgin silver and a jewel of gold and diamonds appraised at four thousand pesos; and the entire guild of quicksilver refiners arranged for another fifteen hundred marks to be presented to him that same night following the festivities that I shall describe below. During the whole of this day he received the visits of priests, prelates, the illustrious guild of refiners, judges, and royal and municipal officials such as officers of the mint; and His Most Illustrious Excellency received them all very kindly.

That same evening the famous miners of the Mountain presented a brilliant and very costly masque in his honor, comparable only to those of the city's very early times, since one so long and so magnificent had not been seen in many years; it had been prepared in a very short time, for they had had only the briefest space to prepare such a show of rich stuffs, French tissues, precious serges, gorgeously colored brocades, satins and costly silks, so much cloth-of-gold, ribbons of expensive materials, gold and silver lace, as well as the finest of white lace, with an incomparable treasure of jewels, chains of gold and of pearls, not to mention a great variety of precious stones and rich trappings for the horses.

First came Don Andrés de la Torre Montellano, chief magistrate of the mines, richly appareled in the most expensive cloth, riding a spirited horse with sumptuous trappings, and accompanied by twenty pages in fine livery bearing torches; then Don Domingo Serrano, an excellent engineer and a native of this city whose mining skill has been so indispensable on the Mountain and who on that same day received from the viceroy by way of restitution (because it was his due) the staff of office as overseer of the Mountain, of which position he had been previously deprived. With him came his associate Don Miguel de Umarán. They were followed by Fame riding on a splendid horse with rich trappings and crests, wearing a beautiful costume, and holding a trumpet in her hand. After her came the twelve famous heroes celebrated by Fame, among them our Caesar, Carlos V, as well as Don Juan of Austria and El Cid, all with lances and shields in their hands and wearing steel breastplates and helmets, fine sashes, tunics, and flying plumes, and mounted on spirited horses with silver trappings. They were followed by the twelve Sibyls dressed in very appropriate costumes of the richest materials in imitation of those seen in old paintings, carrying shields inscribed with their names and prophecies; and the horses' coverings were of brocade and ribbon. Because the Sibyls were represented by handsome youths, it all seemed very genuine, for their costumes and jewels, their precious stones and pearls, reflected the light of the numerous torches (carried by pages in livery). Next came men representing Turks, dressed in the richest of turbans, flowing robes, and other characteristic clothing, astride beautifully caparisoned horses. Then followed famous heroes of the great House of Austria, who went two by two on gorgeously decorated horses and wearing costumes so stunning that the eye could scarcely take in so much richness and so many jewels, so much livery and so many pages bearing torches. After them came the Ethiopians and their crowned king, with beautiful costumes and trappings. They were followed by many nymphs, gallants, and ladies richly dressed, and after them a triumphal float with pleasing music played on various instruments. Under its canopy was a beautiful child representing His Excellency, opulently dressed and seated on a chair with a staff in his hands. At his feet was a representation of the Mountain of Potosí done in its natural colors, and the rest of the float was occupied by six children dressed as angels and another representing an Indian child, a princess of the Incas, splendidly dressed after the fashion of that people.

With considerable difficulty (for the number of spectators was so large that instead of making an estimate that might not be believed I think it better to offer none) the float arrived at a position opposite the principal balcony in the plaza, where His Excellency was already seated in company with the count, his ambassador, the judges of the audiencia, and the nobility of this city; and when the halberdiers whom the captain had appointed as honor guard to His Excellency had taken up their stations, the beautiful float stopped and the children sang with great skill and sweet melody; and in particular the child who represented the Indian princess offered praises to His Excellency. Then two children representing Europe and America performed: Europe spoke of how she had provided his ancestry and been his cradle, America of how she had given him his episcopal honors and government post, comparing his position to that of Moses and Aaron among the Children of Israel, all in the most elegant verse. This was the work of the Reverend Padre Maestro Fray Juan de la Torre, prior of San Agustín, who received enthusiastic applause for these excellent works.

Halfway through this song of praise there emerged from a mine entrance provided for the purpose in the representation of the Mountain a little Indian boy dressed after the manner of those who work in the mines, with his ore bag (which they call *cutama*) over his shoulder, his hat with the candle dangling from it (such as they wear when carrying the ore out of the mines), and as if he were performing this work he poured beaten gold and silver out of his bag and reentered the Mountain with charming grace. This part of the performance greatly pleased His Excellency, the judges of the audiencia, and the other visitors from outside Potosí.

When the song had been sung the float again went on its way and was followed by other persons representing the sun, moon, and other planets, all riding on horses with rich adornments and decorations, and after them many and varied masque figures, some absurd, some graceful, some mysterious. There was a large number of these, and each was accompanied by six, eight, or ten pages with wax torches; and lastly there rode on a wheeled platform one of the incas, or kings of Peru, with his *ccoyas* (a word signifying princesses or queens) under a canopy, dressed with great pomp and magnificence in costumes appropriate to those monarchs.

Much pleased and impressed, His Excellency remarked that he had seen a number of masques performed by gentlemen of the court at Madrid but that none had equaled this one in sumptuousness, ingenuity, and appropriateness of roles; and all the other Europeans were equally complimentary. Indeed, it was a most remarkable thing that it had all been accomplished so quickly and in a time of economic distress, for the most hard-pressed of the miners had spent a great many pesos and those who were richer a great many more. But Potosí accomplished it all as she has ever done, under the influence of the predominant stars of this city, regretting her decline less than the fact that she can no longer display greater magnificence in all things.[10] When public harm is done to provide public pleasure, all men everywhere consider that the harm suffered is greater than the expected good, having in mind their present difficulties as well as the good that may come; and this was what happened in this city, for though there was hope of some benefit from all those demonstrations, the best thing they did was to prepare men's minds for the worst. And yet this did not prevent the city from displaying the utmost generosity.

His Excellency returned to his lodgings at nine o'clock at night, and there he found a present from the guild of quicksilver refiners of fifteen hundred marks of fine silver in thirty cones[11] of fifty marks each, not to mention others that were presented to him privately; indeed, the gift was a most impressive one, considering the fact that many of the refiners hardly had food for their own tables. His Excellency was greatly appreciative of everything, and the performance of the masque pleased him so much that he asked to have it repeated; but since this was not possible (for the engineers' work cannot be interrupted except on feast days) only the song of praise was presented a second time. The banquets as well as visits and gifts to the viceroy went on for several days.

On Wednesday, which was the fifth day after his arrival, all the stands and stagings having been set up quickly in the plaza—for it was only to satisfy the city's good will that he had stayed to receive further demonstrations of loyalty, owing to his haste to reach Los Reyes and take up the duties of his office—bullfights were held. Before they began, the infantry entered the plaza looking very smart in new uniforms and jewels, all different from those they had worn on the first day. After circling the plaza, where His Excellency and the judges and the rest of the nobles had already taken seats on the balconies, they formed battle order, fired a volley, and marched out of the plaza. Then the *toreadores*[12] entered on foot, wearing hideous masks and dressed in wild colors, accompanied by kettledrummers and mules laden with the spears and lances for the fight and covered with rich trappings that had the city's coat of arms painted on them with great artistry. The chief constable, Don Juan Alonso de Mena, entered, sumptuously dressed, riding a fine horse with ornate trappings, and accompanied by pages in splendid livery; he rode around the plaza and His Excellency presented him with the key to the bullpen. Then a handsome youth entered astride a well-trained horse to fight the bulls with his lance; in the course of the afternoon he performed three times, maneuvering so brilliantly that his horses went unscathed. In the midst of the fight with these ferocious bulls another lad, as skilful as he was brave, waited at the exit of the ring on foot, with a sharp knife in hand and with the butt of his lance thrust into the ground. When one of the terrifying brutes noticed him, it made a rush at him and with the violence of its attack was impaled; the lance's metal point went through the bull's throat and came out the middle of his back. After a few steps the bull fell dead, the brave youth having leaped to safety to the applause of all the spectators. His performance was rewarded with gifts of money by all the gentry of Potosí and the gentlemen who occupied the balconies of the cabildo and those who were with His Excellency.

At five in the afternoon scores of servants entered the plaza to the sound of trumpets, all carrying platters of food and a variety of delicious liquors. These were offered to His Excellency and to all the gentry and visiting gentlemen who were with him on the balconies (to whom the cabildo had relinquished their seats); all was served in abundance on behalf of the guild of quicksilver refiners, who, thinking that their gift of silver was insufficient, wished to show His Excellency still more honor with the bullfights and this largesse. There were unfortunate accidents, such as usually take place in this city owing to the large numbers of people who enter the plaza; it has never been possible to prevent too many of them from crowding in. As a result, although few were injured, on this day there were two unfortunate deaths. In addition, three of His Excellency's halberdiers who were posted at the doors of the corregidor's house (where His Excellency was staying) were knocked down and gored by the bulls, despite the fact that their companions wounded the fierce brutes in driving them off.

On the following day, Thursday, there was another bullfight in the same manner, and the ferocity of the brutes caused some injuries among the spectators. Those who fought the bulls from horseback with lances were also less fortunate than the day before, for one was fatally injured as he was wounding the bull with his lance; he was gored in the leg and dragged some distance, still on horseback. The horse was also injured, and the unfortunate youth died a short time after the accident.

That same night, being the eve of San Felipe and Santiago, the day on which the king reached his thirty-third year, there was great rejoicing in the form of bell ringing, illuminations, and fireworks; and on the following day a solemn mass was sung for His Majesty (whom God preserve), attended by His Excellency together with the cabildo, the judges of the audiencia, other judges, and nobles; and on the ecclesiastical side by all of the clergy, the four priests of the mother church, and the fifteen parish priests as well as prelates and monastic communities. This mass marked the end of the festivities. Their cost, beginning with the initial reception of the viceroy, had been 100,000 pesos in costumes, liveries, triumphal arches, banquets, and other expenditures. Another 50,000 was spent in gifts (silver marks and jewels), the approximate sum presented to His Excellency. Thus the total figure was 150,000 pesos, though some estimate it to have been much greater.

On Saturday, at five o'clock in the morning, His Excellency departed from this city with his accustomed briskness, accompanied by the judges of the audiencia and those members of the nobility who were able to go with him, and proceeded to Mondragón, a place of recreation four leagues distant from this city. He took with him more than 100,000 pesos of his own and from the royal treasury 100,000 more in pledges to be redeemed and sent to His Majesty, for at the moment the city had no more money in its coffers; and even this sum was subsequently collected with considerable difficulty by royal officials. And so His Excellency's visit to the city had lasted not quite eight full days.

NOTES

Notes

EDITOR'S INTRODUCTION

1. One of the widely circulated and most imitated coins of Western Europe in the sixteenth century was the German *thaler*. The Habsburg ascendancy in Europe, already maximized through its Spanish connection, was further enriched by an immense flow of silver from Spain's New World possessions. The Spanish peso, or piece of eight, became a standard unit of international exchange and the most common coin in the American colonial world. The eight pieces, or bits, of which the peso was comprised were known as *reales*. English-speaking people referred to the thaler and its imitations (whether they happened to be the Danish *rigsdaler*, the Swedish *riksdaler*, the low German *daler*, or the Spanish peso) as *dallors, dalders, dolors*, and, by the end of the sixteenth century and thereafter, as *dollars*. English colonials grew up with the peso, or Spanish dollar, and with independence the United States adopted it, combining its *reales* into two, four, six, and eight bits, as the American dollar (which was not actually coined until 1794). The Spanish peso sign, a reversed capital *P*, was converted into the dollar sign. Critics of the "Yankee" dollar take note.

2. For the history of the Spanish conquest of Peru (an area including present-day Peru and parts of Ecuador and Bolivia) and for biographical details of the men involved, see John Hemming, *The Conquest of the Incas* (New York, 1970), and James Lockhart, *The Men of Cajamarca* (Austin, 1972).

3. La Plata (originally Chuquisaca), some fifty miles northeast of Potosí in the province of Charcas, was founded in 1538 as a central Andean administrative center. It was here that the revolt against Spanish rule began in 1809. The city was renamed Sucre in 1840 in honor of the first president of Bolivia, of which it is also the capital.

4. *Historia natural y moral de las Indias* (Seville, 1598; rpt. Mexico, 1940), Lib. IV, Cap. 6.

5. In the Spanish occupation of South America, as of the Caribbean and Mexico before it, the *sine qua non* of colonial settlement was the control and exploitation of labor, primarily that of the Indian masses. Control of labor had first been sought by Columbus through institution of the *repartimiento* (from *repartir*, "to divide") in which a Spaniard was simply allotted a given number of Indians who were to do his bidding under their headman. Abuses of the repartimiento caused the crown to replace it with the *encomienda*, which gave the Spanish *encomendero* the right to collect from his Indians the tributes in kind that would ordinarily be due the crown, but did not demand their labor and personal service. In return, the encomendero was required to maintain himself as an armed and mounted defender of the king's

sovereignty and to provide a priest and catechists for the religious training of his Indians. Contrary to the royal intent, the encomenderos commonly decided for themselves how much tribute was due and required the Indians to pay in both kind and labor. In Peru the terms *repartimiento* and *encomienda* appear to have been interchangeable in the postconquest era, suggesting that while tribute in kind was often of great value, as, for example, when it consisted of coca leaves, the chief use of the institution was for the creation of liquid capital through the consumption of Indian labor.

6. For details of the early period in Potosí, see Agustín de Zárate, *Historia del descubrimiento y conquista de la provincia del Perú* (Antwerp, 1555; rpt. Madrid, 1928), or its readily available English translation by J. M. Cohen, *The Discovery and Conquest of Peru* (Baltimore, 1968); Pedro de Cieza de León, *La crónica del Perú* (Seville, 1553; rpt. Madrid, 1928), its most satisfactory English translation being Clements R. Markham, *The Travels of Pedro de Cieza de León*, 2 vols. (London, 1864, 1883); Garcilaso de la Vega, El Inca, *Comentarios reales de los Incas* (Lisbon, 1609), and *Historia general del Perú* (Córdoba, 1617), the most recent and best English translation being Harold V. Livermore, *Royal Commentaries of the Incas and General History of Perú*, 2 vols. (Austin, 1966); Luis Capoche, *Relación general de la Villa Imperial de Potosí*, ed. Lewis Hanke (Madrid, 1959); Pedro Vicente Cañete y Domínguez, *Guía histórica, geográfica, física, política, civil y legal del gobierno e intendencia de la provincia de Potosí* (Potosí, 1787; rpt. 1952); José de Acosta, *Historia natural y moral de las Indias*, a deficient English translation of which may be found in the Hakluyt Society publications, Vols. 60 and 61 (original series, 1878–79); Dr. Don Joseph Baquijano, "Historia del descubrimiento del Cerro de Potosí," *Mercurio Peruano*, 7 (Jan.–Apr. 1793), 28–48, Lima; Antonio de la Calancha, *Corónica moralizada del Orden de San Agustín en el Perú* (Barcelona, 1638); Bartolomé Arzáns de Orsúa y Vela, *Historia de la Villa Imperial de Potosí*, eds. Lewis Hanke and Gunnar Mendoza, 3 vols. (Providence, 1965); "Descripción de la Villa y minas de Potosí, Año de 1603," in *Relaciones Geográficas de Indias: Perú*, 3 vols., ed. Marcos Jiménez de la Espada (Madrid, 1965), I, 372–85.

7. Alexander von Humboldt, *Political Essay on the Kingdom of New Spain*, ed. Mary Marples Dunn (New York, 1972), p. 180. Related estimates and data are provided in Cieza de León, *Crónica*, Pt. I, Caps. 109–10; Acosta, *Historia*, Lib. IV, Cap. 7; *Mercurio Peruano*, 7 (1793), 49 ff.; and Cañete, *Guía histórica*, pp. 51–53. For an appreciation of the difficulties in estimating silver production, see the discussion by Lewis Hanke of the kinds of sources and documentation that are available for study in "Producción de Plata en Potosí," in Arzáns, *Historia*, III, 488–91; and Bailey W. Diffie, "Estimates of Potosí Mineral Production, 1541–1555," *Hispanic American Historical Review*, 20 (1940), 275–82.

8. The *corregidor* was the chief political administrator, chief justice, and principal law enforcement officer of his city and the smaller

towns of the rural districts falling within his jurisdictional sphere (*corregimiento*). Potosí was thus subordinate to La Plata until 1561, when Philip II, grateful for a cash gift of 70,000 pesos, elevated Potosí to corregimiento status, authorized its own municipal administration, and confirmed its imperial title and the famous coat of arms previously granted by his father, Charles V.

9. Concolorcorvo, *El Lazarillo: A Guide for Inexperienced Travelers between Buenos Aires and Lima, 1773*, trans. Walter D. Kline (Bloomington, 1965), p. 165.

10. Garcilaso de la Vega, *Royal Commentaries*, II, 872–73; Cieza de León, *Crónica*, Pt. I, Caps. 107, 110; Arzáns, *Historia*, I, 148.

11. Cañete, *Guía histórica*, pp. 40–41; "Descripción de... Potosí," in *Relaciones Geográficas de Indias: Perú*, I, 374.

12. Cañete, *Guía histórica*, p. 53; Cieza de León, *Crónica*, Pt. I, Cap. 109.

13. In the amalgamation process the crushed ore was spread out on the floor of a walled patio and sown with three reagents: mercury, salt, and copper sulphate. The mass was then covered with hides for a length of time, during which the silver ions united with the mercury. The remaining free mercury was filtered out through canvas bags, leaving an amalgam of mercury and silver, which was then pressed into conical molds and heated sufficiently to volatilize the mercury, leaving a cone of pure silver. For a general treatment of Spanish colonial mining, see Carlos Prieto, *Mining in the New World*, [trans. Frances M. López-Morillas] (New York, 1973).

14. On mercury mining, see A. P. Whitaker, *The Huancavelica Mercury Mine* (Cambridge, Mass., 1941).

15. Garcilaso de la Vega, *Royal Commentaries*, I, 537.

16. "Descripción de... Potosí," pp. 377–78.

17. *Royal Commentaries*, II, 938. The mita was maintained in Potosí until the very end of Spanish dominion, even in defiance of a decree of abolition issued by the Spanish cortes of 1812. On the mita, see Capoche, *Relación*, pp. 116–17; Cieza de León, *Crónica*, Pt. I, Cap. 109; Baquijano, "Historia," p. 37; Cañete, *Guía histórica*, pp. 64–65, 99 ff.; Gabriel René-Moreno, *La mita de Potosí en 1795* (Potosí, 1795; rpt. 1959), pp. 7–11; and Rodrigo de Loaysa, "Memorial de las cosas del Pirú tocantes a los indios," 5 May 1586, in *Colección de documentos inéditos para la historia de España*, 112 vols. (Madrid, 1842–95), Vol. 94, Caps. 52–53, 58.

18. Arzáns, *Historia*, I, 145–71; Cañete, *Guía histórica*, pp. 38–39.

19. Arzáns, *Historia*, I, cxxxi.

20. Most of Toledo's efforts and results are described in "Descripción de... Potosí," pp. 373–85; also see José de Mesa and Teresa Gisbert, "Noticias de arte en la obra de Bartolomé Arzáns de Orsúa y Vela," in Arzáns, *Historia*, III, 450–51.

21. Cañete, *Guía histórica*, p. 41; Capoche, *Relación*, pp. 116–17; Baquijano, "Historia," pp. 35–37.

22. Capoche, *Relación*, pp. 150 ff.; Cañete, *Guía histórica*, p. 54.

23. Arzáns, *Historia*, I, 42–43, 129.

24. Baquijano, "Historia," pp. 35–37; Capoche, *Relación*, pp. 78, 177.
25. Baquijano, "Historia," pp. 35–37. The non-Spanish population would include a very large number of Portuguese. Even though Arzáns frequently mentions the presence of all manner of foreigners in Potosí, the figure of 40,000 seems rather high. This important question is deserving of attention. On the Portuguese, see Lewis Hanke, "The Portuguese in Spanish America, with Special Reference to the Villa Imperial de Potosí," *Revista de Historia de América*, 51 (June, 1961), 1–48.
26. *Historia*, II, 333. See also ibid., pp. 354–62; *Cañete, Guía histórica*, pp. 36–37; Capoche, *Relación*, p. 76; Baquijano, "Historia," pp. 35, 38.
27. *An Account of a Voyage up the River de la Plata, and thence over Land to Peru*, in *Voyages and Discoveries in South America* (London, 1698), p. 46.
28. Arzáns, *Historia*, I, 8.
29. See Gwendolin B. Cobb, "Supply and Transportation for the Potosí Mines, 1545–1640," *Hispanic American Historical Review*, 29 (1949), 25–45.
30. *Historia*, I, 64. For contemporary descriptions of the road from Buenos Aires to Potosí, see Acarète du Biscay, *Account*, and Concolorcorvo, *El Lazarillo*. A penetrating historical account is provided in Charles R. Boxer, *Salvador de Sá and the Struggle for Brazil and Angola* (London, 1952).
31. Arzáns, *Historia*, I, 314 ff. Basques were similarly involved with other Spaniards and Creoles in La Plata, Quito, and several other localities in the Andean world at this time.
32. *Historia*, II, 408.
33. Gwendolin B. Cobb, "Potosí, a South American Mining Frontier," in *Greater America: Essays in Honor of Herbert Eugene Bolton*, eds. Adele Ogden and Engel Sluiter (Berkeley, 1945), p. 53. Also see Garcilaso de la Vega, *Royal Commentaries*, II, 1282; Loaysa, "Memorial," Cap. 43; Cieza de León, *Crónica*, Pt. I, Cap. 113.
34. *Account*, p. 44.
35. Arzáns, *Historia*, I, 258, n. 3.
36. Ibid., 323–24.
37. Lewis Hanke, *The Imperial City of Potosí* (The Hague, 1956), p. 3.
38. For the reader of Spanish, Gunnar Mendoza provides a penetrating critique of the literary aspects of Arzáns's work in "El valor literario de la *Historia*," in Arzáns, *Historia*, I, xcvii–cxxvii. The English reader should consult Lewis Hanke, *Bartolomé Arzáns de Orsúa y Vela's History of Potosí* (Providence, 1965).
39. *Historia*, II, 322–23.
40. Ibid., 322.
41. For discussions of the baroque, see Mario Picón-Salas, *A Cultural History of Spanish America*, trans. Irving A. Leonard (Berkeley, 1963); and Irving A. Leonard, *Baroque Times in Old Mexico* (Ann Arbor, 1966).

42. See Francisco Gómez de Quevedo, *The Visions*, trans. Roger L'Estrange (London, 1904), and Charles Duff's edition of some of Quevedo's work, *Quevedo: The Choice Humorous and Satirical Works* (London, 1926).

PRIVATE LIVES

1. Tucumán (today northwest Argentina) was a frontier province that furnished the mining centers of the high country with textiles, cattle, mules, and wheat.
2. Subsequently known as Lima.
3. According to the register of governors of Potosí, Don Alvaro Patiño was not the corregidor but, rather, was appointed as lieutenant corregidor by the absent corregidor Doctor Gaspar de Escalona y Aguero in 1599. He exercised the full powers of the office until the appointment of a new corregidor shortly thereafter. The following year he was again appointed lieutenant pending the arrival of the viceroy's choice. As lieutenant corregidor, Patiño used the full power and authority of the office to gain his objectives. It would seem pointless, therefore, to correct Arzáns's narrative.
4. Munaypata was the highest hill of the escarpment on which Potosí and her mines were located. According to Arzáns's descriptions it rose about a thousand feet over the city and from its slopes there was little that could not be seen. The foot of Munaypata was apparently a favored place for gang fights and other combats.
5. In Spanish usage a league is the distance a horse can walk in one hour—about three miles.
6. In the Christian tradition, three carnival days before Ash Wednesday. Churchmen usually deplored the revels, probably because of their similarity to the Saturnalian festivals of Rome.
7. Mount Etna, which dominated the landscape and whose eruption destroyed the ancient city.
8. In the Spanish colonial system the *cabildo* was the organ of municipal government. In larger communities its nucleus was comprised of from six to a dozen councilors *(regidores)* who served as chief constable, inspector of weights and measures, public trustee, collector of fines, and royal standard-bearer (the most honored of the regidores and usually the recipient of a double salary). The regidores were originally appointed, but the office was opened to purchase in the sixteenth century and tended to become proprietary and hereditary in the later colonial period. The cabildo also had as members two magistrates *(alcaldes ordinarios)* who, together with the corregidor, held civil and criminal jurisdictions of first instance. Collectively, then, the cabildo controlled land distribution; imposed local taxes; issued building permits; supervised licensing, markets, and public events; maintained public works; and provided local law enforcement. The cabildo of Potosí was further aided in administration by two magistrates of the Santa Hermandad ("Holy Brotherhood," a constab-

ulary of sorts), a chief magistrate of the mines, a chief magistrate of the mint, and a host of royal treasury officials and their agents.

9. In colonial cities Indians lived in their own districts (called *barrios*) and had their own governor, cabildo, and the usual municipal officials. In the early days such offices were commonly appointed by resident friars, but were then made elective (in theory if not always in fact). In course of time the offices tended to become hereditary and proprietary in nature.

10. For some years there had been a widespread conspiracy within the mint and in the royal treasury of Potosí whose end was debasement of the coins that were minted, with the conspirators pocketing the sequestered silver. King Philip IV finally accepted the recommendations of trusted advisors and called in Don Francisco de Nestares Marín and sent him to Upper Peru as inspector general not only of the mint in Potosí but of the entire governmental structure below the office of viceroy that pertained to the silver mining area. He arrived in Potosí in 1649 and soon arrested some forty officials of the mint. The magnitude of the conspiracy can be measured by the fact that one of the conspirators had squirreled away approximately seven million pesos.

11. Condemned criminals ordinarily wore the habit of the Order of Mercy from sentencing until the time of execution.

12. Nestares's authority was based more on the nature of his commission as inspector general (see n. 10 immediately above) than on his title of president of the audiencia of Charcas. But it was of such magnitude that he could decree the execution of an individual by merely shouting the order from his balcony.

13. *Jugar a las bolas* was a very popular diversion in the Spanish world. The game was played over a roadway or in a court, and the two players began from a common point, putting a small iron ball like a shot, each player with his own ball, the object being to return to the starting line first. Each shot was taken from the previous lie, hence the need for skill in selecting the best terrain for bounce and roll, and in judging the angle of flight in order to maximize inertia.

14. The *real* was a coin worth one eighth of a peso.

15. From the Arabic *azaferán*, the name of a plant used to make a yellowish-brown dye. Here it apparently refers to a darkish cast of skin.

16. From the Arabic *alféric* ("horseman"). Originally the *royal alférez* was the king's standard-bearer in battle and held great authority and took command in the king's absence or disability. A simple *alférez*, on the other hand, was but the equivalent of a second lieutenant. Centuries later in the colonial world the title *royal alférez*, having lost military connotation, was employed to designate the most honored of the municipal regidores.

17. The suffix *ote* is augmentative and usually (but not necessarily) depreciative in nature. Hence he was "as big as a castle," or, in our own time, "as big as a house."

18. The fabled kingdom of the Gran Paititi was another El Dorado,

replete with vast metallic wealth—the meanest dwellings had solid gold tableware—and mountains of gold and silver for the taking. And like El Dorado it was sought in many different places, at the cost of hundreds of thousands of real pesos. In the north it was called *Otro México* ("another Mexico"), and in the south, *Otro Perú*.

19. The *audiencia* was a most important judicial body, ordinarily consisting of twelve judges divided into two chambers, civil and criminal, with eight and four justices respectively. Their court was served by crown attorneys, a custodian of funds, and a staff of notaries and secretaries. While their daily business was to hear appeals from inferior tribunals and the sentences of corregidors and governors, they also acted in an advisory capacity to the viceroy or the captain general and governed in his absence.

20. According to Inca reckoning the Potosí area was conquered in 1256, and as Arzáns tells it, by Mayta Ccápac, the fourth of the incas. Eight or nine miles from what became Potosí he discovered the valley of Tarapaya and its natural hot springs. He stayed long enough to oversee excavation and stonework that created a very deep, circular pool and a system of luxurious baths fed by the hot springs. With the founding of Potosí the Spaniards constructed appropriate accommodations and the place became a favored resort for the silver aristocracy. Arzáns walked around the pool one day and found it to be four hundred paces in circumference. The valley was further developed with irrigation, so that gardens, groves, hunting fields, and wild expanses formed a setting for other recreational communities, like Mondragón, Miraflores, and Pucara. Here one found the country homes of Potosí's rich.

21. The coca leaf yields cocaine. Control of the drug broke down with the Spanish conquest, and its production and use proliferated despite all attempts to control or suppress it.

22. *Crónica del Perú* (Seville, 1553).

23. A Spanish weight used in the American colonies equaling about twenty-five pounds.

24. This should be taken as a hyperbolic figure of speech rather than a true comparison. In the age of the horse and before widespread irrigation Trujillo was arid and generally lacking in useful ground cover for grazing.

25. In the Brown University Press edition of Arzáns's *Historia* (2:268, n. 4) Gunnar Mendoza identifies *llipta* as an alkaline substance derived from vegetable ash and used to enhance dilution of the alkaloid cocaine in the saliva. Similarly the Indians of America commonly burned the inner bark of certain trees and leaves of shrubs to obtain alkali products that they mixed with their tobacco in order to increase its narcotic effect, sometimes to a remarkable degree.

26. As used here *cats* is a cant term for thieves.

27. La Chingana (after the Quechua word for "labyrinth") was a suburb in the older part of Potosí.

28. In 1626 the dam forming one of the Ribera's water-power

reservoirs burst, resulting in a catastrophic flood of the city and its mines. Hundreds of lives were lost and enormous material damage was sustained.

29. As Arzáns points out elsewhere, this was a persistent and sometimes stormy issue. The burial fee for infants was at least one hundred pesos for poor people, and for those better off, two hundred pesos and more. Burial of children free of charge by the friars of the mendicant orders was seen by the episcopal clergy to result in a reduction of their income, and they protested accordingly.

PAGEANTRY

1. *Yanaconas* were bound to lifetime servitude under Inca rule. The binding of agricultural workers to the soil continued under Spanish colonial aegis in a variety of forms. The king's yanaconas were tenants, agricultural laborers, domestics, and other workers in service to the Spanish crown.

2. When the Spaniards first landed in the Caribbean they used the native chief, or headman *(cacique)*, to control and exploit the labor of the common Indians. Thereafter in mainland areas of the empire they gave the name *cacique* (pl. *cacicazgo*) to those Indian lords who provided the structure of indirect rule upon which the conquerors were so dependent. In the conquered Inca world the *kurakas*, heads of local kingroups, were so employed. It is interesting and significant that Arzáns uses a term of Carib derivation rather than the local Quechua form.

3. The Quechua *llautu* ("crown") was a headband braided of wool or of woven cotton in splendid colors and worn by Inca nobles.

4. In the Spanish tradition a masque was a torchlight parade in which the nobility, astride fine and richly caparisoned mounts, displayed their wealth and magnificence.

5. The author incorrectly uses *carro* ("cart") and *carroza* ("carriage") interchangeably in referring to what we call the parade float. The precise origins of the float are unknown, but we do know that from very early times some of the circum-Mediterranean peoples annually placed their deities in small boats with wheels and drew them through their streets in a festive spirit that evoked singing, dancing, sexual promiscuity, satire, and even public obscenity. One catches something of this in the Dionysian rites of the Greeks, in Teutonic rites to Nertha, and in Celtic fetes. It emerges more strongly in Rome's Saturnalian festivities. The Latin *carrus navalis* becomes the vernacular *car navale* ("ship cart") and the internal essence of "carnival" in whatever language and culture. The proper *carrus* becomes the Italian *carrozza* and the Spanish *carroza* and *carro*, both of which Arzáns employs for "float" throughout the *Historia*.

6. The defender is the presiding official in a joust or tournament.

7. See n. 3, on p. 205.

8. The author here indicates resentment at the French ascendancy

in Spanish politics that followed accession of the Bourbon duke of Anjou as Philip V in 1700.

9. This is redolent of an old Spanish saying:

> Entre santa y santo,
> Cal y Canto.
>
> Between a female and a male saint,
> Better a stone wall.

10. Silver production was always the immediate barometer of Potosí's economic well-being, although the decline to which Arzáns alludes had a wider basis than the worrisome decline in the quality and value of the ore being taken from its mines. The entire overseas empire had declined under the later Habsburgs and it would require a tremendous effort on the part of the Bourbons to restore its economic vigor.

11. The *piña de fina plata* is the virgin silver that remains in the mold at the end of the refining process. Its name is taken from the shape of the mold, hence "cones" of pure silver.

12. Generically a *toreador* was anyone who fought bulls in the plaza and in any manner. In the present instance the *toreadores* appeared *vestidos de matachines* (from the Arabic *matauachihin*, "enmasked," or "disguised") acting as clowns whose job it was to tease and goad the bulls in preparation for the fight to come. The actual fighting was done, as the story relates, by mounted *toreros*.